Shakespeare and Baseball

Shakespeare & Baseball

Reflections of a Shakespeare Professor and Detroit Tigers Fan

SAMUEL CROWL

1804 BOOKS
OHIO UNIVERSITY SPECIAL PUBLICATIONS
ATHENS

1804 Books
Ohio University Special Publications, Athens, Ohio 45701
ohioswallow.com
© 2024 by Ohio University Special Publications
All rights reserved

To obtain permission to quote, reprint, or otherwise reproduce
or distribute material from Ohio University Press publications,
please contact our rights and permissions department at
(740) 593-1154 or (740) 593-4536 (fax).

Printed in the United States of America
Ohio University Press books are printed on acid-free paper ∞ ™

Paperback ISBN 978-0-8214-2556-5
Electronic ISBN 978-0-8214-2557-2

Library of Congress Cataloging-in-Publication Data available upon request.
Names: Crowl, Samuel, author.
Title: Shakespeare and baseball : reflections of a Shakespeare professor
  and Detroit Tigers fan / Samuel Crowl.
Description: Athens, Ohio : 1804 Books, Ohio University Special Pub-
  lications, [2024] | Includes bibliographical references.
Identifiers: LCCN 2023049418 (print) | LCCN 2023049419 (eb-
  ook) | ISBN 9780821425565 (paperback : acid-free paper) | ISBN
  9780821425572 (pdf)
Subjects: LCSH: Crowl, Samuel—Correspondence. | College teachers—
  United States—Correspondence. | Baseball fans—Michigan—De-
  troit—Correspondence. | Detroit Tigers (Baseball team)—Anecdotes.
  | Baseball—United States—History. | Sports journalism—Author-
  ship. | Shakespeare, William, 1564–1616—Study and teaching (High-
  er) | Shakespeare, William, 1564–1616—Criticism and interpretation.
  | English literature—Study and teaching (Higher) | BISAC: BIOG-
  RAPHY & AUTOBIOGRAPHY / Personal Memoirs | LITERARY
  CRITICISM / Shakespeare
Classification: LCC LA2317.C766 A3 2024 (print) | LCC LA2317.C766
  (ebook) | DDC 378.1/2092 [B]—dc23/eng/20240110
LC record available at https://lccn.loc.gov/2023049418
LC ebook record available at https://lccn.loc.gov/2023049419

This book is for Miranda and Bill and Charlie, Theo, and Miles, and for Sam and Terry and Aidan, Audrey, and Emerson, who are constant reminders of the civilizing pleasures of theater and sport as performers, players, and aficionados.

"If music (and Shakespeare and baseball) be the food of love, play on."

And 'a babbled of green fields.

—*Shakespeare*

It [baseball] breaks your heart. It is designed to break your heart.

—*Bart Giamatti*

Two weeks ago, I was in Spain. I made a pilgrimage to visit the home of one of my great heroes, the Catalan cellist Pablo Casals. . . . I was so lucky to have played for him when I was 7 years old. He said I was talented. His advice to me then: Make sure you have time to play baseball.

—*Yo-Yo Ma*

Contents

Acknowledgments

Like King Lear, I am "Four score and upwards, not an hour more or less." This little book reaches back to my very beginnings as I was born, in 1940, the day after my mother's baseball team, the Cincinnati Reds, beat the club we would come to share, the Detroit Tigers, 2–1 to win the World Series. My Tiger mother gave me baseball. She joined my upland-game-bird-hunting father in giving me Shakespeare. Two generous gifts which still invite and reward penetrating explorations in their realms of gold.

I want to thank all my friends, in and out of the academy, who have shared my passion for the Tigers or for Shakespeare or for both for the pleasure of their company and conversation in ballpark, theater, or tavern. A few must stand for many and they include Jim Cox, Herb Courson, George Wood, Miriam Gilbert, Ed and Carolyn Quattrocki, Bob Demott, Ken Daley, Alan Geiger, Mark and Amanda White, Sandy Elsass, Jim and Beth Bulman, Herb and Judith Weil, Peter Weltner, Michael Shurgot, Charles and Claire Ping, Stuart and Anne Scott, Mike Kaiser, Jim Barnes, Tom Carpenter and Lynne Lancaster, and Lewis and Susan Greenstein.

These friends are joined by a lifetime of great performers who have deepened my love for the game they play and the playwright they perform. In Shakespeare as well as baseball there are stars and utility players, young wonders and old lions, managers and directors. Here are some who have enlightened me about the game they play and the author they serve: Alec Guinness and Al Kaline, Maggie Smith and Mickey Lolich, Brenda Bruce and Willie Horton, Anton

Lesser and Chet Lemon, Judi Dench and Alan Trammell, Martha Henry and Louis Whitaker, Christopher Plummer and Jack Morris, William Hutt and Bill Freehan, Brian Cox and Kenny Rogers, Ian McKellen and Kirk Gibson, Michael Bryant and Tony Phillips, Eve Best and Justin Verlander, Imogen Stubbs and Travis Fryman, Simon Russell Beale and Lance Parrish, Fiona Shaw and Tony Clark, Peter Hall and Sparky Anderson, Trevor Nunn and Roger Craig, Adrian Noble and Jim Leyland, Joe Papp and Mayo Smith, Barbara Gaines and Dusty Baker, James Earl Jones and Bobby Higginson, Mark Rylance and Brandon Inge, Adrian Lester and Curtis Granderson, Kenneth Branagh and Miguel Cabrera.

Hamlet is the Shakespearean character with almost universal appeal to young men. He did not then speak to me, but Falstaff did. I was engaged from the moment he waddled on stage in the dazzling performance of Douglas Campbell at Stratford, Ontario, in the summer of 1958. Here are several other Falstaffs who also delighted me by finding very different approaches to inhabiting the character: John Woodvine, Kevin Kline, Robert Stephens, Michael Gambon, Anthony Sher, and Helen Schlesinger. Proving, at least to my mind, that Falstaff is as mobile, mercurial, and dangerous as the Danish Prince. And funnier and more subversive, though Hamlet gives him a run for his money.

The readers of the manuscript for the press each made improving suggestions (more Shakespeare, fewer letters) and I have attempted to follow their advice by eliminating a few of the letters and adding several sections devoted directly to Shakespeare and baseball, including Falstaff's favorite on Shakespeare, baseball, and beer.

I want to thank Beth Pratt, the director of the Ohio University Press, for making this book possible. She joins a long list of directors of the press I have worked with over the years, including Duane Schneider, David Sanders, and Gillian Berchowitz. They produce handsome books and keep them in print. An author's dream. Much of this book is about the journey out and around the bases, capped, one hopes, by a safe return to home plate. I am particularly pleased that the publication of the book itself enacts that pattern, as the Ohio University Press published my first two Shakespeare books and now, I have returned home, with the last. I want particularly to thank Scott Oancea for his clever and witty cover design and Tyler Balli and John Morris for their work in bringing the book to fruition, and for being avid baseball fans.

This book is about a baseball team, a great playwright, and a family. The dedication speaks to the latter, but not in the detail it deserves. Our children, Miranda and Sam, and their mates, Bill Pistner and Terry Kelleher, have been remarkable companions in sharing in the worlds of baseball and Shakespeare (and much more). Even more amazingly, their kids, Charlie, Theo, and Miles Pistner and Aidan, Audrey, and Emerson Crowl, have joined us in these immersive pleasures of play while also entertaining us with their own fine achievements on diamond, field, court, pitch, links, stage, and concert hall. Two of these madcaps have also raced with the bulls in Pamplona. I am sure Luis Sanguino's massive bust of Hemingway presiding over the ring's entrance broke into a granite grin as they dashed by.

I owe a special debt to Audrey Crowl, who patiently guided her old Luddite grandfather through the agony of computer problems as this manuscript emerged (and disappeared and emerged again), with several stops and starts, over a decade. By the time I, with her expert help, was finally done, she too had produced her thesis in Ohio University's Honors Tutorial College and had won more honors than our ballclub has in the last decade.

Susan Crowl has been a coconspirator in a shared life of teaching, writing, administering, and theater and concertgoing. She has never failed to take time away from her own work to come to my rescue when I have hit a bad patch in mine. As we move gingerly into our octogenarian years, the rich romance of life is often hassled by the physical indignities of growing old. When they become the most bothersome, we take solace in Bogey's famous but slightly amended line, "We'll always have London."

Introduction

This little book has three bases and a longing for home: personal memoir, the game of baseball, and my career as a professor of Shakespeare. It aims to do equal honor to each, but also to explore a field of play and a play of meaning shared among them. As a memoir, this book is less the familiar coming-of-age story than an arrival into old age and retrospective discovery. The discovery of the embedded dialogue between my twin passions of Shakespeare and baseball and my voice as a writer. I have spent my fortunate life teaching and writing about Shakespeare at Ohio University with the writing flowing out of and then back into the teaching. I was not a natural writer. I was happier in company, especially of performers and performances, than in the library. I only became a writer when I discovered that I had some talent in writing about Shakespeare in performance. Writing, I discovered rather late in my career, can also be good company.

My enlightened parents gave me two lasting gifts as a young man. I saw my first Detroit Tiger baseball game at Briggs Stadium in the summer of 1950, and three summers later (at age twelve) I saw my first Shakespeare play under a vast circus tent in the Shakespeare Festival's inaugural season in Stratford, Ontario: Alec Guinness as Richard III. I was twice hooked. It was easier for a midwestern kid to become a passionate baseball fan than a Shakespearean and the Tigers held the upper hand on my attention and affection for much of my teenage years. Even so, my parents and I made repeated summer trips in the 1950s to Stratford, where Shakespeare established his power on my imagination. That power was never more present than in a dazzling performance of *Henry IV, Part One* in 1958 where Shakespeare's Prince Hal became forever linked for me with Detroit's great left-handed pitcher Hal Newhouser (nicknamed Prince Hal) in my eager appetite for the pleasures of play. Baseball and Shakespeare have remained so linked over the past seventy years.

As Shakespeare and baseball, Stratford and Detroit, fed my own youth, so too have they enriched the life of our family from its origins in Bloomington, Indiana. The best academic term of my life was the winter/spring semester of 1963 of my first year in graduate school at Indiana University. I met my future wife, Susan Richardson, in C. L. Barber's seminar on Shakespeare's comedies, the first seminar he taught after coming to Indiana from Amherst College as chair of the English Department in the fall of 1962. Susan was a Jamesian, though like Henry James, she too was drawn to Shakespeare and the theater. She was also a classical pianist and one of her first gifts was to lead me out of dark smoke-filled, whiskey-fumed jazz clubs into the very different illumination and enlightenments of the concert hall. I traded her Monk and Brubeck and Oscar Peterson for Serkin and Ashkenazy and Alicia de Larrocha. Not a bad deal for both teams.

When we met, Susan was the music critic for the excellent local newspaper, the *Bloomington Herald-Telephone*. Soon after we were married, the paper lost its drama critic and Susan persuaded the managing editor to take me on as his replacement. She had already decided to now write under the name of Susan Crowl, so I could not resist stealing her last name for my byline and became Samuel Richardson. For my baseball readers, Samuel Richardson is regarded as the first English novelist. He was also—fittingly for this volume and its series of letters—the inventor of what is known as the "epistolary novel," in which a fictional narrative is developed through a series of letters. Almost three hundred years later the form is still being used, a notable recent example being the Irish novelist Sally Rooney's *Beautiful World, Where Are You?*, where email messages substitute for letters.

Indiana University was rich in theater and music, with the longest-running opera season in the country. It became a natural introduction to stages in London, New York, and Chicago. We also enjoyed the challenge of reviewing. Writing about performance under deadline focuses the mind to recall crucial details and to link them with historical contexts and comparative interpretations to create a coherent account and critical judgment in five hundred to seven hundred words. This practice, tougher than it looks, paid real dividends later in my career when writing about Shakespeare in performance on stage and film became the foundation of my critical work. Baseball remained for me a separate personal passion. Susan has indulged my love of convertibles and springer spaniels, but she has remained immune to my deep attachment to baseball and the Tigers. But she cheered us on when I introduced the game to our children when they hit that magical age of eight to ten, when most fans are born.

Our children, Miranda and Sam, were born in Bloomington in the 1960s and became my baseball companions in the seventies and early eighties, but I lost their company (temporarily) when they went off to college and then to postcollege jobs in Africa and Japan. To compensate I began writing them letters about games I had seen in Tiger Stadium (and elsewhere) as a means of continuing the dialogue about our shared experience of the pleasures and heartbreaks of the game. When they returned to the States and settled in Washington, DC, I continued the practice. No trip (and a trip it was, as Detroit is an almost five-hour drive from our home in Athens, Ohio) to see a weekend series or a significant single game was complete until I returned home and produced and mailed off: the Tiger Letter.

They were amused (and I think pleased) that the old man wanted to keep them in the loop about the glories of the game and our mutual investment in the Tigers. Baseball's inherent narrative quality invites writing and replay to make the experience of the game complete, just as the theater audience completes its reception of a performance in a review. The clock-driven pace of football, basketball, and soccer is a different kind of suspense, one less subject to literary transcription. Baseball and writing like each other. Each takes time. The practice of producing the Tiger Letter continued even when we saw games together and then with their kids as they came tumbling into the world in the late 1990s.

The first letter came in response to a fortuitous but fated coincidence of the annual meeting of the Shakespeare Association of America and opening day of the 1988 Tigers' season, not in Detroit, but in Boston at Fenway, John Updike's "little lyric bandbox of a ballpark." I was in Boston for the Shakespeare meeting. My good Bostonian friend and former Ohio University baseball player Sandy Elsass produced a couple of opening day tickets that made it possible for me to stay over until Monday to catch the game: Jack Morris versus Roger Clemens.

The game was a beauty, especially so for Tiger fans as Alan Trammell hit a two-run homer into the netting above Fenway's Green Monster in the tenth to win it for Morris. When I returned to Athens, I pounded out (I was still using a 1925 Royal typewriter that stamped us both as relics) an account of the game to our daughter, then in Botswana, and our son, finishing his junior year at Lawrence University in Appleton, Wisconsin. That letter became one of seventy written between 1988 and 2018 to children, grandchildren, and eventually Tiger fans and baseball friends who, over the years, asked to join the circulation list. The last letter was written after a visit to Cooperstown (a cultural-melting-pot spot that combines the Glimmerglass Opera House, James Fennimore Cooper's home, and baseball's Hall of Fame) that Susan and I made in July of 2018 during the week that Jack Morris and Alan Trammell were inducted into the Hall. The 1988–2018 Trammell-Morris symmetry was irresistible.

I began to think about gathering the letters together in a collection that might be of interest to other baseball addicts. This account began as a brief autobiographical introduction to explain the origins of my love of the game, my attachment to the Tigers, and the history of the letters. But as I mention perhaps too frequently, baseball loves writing, and the introduction became a little book of its own, swamping its original intentions. Like those novels where authors report that their characters took over in midstream and finished the job, often producing a narrative not at all in line with the author's initial plan, I discovered I had produced not an introduction to a collection of letters, but a novella-length account of a life enriched by the interaction between baseball, Shakespeare, the Tigers, and our family. Without quite intending to, I realized that I had created in this inter-weaving not an intellectual analysis but a lived description of the pleasures of play. *Pleasure* and *play* are two terms not often enough invoked in academic discourse, and the book became a rare opportunity to demonstrate a case for their inclusion in a professor's lexicon.

The Tiger Letters were long and detailed, the life brief and breezy. The answer to restoring a balance between the two was to merge the marriage at the end of a Shakespearean comedy with the thrilling walk-off home run to conclude baseball's equivalent of a comedy: both the marriage and the homer a sweet triumph of dream over reality, holiday over everyday. Those seventy letters covered over one hundred Tiger games and three hundred pages of text. Perhaps someday they will become a volume of their own, but for now several representative letters are included at appropriate moments in this narrative. The autobiography is only a partial account of a Shakespeare professor's life, while the letters are overloaded with what cultural anthropologists call "thick description." Together I hope they reveal something of my fascination with the pleasures of performance in ballpark and playhouse.

A version of what might be called my "Shakespeare Letters" exists in the many reviews I have written of stage and film versions of Shakespeare's plays. Some of those reviews were then expanded into more reflective and polished essays that became chapters in my books on Shakespeare in performance. Those essays and chapters, as in the case of the Tiger Letters, employ the device of thick description both to capture the pleasures of performance and to support patterns of informed interpretation.

My effort to keep the game and the Shakespearean comic romance alive in our family life has been rewarded far beyond deserving. Our kids married baseball fans. Miranda's husband, Bill Pistner, grew up rooting for the Pirates, while Sam's wife, Terry Kelleher, was an Orioles fan. When Sam and Terry lived and worked in Washington, DC, they managed to see the Oriole games leading up to and including the game when Cal Ripken Jr. broke one of baseball's seemingly insurmountable records: Lou Gehrig's 2,130-consecutive-games-played streak, a streak that had ended in April of 1939 against the Tigers in Detroit in Briggs Stadium. Sam and Terry eventually settled in Athens, reuniting father and son (and eventually his sons and daughter) in following the Tigers.

Miranda and Bill managed to go them perhaps one better by taking jobs as English and American lit teachers at Cranbrook, an esteemed K–12 school in Bloomfield Hills, Michigan, just twenty miles north of Comerica Park. Both school and park have their addresses on Woodward Avenue, which runs from the heart of downtown Detroit all the way to Pontiac. Bloomfield Hills is a small suburban town they have shared with many past and current members of the Tigers, from Al Kaline to Miguel Cabrera. In keeping with the spirit of this account, Bill teaches a senior seminar in sportswriting and Miranda one on Shakespeare. Their three boys proved to be fine high school athletes, and one an award-winning national champion lacrosse player at Michigan State. They came of age just as the Tigers were having perhaps the finest ten years (2006–15) in their long history.

I have taught Shakespeare at Ohio University for the better part of the last fifty years, spent a decade as a dean, published several books primarily on Shakespeare on film, and nurtured a lifelong love of baseball and the Detroit Tigers. My wife, Susan, was as a fellow professor in Ohio's English Department, writing on and teaching in the fields of Victorian and American literature, with a concentration on Henry James and Robert Browning. We were and are also fellow followers of Shakespeare in performance on stage and screen.

Baseball is the writer's game. Poets, novelists, essayists, biographers, historians, and even Shakespeareans have found the game irresistible. Writers love the pace and grace of the game and the way it invites its history to seep into the watching of any individual encounter. What other game has its own national anthem (played not at the beginning, but as the game reaches its climax), an Iowa field of dreams, and mock-epic poem? Baseball is played on a diamond set in a green field and is replayed in stories and statistics as well as in the mind's eye. In no other sport are images so surrounded and augmented by numbers and memories. Batting averages, runs batted in, won-loss records, earned run averages, errors, fielding averages, the list is endless and now expanded by sabermetrics, especially OPS (on-base plus slugging) and WAR (wins above replacement). Does a quarterback's number of touchdown passes become part of the fan's conversation the way a slugger's home runs do? Are a tennis player's aces recorded in the same fashion as a pitcher's strikeouts? Does Michael Jordan's field goal percentage register in the same way as Ty Cobb's lifetime batting average? Is a soccer goalie's name always followed by his won-loss record as a pitcher's is? Do other sports provide such a rich history written in statistics? Does any other sport incorporate the virtues of small ball—the bunt, the stolen base, the runner on second with less than two outs moved over by a grounder to the right side, the pickoff, the well-timed pitchout? The answer, as King Lear and Samuel Beckett might say, is "No."

Baseball fans can be heirs in a literal as well as a literary sense, as I can attest. Shakespeare's Henry V justifies his claim to the French throne by insisting that he, by Salic law, inherits through the female, from his mother's genealogical line. I, too, inherit my love of baseball and the Tigers from the female line, formed by listening with my mother to Harry Heilmann's broadcast of the Tigers games in the long swim-sweet summers we spent together in a cottage on West Twin Lake near Lewiston in northern Michigan from 1945 to 1949.

She was recuperating from a near-fatal experience with tuberculosis contracted in 1942 that confined her for almost two years in the TB ward in the University of Michigan's hospital in Ann Arbor, where the doctors saved her life. Although the Cincinnati Reds were her favorite team, she also became a Tigers fan then, listening to the Tiger games in the hospital. Her doctors believed the clean, crisp air of the north woods would strengthen her recovery, thus the summer cottage on the lake. In those summers I learned to swim, fish, and eventually handle a beautiful sixteen-foot Lyman runabout with a small Johnson motor on the stern, and even though I was born, raised, and have lived most of my life in Ohio, in those north Michigan woods I became a Tiger rather than an Indian. Baseball and the Tigers became a natural part of a boy's summer pleasures.

Other than warm memories, little of those Hemingwayesque summers survived into my later life. They ended when I began to play baseball and did not desire to trade it for lakeside pleasures. I no longer fish, and I do not have a boat or a cottage, but I still have baseball and the Tigers. They became my team and have remained so even as life has revealed other pleasures undreamt of by a young kid on West Twin Lake in the late 1940s. Susan and I do share a big lake, but it is called London, where we have swum and fished dazzlingly in its many museums, libraries, theaters, concert halls, and pubs over the past fifty years. Our children too have splashed about in those waters and introduced us to new ones as well in Paris and Africa and Japan. But baseball and Shakespeare have been among the continuing joys we have shared with them and now with their children. Baseball, most often dressed in the uniform of a specific team, becomes a part of one's wardrobe. For our family, the Detroit Old English Ð is as ancient and iconic as Dodger blue or Yankee pinstripes.

Our move from Bloomington and Indiana University, where we met, married, completed our PhDs, and welcomed our kids into the world, to Athens in 1970 put us within striking distance (two and a half hours by car) of Cincinnati and the Reds. Perfect timing, as the Reds were just entering the decade of the Big Red Machine, multiple appearances in the postseason, and two World Series championships in 1975 and 1976. Sam and Miranda followed my mother's lead by first becoming Reds fans. Later, after they experienced baseball in an aging temple where the game was meant to be played, rather than in a concrete multipurpose oval without tradition, charm, or grass, they abandoned the powerful Reds for the struggling Tigers. Sparky Anderson's Reds were a rare treat to watch, but they succeeded despite their antiseptic surroundings in Riverfront Stadium.

The three of us made the trip to Riverfront several times a summer, often in the company of some of their close pals. On the drives home, I became a broken record by grousing, "It was a great game, but wait until you see baseball played in a real ballpark like Tiger Stadium." As it turned out—again serendipitously—we saw our first game there the summer of 1976 on our way back to Athens from a long weekend of playgoing at Canada's Stratford Shakespeare Festival. The Tigers were in a funk as a team but were momentarily brought alive as a national phenomenon by the brilliant performance that summer by their mop-haired rookie pitcher, Mark Fidrych. We missed the Bird, and the Tigers lost 5–4 to the Red Sox, but the inner glories of Tiger Stadium became firmly implanted in their imaginations.

"You can't know the players without a scorecard" barks the vendor as you enter the ballpark. This account is my scorecard with notes scribbled in the margins. Some of it will seem digressive. But even if it is, the beauty of a good digression is that, like a baseball game or a Shakespeare play, it circles out only to eventually find its way back home, sometimes with a nifty hook slide or a lively comic dance or sometimes tragically with an out or a death, but always enhanced by the journey. I undertake this sharing of my journey aware of the sublimely subversive warning of our friend Jim Cox, the great Mark Twain scholar and fellow Tiger fan, that "biography is murder; autobiography suicide."

Part 1

The 1940s and 1950s

THE 1940S

I am a World Series baby. I was born on October 9, 1940, the day after Paul Derringer and the Cincinnati Reds defeated Bobo Newsom and the Detroit Tigers 2–1 in the seventh game of the Fall Classic. I am sure my mother felt twice blessed: once for relieving herself of an eight-pound, twelve-ounce burden and second in rejoicing that her Reds had just won their first legitimate World Series. Their only previous triumph had come in 1919, when the White Sox became the Black Sox by taking a dive. My mother was a baseball fan and came from Findlay, Ohio, located on a direct line (now I-75) between Cincinnati and Detroit. The Reds were her National League team, while the Tigers later became her American League club during her long, lonely months in Ann Arbor.

I grew up in the tiny (pop. 1,000) old canal town of Waterville, Ohio, about fifteen miles up the Maumee River from Toledo. My father was a printing and advertising executive and an outdoorsman. His happiest hours were spent wading a trout stream or tromping the autumn terrain with one of our English setters in search of pheasant, woodcock, grouse, or quail. He had a casual interest in baseball; football was his sport, but he was more an impartial observer than a fan. My father admired Paul Brown, and when the Cleveland Browns were powerful he followed the Browns. When the Detroit Lions roared in the Buddy Parker years, he enjoyed their success. The 1950s provided him with some remarkable football pleasures, as first the Browns dominated the professional game and then were challenged and eclipsed by the Lions. He took equal delight in Otto Graham's professionalism and Bobby Layne's swagger. And, like most Ohioans, he often spent his fall Saturday afternoons tuned in to the Buckeyes.

My father taught me to fish and hunt and followed closely my high school football and baseball careers, but I do not recall that we ever played catch in the classic father-son baseball formula. I did not play catch with my mother either, but I inherited my love of the game and passion for the Detroit Tigers from her. In her long convalescence recovering from TB at the University of Michigan hospital in the spring and summer of '42 and '43, the Tigers became her daily companions via the radio voices of Ty Tyson and the former Tiger great and Hall of Famer Harry Heilmann. When she emerged two years later out of danger and on the road to permanent recovery, the Tigers had joined the Reds as members of her baseball pantheon. Her young son and only child became heir to her idols, which included Shakespeare as well as baseball.

However, my first direct contact with the Tigers came through my father. Sometime in '45 or '46 he took me with him on a business trip to Detroit. I was to stay with family friends there, the Munns, while he made his calls. I was a rambunctious child, and as a bribe for good behavior I was promised an afternoon visit to the J. L. Hudson department store, a Detroit landmark now long gone, where the great Tiger left-hander Hal Newhouser was making a promotional appearance. I behaved, we made the visit, but I only got a glimpse of Newhouser, surrounded by a crush of fans, because I was perched on Mr. Munn's shoulders. Even from a distance I could see that he was tall and lean with a

narrow face, a sharp, prominent nose, and a thin smile. He
resembled many players of his generation in the republic
of baseball, who all had a lean and hungry look. I imagine
it came from having grown up in the Depression and, for
many, having served in World War II. That was one reason
Babe Ruth stood out among his fellow players, as he lacked
their small waists and hollow cheeks. His round face and
barrel chest were immediately recognizable. Newhouser
was as out of place in a department store as he was at home
on the mound. Mr. Munn told me his nickname was "Prince
Hal." I asked why, but Mr. Munn confessed he did not know.
A decade later, I learned why and made my first critical connection between baseball and Shakespeare.

In 1948 my mother learned to drive. We had moved into
a wonderfully eccentric home built in the 1930s by an archi-
tect for himself and his wife on the Maumee River next to
the Waterville Bridge. Waterville was fifteen miles from Toledo, where my father worked, and six from Maumee, where
I went to school. There was no public transportation. My
mother, always a determined and pragmatic woman, realized she had to learn to drive if she wished to bridge the gap
between her idyll on the river and a wider life. And she did.
Her first car was a gray 1947 Ford coupe that looked something like a baseball with a snout on it.

THE 1950S

That car not only got my mother back and forth to shopping,
community service meetings, and friends, but it also got us
both to Detroit once a summer to see the Tigers (and more
often to Toledo's Swayne Field to see the Mud Hens). Our
first foray was for an afternoon game sometime in the summer of 1950 against the White Sox. My only request was that
we see a game in which Newhouser was to pitch. I have forgotten the game's details (sadly, my mother's scorecard has
not survived) except that the Tigers and Newhouser won,
George Kell got a couple of hits, and Hoot Evers hit a home
run. But no one ever forgets the impact of first seeing Briggs

Stadium. It loomed at the corner of Michigan and Trumbull and occupied the equivalent of an entire city block. Al Kaline thought it resembled a huge gray battleship when he first saw it in 1953, several years after I did. Kaline, having just turned eighteen, joined the team right out of his Baltimore high school and never left. He remembers that the veteran infielder Johnny Pesky, who first took him to the stadium, called it "the old lady," when she was barely forty.

The poet Donald Hall, who visited often in the years he taught at the University of Michigan, called it an "old green and gray, iron and concrete fort." He admired its age as the oldest park in the country, along with Fenway; both opened in 1912. For Hall, Briggs Stadium was not Pesky's "old lady" but more like her husband, "an old grocer who wears a straw hat and blue necktie and is frail, but don't you ever mention it. It's the old world, Tiger Stadium, as baseball is."[1] It had little charm from the outside. The stadium's appeal registered only after you entered. The lower-deck concourses that contained the concession stands and tunnels that led out to the field were so narrow that when you emerged from those dark, cramped, people-packed quarters and into the vast interior of the stadium itself you were dazzled. Suddenly you confronted a huge expanse of sun-drenched greensward and dirt base paths surrounded by two and, out in right field, three decks, all painted in what Maine's most famous baseball fan, Roger Angell, dubbed "canoe green." Your eyes danced trying to absorb all that green majesty in one glance. And it sure as hell took your breath away. And made your heart race, at nine or nineteen or almost fifty-nine, when I walked into it for the final time on September 29, 1999, for the last game at the corner of Michigan and Trumbull. The place of play matters, whether the play takes place in a stadium or theater.

SHAKESPEARE AND BASEBALL I

One of the keen pleasures one takes from professional performances, dramatic or athletic, comes from the built environment and communal atmosphere which surrounds them. Having had the pleasure of roaming the playing field at Tiger Stadium, awed by the massive superstructure that encloses it, and having had the opportunity to play catch with son and grandson on that very field after the stadium was torn down, I can confirm the obvious: the stadium (or park or field) is crucial to the experience of the game it contains. So is the audience. The same holds true for the theater. Actors have long known that a play is only completed by a performance in a particular space before a particular audience. Hamlet performed in a small black box theater for an audience of two hundred is never the same Hamlet performed in a theater before a thousand spectators. And neither is ever the same performance as the one the night before. You can't step into the same Hamlet twice.

Space and superstructure and tradition matter. The Shakespearean actor standing on the stage at the Old Vic, the new Globe, and the Festival Theatre in Stratford, Ontario is not the same actor in each. The house, like the audience, has a crucial role to play in the performance. The fine English actor, Anton Lesser, who played Romeo and Richard III and Petruchio for the Royal Shakespeare Company in the 1980s, told me that after a performance in the Shakespeare Memorial Theatre he would wait until everyone else had left, and then he would go down from his dressing room to stand on the stage alone for five or ten minutes, just absorbing the atmosphere and history of the place. I am sure he is not unique in that experience, and I would argue that something similar happens in baseball. Baseball players have always been aware of the differences in playing in front of small or packed houses and in historic or commonplace ballparks. Playing in Wrigley Field, Fenway Park, or Yankee Stadium creates an atmosphere that cannot be replicated in mistakes like Tropicana Field (the Rays) or the Oakland Coliseum (A's) or even new retro spaces like Citi Field (the Mets) and LoanDepot Park (the White Sox). The game provides its own electricity, but tradition boosts the voltage.

The theater audience helps shape the performance by its reaction to the unfolding of the narrative. It completes the performance of the play. Actors are keenly aware of the audience and its response and instinctively know which audiences are "dead" or "alive," "dull" or "attentive." Nowhere is this more obvious than in the new South Bank Globe, where the seven hundred "groundlings," standing in the pit and sharing the same light as the actors, become essential to the performance, reminding us of the interactive nature of Shakespeare's theater. Baseball players have always acknowledged that playing before packed houses in a pennant race raises the stakes and often their level of performance. What they learned in the COVID-shortened season of 2020, played before empty stadiums, was just how crucial the fans had always been to each individual game, however large the attendance. The players confessed they missed the jeers almost as much as the cheers. The audience mattered.

We tend to think that plays have an audience (where the ear is key), while games have spectators (where the eye is key). But ear and eye are crucial for both experiences. We see a play as well as hear it; we hear a game (especially baseball) as well as see it. Shakespeare in the theater is poetry in motion, and the motion matters. Baseball is heightened by its sounds: the crack of the bat, the thump of the pitch arriving in the catcher's mitt, the slap of the well-hit one-hopper into the shortstop's glove, the thud of the outfielder crashing into the fence in pursuit of a flyball, the roar of the crowd.

The playing space also helps shape both the play and the game. When Shakespeare's company began to perform a winter season in the small indoors Blackfriars Theatre (fashioned out of a former monastery) his plays changed to fit their new surroundings. While the Globe held almost three thousand spectators, the Blackfriars held only six hundred. The plays that are commonly referred to as Shakespeare's "Late Romances," *The Winter's Tale*, *Cymbeline*, *Pericles*, and *The Tempest*, all are infused with masque-like magical elements easier to produce in an intimate indoor playhouse lit by candles rather than natural lighting. These plays were also easier to transfer to the smaller playing spaces at court, where King James and his theater-loving wife were enamored of the masque, with its combination of music, dance, and magic to enhance and propel the narrative.

Baseball teams are also built to meet the physical dimensions of the parks in which they play. The dimensions of all baseball infields are the same, but outfield distances can vary greatly from park to park—often with interesting and unique elements like Fenway's Green Monster wall in left field and Wrigley Field's ivy-covered outfield walls. Some are known as "hitter's" parks, others as favoring pitchers. Yankee Stadium's short porch in right is a left-handed pull-hitter's delight. It's no surprise that the two most prolific home run hitters in the pre-steroid era, Babe Ruth and Roger Maris, were Yankee left-handed hitters. Several generations later, when the former Tiger Curtis Granderson joined the Yankees, his yearly home run totals almost doubled from his years playing in Detroit's more spacious Comerica Park. It should be noted that Aaron Judge, a right-handed hitter, received no home advantage from Yankee Stadium's "short porch" in hitting the American League record for home runs (62) in 2022.

Baseball is a country game played in the city in an enclosed enclave with lots of green space and no clock. In America's great urban centers, it kept the idea of the garden alive in the age of the machine. What other major professional sport has garden tools like rakes and shovels and lawnmowers as part of its necessary equipment? Now even some of the head groundskeepers at ballparks have degrees in agronomy, reminding us that farms and farming produced some of our first great ballplayers. The evocation of the garden in the city is even reflected in the names of such indoor playgrounds as the Boston Garden and New York's Madison Square Garden, homes of winter sports like hockey and basketball.

In Detroit, major league baseball was played at the corner of Michigan and Trumbull from 1912, even as the stadium itself expanded and changed names, from Bennett Park to Navin Field to Briggs Stadium and finally to Tiger

Stadium. "The Corner," as it was nicknamed by Ernie Harwell (the Tigers longtime Hall of Fame radio broadcaster), was a long mile southwest of the heart of downtown Detroit in an area called Corktown. Corktown was known for its Irish immigrants, their modest Victorian houses, a few taverns, the Saint Boniface Catholic church, the Checker Cab garage, and the DeWitt–Spaulding lumber company. Pictures from the 1930s show the Corner packed on game days with cars and streetcars and pedestrians as the city, spurred by the success of the auto industry, grew into one of America's economic powerhouses.

The impact of discovering a green oasis in the middle of Detroit's industrial might was even greater if your seats were in the stadium's upper deck. To reach the upper deck, you walked up winding ramps to enter from the crowded concourse not through a tunnel but down a bridge suspended over the lower deck lined with wire mesh, as though you were walking in a long narrow cage. Suddenly you met the vast interior expanse from a privileged perspective above the field. The first rows of the upper-deck boxes hung out over the field itself. This is where the baseball gods sat in Tiger Stadium. At Shakespeare's Globe, they sat on the stage.

What I remember most about that first experience in 1950 has as much to do with sights and sounds and smells as with the score. The visual memories included the striking impact of the place, the dirt path that ran from the pitcher's mound to home plate (an unusual feature of the field back then that disappeared sometime in the late 1950s but was restored by Mike Ilitch when he bought the club and remains a unique feature of the Tigers' new home at Comerica Park), the late afternoon shadows, cast from the tall first base–side light towers, that spread out over the pitcher's mound. In the middle innings the mound was in the shadows while the batter's box was still in the bright sun. Even then I thought how tough it must be for the hitter to see that ball coming out of the dark and hurtling towards the light. Eventually the shadows of the upper deck would reach the plate and a balance would be restored, but not before the pitchers had an inning or two of decided advantage.

I remember the crisp slap of ball meeting glove, the solid crack of ball meeting bat before it streaked out in a straight white line over the green grass. At first I found it hard to pick up the flight of high fly balls and often misjudged their distance from the sound they made on contact. I thought they were all headed into the seats. I can still be so fooled especially when the game is on the line, my hopes are high, and a Cash or Fielder or Cabrera is at the plate. I also was enamored with the wonderful flavor of the players' names: Jerry Priddy, Johnny Lipon, Hoot Evers (an early favorite), Vic Wertz (sounds just like a power hitter), George Kell, Dizzy Trout, and, best of all, Virgil Trucks. In 1952 Trucks only won five games, but two of them were no-hitters. And, finally, the smells: of hot dogs, onions, and green peppers on the grill, peanuts newly liberated from their shells, and beer.

I picked a good year to get hooked on the Tigers as that 1950 crew was solid. Kell hit .340 and had 218 hits; Hoot Evers hit .323 with 103 RBIs; Vic Wertz hit 27 home runs with 123 RBIs; and Johnny Lipon played a steady shortstop. The starters were an impressive mix of youth and age, led by the young Art Houtteman, who went 19–12, followed by Fred Hutchinson at 17–8, Hal Newhouser at 15–13, Dizzy Trout at 13–5, and Ted Gray at 10–7. The Tigers engaged in an exciting first-place battle with the Yankees, trading the lead back and forth from May until August. They had a slim lead heading into September but faltered down the stretch, and even though they won ninety-five games (seventh best in club history) they finished second, three games out.

But 1950 was the end of a glorious Detroit competitive run that began in 1934, during which they appeared in the World Series four times and boasted their greatest players between Cobb and Kaline: Gehringer, Greenberg, Kell, Cochrane, and Newhouser, all Hall of Famers. The collapse was quick, decisive, and long-lasting. By 1952, after several disastrous trades, the club had crumbled and finished 50–104 for the then-worst record in Tiger history. But there were players to root for and follow. One of my favorites was Ray Boone.

Boone had the unenviable task of following Lou Boudreau as the shortstop for the Cleveland Indians. Boudreau, as player-manager, had led the Indians to their last World Series victory in 1948. Boone wasn't Boudreau, for which the Cleveland fans refused to excuse him, and he was soon traded to the Tigers, who moved him to third base, where he was more comfortable, and he prospered. Boone was a solid, not flashy, infielder but hit with modest power (20-plus homers a year) and was a reliable RBI man (he drove in 116 runs in 1955) even on poor Tiger teams.

He is, of course, noted for founding the most successful baseball family dynasty in the history of the game. His son Bob was a standout catcher for the Phillies and then managed both the Royals and the Reds. Bob's sons Bret and Aaron fashioned their own successful major league careers: Bret drove in 141 runs for the Mariners in 2004 and Aaron hit a crucial eleventh-inning walk-off home run against the Red Sox in 2003, sending the Yankees to the World Series and the Red Sox to yet another crushing defeat. Fifteen years later he became the manager of the Yankees. Ray Boone created a unique baseball legacy, but I remember him best for his habit (the first player I noticed doing so) of pushing the left sleeve of his jersey up almost to his shoulder when he was at the plate.

I wish he had pushed the Tigers up as high as they continued to chase the Yanks through the rest of the fifties and sixties and year after painful year they came up short until Kaline, Cash, McLain, Lolich, Horton, Freehan, and company finally brought them back to the World Series in 1968. My long ('45–'68) world championship drought was not as extended as that of Red Sox, Cubs, and Indians fans, but I took no solace from that; in fact, it never crossed my mind, as one cruelty of fandom is being oblivious to the sufferings of others.

If 1952 was the nadir in the decade-long decline in the fortunes of my Tigers, it was also my first encounter with the ways baseball (and even the Tigers) has worked its way into the fabric of American literary culture. Perhaps because I was an only child and spent those long summers in Michigan with my mother, who was an avid reader, I became one too. I was a binge reader who skipped the Hardy Boys and went straight to Erle Stanley Gardner's Perry Mason mysteries. I think I read them all, courtesy of the Lewiston, Michigan, town library, in the summer of 1951. I read everything from comic books to the Landmark series of biographies of great American historical figures written for kids to sports novels and biographies written for the same audience, such as *The Kid Who Batted 1.000* and *Player-Manager*.

Though home in Waterville and playing baseball in the summer of 1952, I discovered baseball and my team in an unexpected source: Hemingway's *The Old Man and the Sea*. My parents were both avid Hemingway readers, and they decided, rightly, that his new novella was the perfect introduction to his world for me. Like Santiago's great marlin, I was hooked and have been towed around by Hemingway ever since. It seems everywhere I have traveled, he has been there first: northern Michigan, Cuba, Paris, London, Venice and the Po Valley, Pamplona and San Sebastian, Nairobi and Kenya, Normandy. Shakespeare has taken me to most of those spots and even Japan, but not China. But if he had, Hemingway was there first.

Hemingway immediately engaged my young imagination in the novella's opening pages when Santiago's teenaged friend Manolin is trying to boost the old man's spirits after a long run of fishing bad luck. When Manolin tells Santiago that he will go net some sardines as bait for the day's fishing, the old man replies that he will sit in the sun with yesterday's newspaper, "and I will read the baseball."

"I'll be back when I have the sardines. . . . When I come back you can tell me about the baseball."
"The Yankees cannot lose."

"But I fear the Indians of Cleveland."

"Have faith in the Yankees, my son. Think of the great DiMaggio."

"I fear both the Tigers of Detroit and the Indians of Cleveland."[2]

As early as 1952 Hemingway was aware of the Cuban fascination with baseball, which subsequently spread throughout the Caribbean, with Latin ballplayers eventually coming to dominate American professional baseball. Manolin was right to fear the Indians, who won it all in 1948 (and for the last time) and had a brilliant team in 1954 that won 111 games but lost the World Series to the Giants in four games, thanks to Willie Mays's iconic catch of Vic Wertz's drive to deep center field in the Polo Grounds in the first game. But he was wrong about the Tigers, powerful from the mid-1930s to the early 1950s but about to embark on a decade of decline. As the Tigers swooned, Shakespeare came to my rescue.

SHAKESPEARE AND BASEBALL II

While I followed the team faithfully with my ear pressed close to the radio as the Tiger play-by-play announcer passed from Harry Heilmann to Van Patrick to the incomparable Ernie Harwell, and from WWJ to WJR, I discovered other compensations as one middling season gave way to another. They all arrived in the summer of 1953. After two seasons of softball, I graduated to hardball teams in what passed for Little League play in Waterville. Though not a natural athlete, I loved it. On a family vacation trip to a fishing camp in northern Ontario, my parents and I stopped at Canada's Stratford Shakespeare Festival to take in one of the plays in its inaugural season performed on a revolutionary thrust stage designed by Tanya Moiseiwitsch and constructed under an enormous circus tent.

We saw Alec Guinness as Richard III under Tyrone Guthrie's vivid direction. Though only twelve, I was engrossed.

As with my first visit to Briggs Stadium, the venue mattered. Seeing Shakespeare under a circus tent was immediately appealing. Actors scurried up and down the theater's aisles, often waving large banners. Sometimes they shouted out lines from the back of the auditorium, and other scenes were played on an upper-level playing area that jutted out fifteen feet over the lower stage, which itself poked out into the audience, who surrounded it on three sides. This was a space, under Guthrie's deft direction, that quickened the imagination. Shakespeare, from that still vivid moment, became linked with the Tigers (and fishing) as a summer pastime. Finally, Al Kaline, fresh out of his Baltimore high school, was signed by the Tigers that spring and joined the club immediately, never to leave until his death at eighty-five in 2020.

Alec Guinness and Al Kaline. What a pair. Both were consummate professionals who modestly preferred to let their play do the talking rather than their celebrity. I never met Kaline, but I admired the grace and beauty of his performance over his long and productive career. Our family did get to meet Guinness, though, when he warmly welcomed us (with a cup of tea) in his dressing room after his matinee performance in Alan Bennett's *Another Country* in London in 1977. A head-and-shoulders oil portrait of him as Richard III, painted by the noted Canadian portrait painter John Coppin, hangs in our living room, a generous wedding gift from the artist, who was a friend of my parents. A larger full-length Coppin portrait of Guinness, painted in the summer of 1953, hangs in Stratford's Festival Theatre. Guinness remembered Coppin fondly and was pleased and amused that his wry smile as Richard peered down from the walls of an Ohio family of Shakespeareans who lived in a place called Athens. We did not talk baseball, or cricket.

I played summer baseball for five years, the last three on the Waterville American Legion team. I was large and clumsy but loved being at the center of the action. No surprise that I was a catcher. My best friend in Waterville was our pitcher. Tommy Dressler was a lefty, cut from the Koufax mode. He was quiet, modest, and good. I was his opposite, a dirtbag with a big mouth. The summers we played together were baseball-rich, topped in 1956 by his only no-hitter.

We were playing a team from a Toledo suburb on their field. We took a 2–0 lead in the top of the seventh (the last inning in our league). In the bottom half, Tommy struck out the first hitter on three fastballs; the second batter hit a soft liner to second; one out to go. Tommy was as calm as I was agitated. When the next batter, a pinch-hitter, stepped into the box, I whispered that Tommy's fastball would eat him up. He shut me up by working the count to 2 and 2. I called for the curve. Tommy shook me off. I put two fingers down again and he reluctantly nodded. He broke off a beauty and the hitter waved helplessly at a pitch that ended up in my glove way wide of the strike zone. I leapt up and rumbled towards the mound. I was too big to jump into his arms and he too polite to jump into mine, so we just hugged and slapped each other on the back before our teammates joined the celebration. I have never forgotten the sweet pleasure of that moment; I was dirty hot and sweaty; he appeared as cool as frozen custard but with a shy grin on his face. He was a fine pitcher and a great batterymate and to make this tale complete, he graduated from Ohio University and became a college professor.

Shakespeare turned out to be a great batterymate too, and we have played a version of pitch and catch for over sixty-five years. My parents and I made return trips to Stratford in subsequent summers as the theater grew out of its tent and into a magnificent permanent home overlooking Canada's version of the Avon (with the requisite swans). And, as though designed for this account, several youth baseball diamonds are nestled between the theater and the river. Seeing Shakespeare on stage before I read him in high school made the text come alive. I realized that Shakespeare's rich language miraculously created character, landscape, and action in an instant. And I learned early, when confused, to read him aloud. It was magic to discover that iambic pentameter verse was meant to be spoken and followed the natural rhythm of the English language and the beat of the human heart.

Shakespeare, like baseball, transformed my teenage Waterville life in the summer of 1956. The man perhaps most responsible for the post–World War II summer Shakespeare festival explosion in America was Arthur Lithgow. He had attended Antioch College in the 1930s, went on to take an advanced degree from Cornell, and returned to Antioch after the war as a drama professor. In 1952 he created the summer Antioch Shakespeare Festival at an outdoor theater constructed at the college. In his seasons at Antioch Lithgow became the first American to direct productions of all of Shakespeare's plays. In 1956, looking to expand the festival's audience base, he headed to Toledo to perform a season of plays at an outdoor theater at the city's impressive zoo. He and his wife and family, always attracted to living off the beaten track, settled in Waterville. I don't recall being aware of their presence in our little village, but I do have vivid memories of Lithgow's productions of *Henry VIII* (the only stage production of the play I've ever seen) and *The Tempest* (my first of many).

While I met some of the actors in Lithgow's Shakespearean family, I did not meet any of his own. As an adult, I don't think it ever registered on me that John Lithgow the actor might be connected to Arthur Lithgow the producer-director until I read his autobiography. I was, of course, saddened that our paths had not crossed in Waterville when we were kids. I was five years older and caught up in playing baseball in the summer of 1956, and he, it turns out, was already working as a stagehand for his father. During the year we attended different schools. But our paths did eventually cross. In December of 2012, Susan and I were in London for several weeks when Lithgow was starring in a production of Arthur Wing Pinero's farce *The Magistrate* at the National Theatre. The National sponsors a series of Platform performances and talks, perhaps one or two a week, where actors and directors and playwrights and authors are interviewed before performances. Though ignorant of his history, we were delighted to learn that Lithgow would be interviewed about his varied and distinguished career by the National's director, Nicholas Hytner, one evening before a performance of The Magistrate.

We got tickets for both. Lithgow talked lovingly about his father and growing up with Shakespeare. In the question session after his interview, a questioner identified herself as being from Ohio and as having seen one of his father's productions. When it came time for the last question, I rose and announced from the front row of the balcony that not only was I from Ohio too, but from Waterville. Immediately Lithgow's hand flashed to his forehead to shade his eyes from the bright stage lights to see if he could pick me out. No luck. But when Susan and I came out into the lobby, there was all 6′4″ of John Lithgow beaming at us. His face fell when he realized I wasn't one of his old pals from his deep past, but he quickly recovered and was brilliantly animated as we chatted on about Waterville, his father, his early theatrical experience, and especially two of the actors (Clayton Corzatte and John Scanlan) who were regular members of his father's company and had played Ariel and Caliban in The Tempest in 1956. As he was starring on the National Theatre's Olivier stage, and its bookstore had several of my books on its Shakespeare shelf, we decided that was pretty good for two boys from tiny Waterville, Ohio. Eighteen months later Lithgow was playing King Lear in a production at New York's Delacorte Theater in Central Park, proving his remarkable versatility and range as an actor.

In the summer of 1958, my parents and I were back in Stratford for a production of Henry IV, Part One. I must confess that I had not read the play in preparation. In fact, I rarely did, a victim of teenage laziness that turned into a virtue as I first experienced Shakespeare as the Elizabethans did: in performance. Henry IV, Part One was love at first sight, though not because of Prince Hal but because of the fiery rebel Hotspur (Jason Robards Jr.) and even more so the great subversive clown Falstaff (Douglas Campbell). Falstaff was the first Shakespearean character who spoke directly to my teenage hunger to be reckless and carefree and witty. It was love at first laugh. Falstaff provides rich and rare pleasure, and I was an eager consumer. As the play unfolded, I only wanted more of fat Jack one-upping the prince and mocking the powerful.

I got more when I went off to Hamilton College that fall and discovered that two of the texts in the freshman writing seminar were Henry IV, Parts I and II. Reading both plays made me realize Prince Hal's centrality to the developing narrative and the way each part ends with his triumph over one of his two dazzling rivals, Hotspur on the military battlefield at Shrewsbury in Part I, Falstaff on the political battlefield at Hal's coronation as Henry V in Part II. I celebrated him for the former but felt betrayed by the latter. However, I began to understand why Detroit's great lefty, Newhouser, was nicknamed "Prince Hal." Like Shakespeare's Prince, Newhouser had a wicked fastball and a reputation for wildness, but just as he had the hitter expecting the heater, he'd dispatch him by throwing a wicked curve. The wicked curve with which Hal dispatched Falstaff, the brilliant old rogue never saw coming. Neither did I.

Newhouser, the dominant American League pitcher of the 1940s, had to wait until 1992 before the Veteran's Committee elected him to the Hall of Fame. I went up to Detroit several years later for the game in which he was honored by the Tigers and his number (16) retired, joining those of Gehringer, Greenberg, Kell, and Kaline displayed on the facing of the third deck above right field (no Ty Cobb number as the players did not wear numbers in his era). Newhouser was driven around the warning track sitting on the back of a convertible. He had grown frail and wore sunglasses to protect failing eyes, but the face had not changed from our first encounter over forty years before; it was still sharp and thin and crafty. I next saw that face on his plaque in Cooperstown and was pleased to discover that underneath his name, in parentheses, was his nickname: Prince Hal.

Part 2

The 1960s

Part of baseball's allure is the way in which its past is always present. No Tiger fan of my generation came of age without the awareness of Harry Heilmann and Ty Cobb, Mickey Cochrane and Schoolboy Rowe, and Hank Greenberg and Charlie Gehringer. They were all gone by the time I pledged my allegiance, and soon George Kell and Hal Newhouser would depart, but the momentary vacuum of Tiger greats was quickly filled when Al Kaline joined the team in 1953. Kaline got me through high school, college, marriage, kids, and graduate school. Then, after a long and eventful career, he departed directly into the Hall of Fame on the first ballot. At almost the same moment the kids, Alan Trammell and Lou Whitaker, arrived at the Corner, and they took me deep into my maturity.

Baseball is a game made for radio much as football and golf belong to television. Radio diminishes the distance between the fan and the park. For those of us in the neighborhood or far away in exile, the game came to us in our ears and played out in our mind's eye. Announcers often became the club's most valuable player: Red Barber, Mel Allen, and Vin Scully are classic examples. The Tigers had a Hall of Fame voice in their league: Ernie Harwell. Like many fans, most of my experience with my club was via the radio, and from the time I headed to Indiana for my graduate work in 1962, until that game in the summer of 1976, I was absent from Tiger Stadium. Absent but not missing in action thanks to Detroit's WJR, a powerful fifty-watt station, and Ernie Harwell's soft Georgia lilt in my ear. Sometimes, given the wind and the weather, it arrived through static and crackle, but the way it faded in and out only contributed to the excitement and tension of the game experienced in the gaps of clarity between the static.

Between September of 1961 and September of 1972, I only saw four major league baseball games in person. None were in Detroit and only one featured the Tigers. But that one was a heartbreaker. Between 1950 and 1968 the Tigers made only two serious runs at the American League championship: 1961 and 1967. In '67 they chased the Red Sox to the last games (a doubleheader) of the season before losing. In the great summer of '61 they had a season-long battle with the Mantle-Maris Yanks. Mantle and Maris provided a remarkable long-ball competition culminating in Maris breaking Babe Ruth's record of 60 home runs, which had stood for thirty-four years. Maris was the first to topple one of the game's iconic records. He would be followed by Hank Aaron, who broke Ruth's career home run record of 714 in 1974; by Pete Rose, who broke Ty Cobb's all-time hit record of 4,191 in 1985; and Cal Ripken Jr., who topped Lou Gehrig's seemingly invincible consecutive-games-played record of 2,130 in 1995. I leave what to say about McGwire, Sosa, and Bonds to the baseball historians.

The 1961 American League race was baseball at its best. If the Yanks had the "M and M Boys," the Tigers matched them with the "Cannon Corps": Kaline, Cash, and Colavito. Because Maris's feat was accomplished as a Yankee in the country's biggest media market, most baseball fans know that Maris not only hit 61 home runs but drove in 141, while Mantle hit 54, drove in 128, and hit .317. But few probably remember that Norm Cash led the league in hitting with a .361 average while slamming 41 homers and driving in 132, that Rocky Colavito hit .290 with 45 home runs and 140 RBIs, and that Kaline chipped in with a .324 average, 19 homers, and 82 RBIs.

The race was decided by a three-game Labor Day series in Yankee Stadium, which started with the 88–45 Yanks holding a two-and-a-half-game lead over the 86–48 Tigers. The Tigers came into the weekend on an 11–4 roll. I had been invited by a couple of friends to spend some time in that late August sailing (with the help of a captain and first mate) a fifty-four-foot gaffe-rigged schooner up the Eastern Seaboard from New Bedford, Massachusetts (Melville territory), to Maine and back again. I convinced them at the end of our sail that we should return to Ohio via New York to catch at least a game of the big showdown. My Hamilton College roommate was a New Yorker, and his generous father managed to get us first-row box seats out in the second deck in left field.

Though the season still had almost a month to go, it was clear this was to be the big series between the two clubs. The buzz of the huge crowd that greeted us when we arrived at the stadium had the aura of an exciting stretch-run encounter. Whitey Ford versus Don Mossi. Two smooth left-handers, each having a strong season. Ford's distinguished career was at its zenith (he would go 25–4 in 1961, his greatest season), while Mossi's had been revived by a trade from the Indians to the Tigers in 1960. The Tigers had taken him out of the bullpen and made him a starter, and he had a 14–3 record when he matched up against Ford. Yogi Berra was in his sixteenth season with the Yanks and no longer catching but getting most of his playing time in left field. The Yankee lineup was filled with familiar names: Boyer, Kubek, Richardson, and Skowron in the infield, Elston Howard, the Yankees' first African American player, behind the plate, and Maris and Mantle joining Berra in the outfield.

The Tigers were anchored by Kaline, Cash, and Colavito, but they were supported by the wonderful center fielder Billy Bruton, whose great days had been with the Milwaukee Braves, the young, promising second baseman Jake Wood, and Steve Boros at third. The game remained scoreless into

the seventh, when, with one out and a runner on first, Kaline
hit a sharp line drive down into the corner in left directly
below us. I thought that he had a certain double, especially
with Berra—not a natural outfielder—having to the dig the
ball out in the corner. But Yogi proved again why he was to
be a Hall of Famer by getting to the ball quickly and making
a clean line drive catcher's peg to Richardson at second to
nail Kaline. The fans around us stood and erupted, chanting
"Yogi . . . Yogi . . . Yogi" as Berra humbly repositioned himself in the field. Colavito walked but Norm Cash popped up
to end the inning. Mossi continued his mastery by retiring
the Yanks in the eighth. In the bottom of the ninth he got
Maris on a fly to right, struck out Mantle, and then Howard and Berra singled and Skowron singled home the game-
winning run, and just like that the game was over.

I knew before the game that this one was crucial. If they
lost, the Tigers would need to win the next two. And I knew
that a close loss might prove devastating. And so it was, for
me and for the Tigers. Despite a brilliant game by Mossi,
when for eight-plus innings victory was just within our
reach, the Yanks went on to sweep the series, beginning a
thirteen-game winning streak for them and an eight-game
losing streak for the Tigers. The pennant race was over, as
the Yankees finished the season with a 109–53 record, second in team history at that time only to the famed 1927
team, which won 110. But the Tigers rebounded to go 10–2
down the stretch to finish 101–61, the most wins in their
history, topped eventually only by the World Series winners
in 1968 (103) and 1984 (104).

The long drive back to Toledo the next day was miser-
able. I sulked in the back seat while my two non-Tiger-fan
pals, oblivious to the ways in which baseball can break your
heart, chatted away about the great sailing we had had, the
wonders of Provincetown, the gustatory glories of fresh
lobster shorts, and the allure of the nubile young lasses on
Nantucket. Who gave a honk about sailing (or lobsters or
lasses) when the Tiger season had just been torpedoed by an
old catcher finding new life in left field?

The Tigers weren't serious competitors again until the summer of '67. They had continued to build around Kaline and Cash with important additions in Bill Freehan behind the plate, Jim Northrup and Mickey Stanley in the outfield, and Mickey Lolich and Denny McLain on the mound. Colavito was gone, replaced by Willie Horton—Detroit's first great homegrown Black player—in left. They engaged in a season-long three-way struggle for the pennant that came down to the final game of the season, when they were nipped by the Red Sox. The Red Sox were led by Jim Lonborg on the mound and Carl Yastrzemski at the plate. Yaz won the AL Triple Crown and remained the last person to do so until Miguel Cabrera's magnificent 2012 season for the Tigers. Both hitters got their clubs to the World Series, but both lost.

Nineteen sixty-seven was not the Summer of Love in Detroit, when the city went up in flames and the Tigers lost the pennant to the Red Sox on the last day of the season. The devastating race riots were provoked by a police raid on a blind pig, an after-hours joint. The cops, rather than discovering the usual dozen or so drinkers and card players, found the pig packed with men celebrating the return of several locals from service in Vietnam. The police got rough, the place exploded, and the melee spilled out into the street. Suddenly the neighborhood and then the city were on fire.

The next day, with smoke from those fires visible from the Corner, Willie Horton, the Tigers' fine outfielder and Detroit native, left Tiger Stadium after a game with the Yankees and, still in his uniform, drove to the Twelve Mile Road area, where the trouble had begun and where he had once lived. He climbed up onto his car's roof and tried to calm the crowd. But his brave pleas went unheeded and the riot spread. The next day his teammate Mickey Lolich, a member of the Michigan National Guard, was called up and was soon patrolling the streets in downtown Detroit. A unique moment in baseball and American social history. Over the next five days the city burned. Forty-three died and over fourteen hundred buildings were destroyed. A year later, perhaps, as many think due to the success of the '68 Tigers, Detroit did not repeat such carnage even as many other American inner cities went wild in response to the assassinations of Martin Luther King Jr. and Robert Kennedy and the escalating protests about the war in Vietnam. While Detroit burned, my life thrived, with Shakespeare very much at its center.

SHAKESPEARE AND BASEBALL III

My fifteen-year absence from Tiger Stadium was a result of having turned a major corner in my life, into graduate work, my marriage to Susan, our years together in Bloomington completing our PhDs, the arrival of our children, and the start of our careers at Ohio University. Those years were often baseball-poor but were always Shakespeare-rich. I met Susan in a seminar on Shakespeare's comedies taught by C. L. Barber. Shakespeare and his contemporaries became a prime focus of my graduate work, and Barber became a mentor to us both. He arrived at Indiana in 1962 as the new chair of its English Department with his prize-winning book *Shakespeare's Festive Comedy* just out (1959) from the Princeton University Press.

At the same moment I arrived fresh from Hamilton College with no prizes and little notion if I had the talent or the discipline for graduate work. I wanted to teach but had only marginal confidence that I had the intellectual skills to complete a PhD in English so I could qualify to teach at the university level. My only claim to modest college fame was that, as a senior, I had been the director of the college's dramatic society, the Charlatans. Alexander Woollcott, a noted New York City drama critic and a member of the famed Round Table group who met regularly at the Algonquin Hotel, was one of my predecessors. Hamilton, like Oxford and Cambridge, had no drama program and entrusted the selection and production of the year's plays to the Charlatans. I had the pleasure of selecting, producing, and directing a season ranging from Ben Jonson's *The*

Alchemist to a powerful double bill of one-act plays, Clifford Odets's *Waiting for Lefty* and Edward Albee's *Zoo Story*, to Sam and Bella Spivak's Broadway comedy *We're No Angels* to a shortened version of *A Midsummer Night's Dream*.

I loved Shakespeare, admired several of my professors, and enjoyed the rhythms and routines of college life. I was self-aware enough to realize that I did not possess the talents as an actor or director to find a life in the American professional theater as it existed in the 1950s. But I thought those same modest talents might make me a successful classroom presence, where, as one wit once cracked about teaching Shakespeare: "It's the ideal job. You get to play all the parts and grade the audience." I also knew that if I wanted to teach at the college level, the PhD was the union card. I applied to graduate programs in English at several midwestern universities, and Indiana took a chance on me. I headed to Bloomington having never heard of C. L. Barber, who turned out to be among the most noted American Shakespearean critics of the second half of the twentieth century, and a remarkable man and mentor.

Barber graduated from Harvard in the mid-thirties, spent a year at Oxford, and then returned to Harvard as a Junior Fellow (a three-year fellowship program meant to replace or rival the PhD degree). He was mentored, as an undergraduate, by F. O. Matthiessen, who had just published his book on T. S. Eliot and was beginning to work on his monumental *American Renaissance*, focusing on the leading American authors of the mid-nineteenth century: Hawthorne, Melville, Whitman, Emerson, and Thoreau. Matthiessen had a capacious mind which moved with ease and critical sophistication from Shakespeare and the Elizabethans through the writers of the American Renaissance to Henry James and T. S. Eliot. He also included students in his circle of friends and announces in his preface to *American Renaissance* that the three readers he had most in mind while writing it were Harry Levin, Howard Baker, and C. L. Barber—all former students. One would be hard pressed to discover another major work of literary criticism whose author confessed that his ideal readers were three recent undergraduates. Matthiessen was also a noted social and academic harbinger as he was both gay and socialist.

Barber had a similar capacity to carry on a spirited critical conversation between past and present, and his mind, like Matthiessen's, moved powerfully between a literary text and its cultural and historical context. He too moved easily between Shakespeare and Eliot, Marlowe and Joyce, cultural anthropology and Freud. His own student years at Harvard and then post–World War II years as a faculty member at Amherst had been founded on stimulating social and intellectual interaction between faculty and students. Such exchanges were a necessary ingredient of the natural rhythm of his life. He was socially gregarious and wore his substantial learning lightly. He loved books and ideas and conversation gently lubricated by strong drink and good wine, but unlike Matthiessen he was not a prolific publisher, though he wrote all the time. He only published one book in his lifetime, with two others appearing posthumously. His only flaw, for me, was his inability to embrace Dickens's genius, a fate true of many New Critics, who found Dickens hopelessly mawkish and sentimental. James Joyce was his man, and he taught a senior seminar on *Ulysses* every year at Amherst.

We were immediately compatible. Barber loved engaging with students, and my Hamilton experience had made me comfortable interacting with faculty in office chats and social situations. And we had Shakespeare to share. I had a vivacious and challenging Shakespeare professor at Hamilton, Edwin Barrett, who had been particularly good in his reading of the comedies, often treated as lesser works than the tragedies. Not for Barrett and not for Barber. Barrett was a dynamic classroom presence with beautifully expressive hands and an infectious laugh. Barber worked best at the head of a seminar table, where his gracious manner, quick mind, and uncanny ability to latch onto short passages from Shakespeare (often quoting them from memory) and then to expand on their interpretive reach to speak for larger issues at work in the play was impressive. He encouraged us to do likewise (including asking us to read our passages out loud) and had an unerring instinct for helping us to see how our passages related to other moments in the play and in contemporary Shakespeare criticism as well.

In our seminar, I often offered up ideas I had first encountered in Professor Barrett's class. Barber's response was almost always positive. Hamilton had certainly prepared me for Barber, while Amherst, I think, had prepared Barber for me. We shared not only Shakespeare but also a rich appreciation of comedy in literature and life. I did not regard myself as a great student, but I somehow had little difficulty interacting with my professors as though we were colleagues. I did not hesitate to challenge their ideas in the give and take of social conversation. This, of course, was sheer folly in many of my encounters with most profs, but not with Barber, who seemed to delight in my chutzpah. Like Shakespeare, Barber could be ironic, and he was alive to Shakespearean ambiguity (irony and *ambiguity* being key critical terms for the New Criticism), but also like Shakespeare he was naturally generous and rarely cynical. I was a naive kid, but instinctively shared an innate suspicion of cynicism as demonstrating the defensive mechanism of a damaged ego. It is a pose often struck in the academy (and in the Forest of Arden when Jaques is presiding), and I rarely found it appealing.

Sometime in the middle of the term Barber asked me to be his research assistant on a new edition of the comedies he was working on for *The Riverside Shakespeare*, one of the leading single-volume editions of the complete works. Even though Barber's participation in this project ultimately came to naught, we spent several hours each morning in the early summer of 1963 going through each of the early comedies deciding which of the former editor's notes to keep, which to eliminate, and what new ones to add. We read passages aloud to each other, discussed for far too long decisions about notes, and reveled in Shakespeare's achievement even in his two earliest comedies: *The Comedy* of *Errors* and *The Two Gentleman of Verona*. It was a wonderful and unique master-apprentice relationship, but it was also a short-lived folly. In mid-July he went off to vacation with his family on an island off the coast of Maine, and I worked away on the annotations but spent most of my time wooing Susan Richardson.

What I did not know was that *The Riverside's* publisher, Houghton Mifflin, was expecting all of Barber's introductions and annotations to the comedies to be completed by the end of the summer. Some of the other editors (Frank Kermode, for example, who was doing the tragedies) had already finished their assignments and had shared them with us. Instead, by the end of August he had only completed the intros to two plays and I the annotations for just three. Barber rightly sensed that I was not the man who would manage to whip through the annotations for the rest of the comedies while teaching and taking courses in the fall. He was also acutely aware that he had the administrative demands of the chair's job as well as the desire to begin reworking a book-length manuscript on Christopher Marlowe and Freud he had completed the year before while on leave at the Institute for Advanced Studies at Princeton, and so he withdrew from the project.

I was filled with a mixture of guilt and relief. Barber was his usual generous self in taking all the blame, saying he had reservations about his participation in the edition from the start and that he knew, given the pace at which he worked, it would take several more summers for him to complete the introductions. He was happy and relieved to be free of the project, and our relationship became even stronger when he learned that my wooing of Susan had been more successful than our collaboration on the comedies and that we were planning to marry. Barber was delighted as Susan possessed a nuanced critical mind which expressed itself in prose like that of her dissertation subject, Henry James. So, for Barber, our summer of work was ending as a comedy should: in a wedding. I must confess it was not until late in my own career that I came to realize, when working on a project for

The Norton Shakespeare, how much potential royalty income Barber had sacrificed.

Barber and his wife, Betty, continued to include us in mixed graduate student-faculty receptions at their house for visiting speakers. At such gatherings one or both of us met Stanley Edgar Hyman and Shirley Jackson, Robert Brustein (then a young modern drama professor at Columbia and the author of *Theater of Revolt*), the poet Richard Wilbur, and, most engagingly, Joseph Papp, the founder of the New York Shakespeare Festival. We also were invited for small dinner parties, where inevitably, as the six or eight of us were finishing the last bottle of wine, the T. S. Eliot came down off the shelf and we all took turns reading passages from *The Waste Land* and *Four Quartets* aloud. And we entertained the Barbers in return. During our friendship Barber and I spoke of many things, from Wagner's *Parsifal* to experimental education and his role in the creation of Hampshire College, to Joyce and Pound and Eliot, to Shakespeare in performance, and to Indiana basketball, in which he had developed a keen interest. But never baseball.

I once played against him (graduate students versus faculty) in a departmental softball game (the grad students lost; we weren't stupid and the faculty were wired to win), but I don't recall that he and I ever talked baseball. He died, way too soon, of throat cancer in 1980. I never got to ask him if, given his years in Cambridge and Amherst, he was a Red Sox fan. Even if he was not, I like to think that he must have admired Ted Williams, surely along with Babe Ruth the most Shakespearean of modern ballplayers: the Babe, a version of Falstaff in spikes, and Williams (himself a warrior), a proud, defiant embodiment of Coriolanus refusing to show his scars (or tip his hat) to the Boston fans and sportswriters.

My early fascination with Falstaff was deepened by Barber's work on *Henry IV, Parts One and Two* in *Shakespeare's Festive Comedy*, where the character is associated with the Lord of Misrule figure in holiday carnival. Barber's book exposes and explores a rich vein in the relationship between social ritual and Shakespeare's sophisticated comic art. Falstaff

and his subversive relationship to power in the persons of
the king and his son, Prince Hal, becomes a central figure in
Shakespeare's development. Here is how Barber concludes
his analysis of this material, in a passage revealing the power
and grace of his prose and the depth of his thinking about
Shakespeare, literature, and life:

> Historically, Shakespeare's drama can be seen as part
> of the process by which our culture has moved from
> absolutist modes of thought towards a historical and
> psychological view of man. But though the Renaissance
> moment made the tension between a magical and
> empirical view of man particularly acute, this pull is
> of course always present: it is the tension between the
> heart and the world. By incarnating ritual as plot and
> character, the dramatist finds an embodiment for the
> heart's drastic gestures while recognizing how the world
> keeps comically and tragically giving them the lie.[3]

After his years as chair, Barber left Indiana, lured for
a year to Smith College, where his only responsibility was
to give a series of lectures based upon his expansion of his
manuscript on Marlowe's plays into a work on the origins of
Elizabethan tragedy. He eventually headed back to his own
origins in northern California by becoming the vice provost for the humanities at the newly created University of
California at Santa Cruz, allowing him the opportunity to
influence new ideas about educational structures and cur-
riculums he had first explored in The New College Plan that
had led to the creation of Hampshire College.

While he was engaged with imagining UC–Santa Cruz,
I was settling into my teaching career at Ohio University,
where I developed an early (perhaps the first) course devoted exclusively to Shakespeare on film in the country.
That course, via Orson Welles's great film using the Falstaff
material, Chimes at Midnight, linked my Shakespearean beginnings at Stratford and Hamilton with my work with Barber
at Indiana, and led to the writing of my first mature essay,
"The Long Good-Bye: Welles and Falstaff."

A version of that essay was accepted to be presented at the Shakespeare Association of America meeting held in San Francisco in April of 1979, with Barber presiding as president of the association that year. He was delighted; I was thrilled. My paper session was chaired by Al Kernan, a distinguished Shakespearean who had taught at both Yale and Princeton. The audience was filled with major figures in the field and many younger scholars interested in the nascent field of Shakespeare on film, many of whom would go on to be among my closest scholarly friends.

One of our closest graduate student friends in Bloomington, Peter Weltner (also a Hamilton graduate), was also in attendance as he was now an English professor at San Francisco State. He generously shared his apartment up near Coit Tower overlooking the bay with us while we were in town. The casual and sometimes intense conversations I had with Peter at Indiana, especially when we were both teaching the Great Books course, were inspiring because they were so natural and transparent. The two-course sequence included works from the ancient Greeks to the American present, ranging from Plato and Sophocles to Dante and Shakespeare to Joyce and Faulkner. In my teaching, I probably stole as much about Shakespeare from Weltner as I did from Barber. They still resonate, though as with Barber, we never talked about baseball. That experience reminds me that we often learn as much from our friends and fellow students as we do from our profs.

The paper turned out to be a success because it explored terrific material (Welles and Shakespeare), made hyperbolic claims for *Chimes at Midnight* as being the foundational Shakespeare film, and was delivered by a former actor performing at 9 a.m. on a Saturday morning before a crowd of slightly woozy Shakespeareans. Welles and Falstaff and I roused them from their late-night revels, where they, too, had heard the chimes at midnight. One of the audience members was John Andrews, the editor of *Shakespeare Quarterly*, the most prestigious journal in the field. He introduced himself after the session and suggested I send SQ the longer essay from which the paper was derived. I did. The essay received positive responses, with suggestions for revision from its readers, and was subsequently accepted for publication. It was the first essay on a Shakespeare film to be published by the journal. A still of Welles as Falstaff graced the cover of the Fall 1980 issue and heralded a new genre in Shakespeare studies.

As the poet Keats rightly understood, the Shakespearean fruit is bittersweet. As the essay was undergoing the final review process in the early winter of 1980, C. L. Barber was diagnosed with throat cancer and died suddenly in April. When he had stepped down from his administrative duties at UC–Santa Cruz the previous summer, he had written to me with his customary optimism: "My days used to be an alley to get through; now they are a space to move in." The space he planned to move in included co-teaching a Shakespeare seminar at Berkeley with Norman Rabkin and beginning to assemble, in collaboration with his former student Richard Wheeler, the work he had already done on his long-planned study of Shakespeare's career as a playwright, The Whole Journey: Shakespeare's Power of Development. It was not to be, though in a generous act of scholarly cooperation, Wheeler did manage to bring the manuscript to fruition, and it was posthumously published by the University of California Press.

I later learned that Barber spent his last sessions with his doctors, who were devastated that the cancer was inoperable, consoling them about their concern for his condition. But the bitter Shakespearean magic sometimes can be sweet. More than twenty years later, I arrived at my Ellis Hall office to discover a package from W. W. Norton and Company in my mailbox. Norton, the largest publisher of literary texts and anthologies in America, had long published a series of major individual texts called the Norton Critical Editions. Such editions contained the text, a section called Contexts and Sources, and another called Criticism, which reprinted what the editor of the individual volume regarded as the best of the critical responses to the work since it was written.

My package contained a new third version of the Norton Critical Edition of Shakespeare's 1 Henry IV. I smiled, pleased that our Norton representative had sent the new edition to me even though I had an earlier one, and put it on my desk. It soon got covered with other books and papers. Several days later I tried to bring some order to my desktop and discovered the Norton. I opened it to the table of contents and glanced down the list of essays included in the Criticism section, which began with excerpts from John Dryden and Samuel Johnson and continued with seminal essays by J. Dover Wilson, E. M. W. Tillyard, Sigurd Burckhardt, Stephen Greenblatt, and Coppelia Kahn, among others. I was stunned to discover my Welles and Falstaff essay included in such ravishing company. Better yet, it was cheek by jowl with Barber's great essay on the play, "Mingling Kings and Clowns."

As deeply satisfying thrills go, I did not think anything could top Kirk Gibson's eighth-inning home run in game 5 of the 1984 World Series, but in the world of professional Shakespeareans this moment was more than the equivalent of a Series-clinching home run. I looked back to see who the new editor was. It was Gordon McMullan, a young Shakespearean at King's College in London, and he immediately became, for me, the best young Shakespearean in the world. A year later we had lunch together at Orzo (Joe Allen's sister restaurant just off the Strand in London), where he was pleased to learn that I had been a student of Barber's and that he had played an unexpected role in bringing our relationship full circle. McMullan scripted one of those rare moments where the personal and the professional mingle, like Shakespeare's kings and clowns, to enrich the drama of a literary life.

My intellectual and cultural experience at Indiana was deeply engaging, but what made it all possible for me was our marriage and the opportunity to teach. In large PhD programs the graduate students teach the freshman composition courses, and then some move on to teaching sections of the beginning literature courses as well. I knew from the first class I taught that I had found my space. I had to grind out almost every seminar paper I wrote, but I was a natural as a teacher. It took me years to find my voice on paper, but I had it from the start in the classroom. It was my green field. On the other hand, I labored over the dissertation. Barber had left and because I dawdled two other directors who had agreed to take me on had time to leave to be the chairs at Michigan State and Rutgers. I was rescued by Don Gray, as were many others over his years at Indiana, who was an ideal director. He returned chapters promptly, always with improving suggestions. He taught me in the margins.

I never shared my passion for the Tigers with Barber or with Don Gray: for that I had another Indiana prof, James Cox. The same term Susan and I met in Barber's class she was also taking a seminar in the nineteenth-century American novel from Professor Cox. Cox was already a legend among the graduate students. He was the most dynamic lecturer in the department and known to be working on what would become the definitive critical work on Mark Twain: *The Fate of Humor*. If Barber was a product of the New England educated elite, Cox came from old farming stock in the Virginia mountains. The family farm was located outside of Independence, tucked into the southwest corner of the state near the borders with both North Carolina and Tennessee. Cox used to joke that he came not from the Deep South but from the High South. Barber went from Phillips Exeter Academy to Harvard to Amherst to service as a naval officer in the Pacific during World War II and back to Amherst. Cox, twelve years his junior, went directly from high school to the war, also seeing service in the Pacific, but as a sailor. After the war, Cox went to the University of Michigan on the GI Bill. Like many of his generation he found the study of American literature a new field to be fought and won. And like my Tiger mother, Cox became a Detroit Tiger fan in his Ann Arbor years.

On the surface it might appear that Barber and Cox came to the profession from two different directions. But Barber was not strictly a product of the Eastern establishment. C. L. stood for Cesar Lombardi (he was universally known as "Joe"). He was born in California, not New England. His father was an officer in the First World War, was fluent in several European languages, and was sent back to Europe after the war as a diplomat. He and the family eventually settled in Washington. As I mentioned, Barber's mentor at Harvard, F. O. Matthiessen was an Americanist and, along with John Crowe Ransom and Lionel Trilling, was one of the founders of the Kenyon School of English. Another was Michigan's Austin Warren, who recommended to Cox that he attend the Kenyon program in the summer of 1952, when he took a seminar from the greatest of all American critics of his age, Kenneth Burke. Cox loved Burke and so did Barber. Burke thought that the study of literature was "equipment for living," a proposition Barber openly embraced, as did Cox, though more cautiously. Several years later, when Cox debated about returning to school to work on a PhD, he thought of the Kenyon program, which had relocated to Indiana University and been rechristened the School of Letters. So he headed to Bloomington. The first School of Letters course Cox took was taught by Leslie Fiedler, for whom *Huckleberry Finn* was a key mythological archetype of American literature.

When Cox graduated from Indiana he was hired as a young nontenure track faculty member at Dartmouth. When his three years in Hanover were up, Indiana immediately hired him (a rare phenomenon, as most graduate programs do not hire their own), and by 1962 he had been tenured and promoted to associate professor and had just finished a year at Berkeley working with its extensive collection of Mark Twain's papers. He had a broad, open face with a mop of curly, sandy-colored hair. His speaking style was reminiscent of a southern evangelical preacher, but his subject matter was the democratic promise and peril of nineteenth-century American literature. His lectures created a stunning American drama played out between Hawthorne, Melville, Emerson, Thoreau, Whitman, and Twain (with Jefferson and

Lincoln in key supporting roles) and were standing room only. Befitting a Twain scholar and one bold enough to title his book *The Fate of Humor*, his own sense of humor was powerful and playfully subversive. He enjoyed Twain's humor and his own in equal measure. Many of the graduate students (including Susan, who had planned for Cox to direct her dissertation) were crushed when he announced in the spring of '63 that he was leaving Indiana to return to Dartmouth, where he taught for the rest of his professional life.

In 1996, years after leaving Indiana, I was giving a paper at the Shakespeare Association of America conference, being held that year in Los Angeles. One of the Shakespeareans I most enjoyed sharing time with at these gatherings was also one of its most unique, Ralph Cohen. Cohen managed to juggle two careers, one as an academic, the other as the founding director of the Shenandoah Shakespeare Express, now known as the American Shakespeare Theater. Cohen and I shared a passion not only for Shakespeare in performance but for baseball as well. We could not resist playing hooky, along with professors Herb and Judith Weil, from the conference and taking in a Dodgers game at their inviting home in Chavez Ravine.

Baseball's pace, as Bill Veeck so wisely noted, provides a setting for "the American love of gregariousness." Baseball invites conversation, and, as the game was not tight, it allowed us to catch up with one another between pitches. He wanted to know what it had been like to study with Barber, whose reputation as a Shakespearean had only grown after his early death, at sixty-seven, in 1980. When I asked Cohen where he had done his undergraduate work, he said, "Dartmouth."

I immediately responded, "Did you have Jim Cox?"

"He's the reason I'm sitting here." He laughed, a bit stunned at a name I had plucked seemingly out of the blue. Cohen went to Dartmouth in 1963 as a business major, but, as he went on to reveal, "I did take an American lit class from Cox and at the end of that term I switched my major to English. His example, the penetrating vitality and extravagant good humor of his teaching, was so powerful and persuasive it made the study of literature seem irresistible. I then took a Shakespeare class and was hooked, but it was Cox who got me to Shakespeare." It seems fatefully fitting that when Cohen came to establish a permanent home for his Shakespeare company (which had been initially a traveling group of players), he did so in Staunton, Virginia, only a two-hour drive away on the Blue Ridge Parkway from Cox's farm at Independence. Baseball and Shakespeare now linked, at least for me, with Virginia, Cox, and the American experience.

Jim Cox's American journey from post–World War II GI Bill college degrees to eminent scholar and charismatic professor of American literature comes to vivid life in this tribute to the New Criticism in his last book:

> After the war, when the schools rapidly expanded, the New Criticism—as we have come to know it—was in an ideal position to be recognized. Freeing the text from the social, political, and national interests that had held it in bondage, the New Critics offered what was essentially a practical criticism, affording what seemed—after a surfeit of propaganda—a chance for both student and text to speak to each other. The text thus became a space of volatile energy, generating not only potentialities of interpretation but also possibilities of power for the individual reader.[4]

My good friend from Hamilton and fellow graduate student at Indiana Mike Kaiser had Cox's survey course in the fall of '62 and was mesmerized; Susan had his graduate seminar in the winter of '63 and wrote the paper on Henry James that became the core of her dissertation; I only had Cox for the Tigers. In the few encounters we had at faculty–graduate student parties, I quickly realized that Cox was relieved to be talking baseball and the Tigers rather than Hawthorne and Melville (or Hemingway and Faulkner) with current or former students wanting more from the oracle. We went back and forth on about the accomplishments of Greenberg and Gehringer (whom he had seen) and Newhouser and Kell (whom we shared). We both were great fans of a terrific, but little-known, Tiger pitcher in the 1950s, Frank Lary, who had a special talent for defeating the Yankees.

He was pleased, and a bit astounded, that I had been in Yankee Stadium for that fateful game in early September of 1961 when the Yanks and the Tigers were locked in a tight pennant race and the Yanks won 1–0 on a walk-off single by Bill Skowron. He, in his best definitive manner, declared it the most crucial game in Detroit baseball history between 1945 and the last game of 1967 (when by losing they lost the pennant to Boston). There was also a shared sense that we both felt slightly out of place in academia, Cox because, like Falstaff's, his subversive humor could not be contained, and me because while I felt at home with Shakespeare, I still felt a bit out of my league with the rest of the literary enterprise. Baseball and the Tigers let us both return to the world of Huck and Jim on that raft floating down the Mississippi and into trouble. Though truth be told, we probably were much closer to the King and the Duke.

When John Seelye (a noted American lit prof at the University of Connecticut) presented Cox with the Hubbell Medal, the American Literature Association's greatest honor, at the Modern Language Association meeting in Toronto in 1997, Susan and I were there. The room was packed, and Seelye reminisced about his first meeting with Cox at Berkeley back in 1961. Seelye was then a young assistant professor whom Cox immediately befriended and absorbed into his world. Seelye got Cox just right when he observed that "he somehow made you feel part of a conspiracy against the dunces who made up the large part of the department [laugh], indeed any department [bigger laugh], indeed the entire profession [biggest laugh]. He made you feel that you and he were part of a knowing and affectionate community, a kind of low-wattage illuminati, like that immortal pair on the raft." This is how Cox made me feel as a beginning graduate student, as if we constituted a small (just large enough for a raft) secret society of Tiger fans while the "dunces" in the room "come and go talking of Michelangelo." Cox was in the navy in World War II, and his raft was a submarine in which he undoubtedly made his affectionate but subversive humor work in a submerged and tense environment.

Susan and Mike were of course sad to lose their favorite prof; I was sorry to miss the opportunity to have a class from Cox, but even sadder that I had lost a Tiger fan. We did exchange a few letters over the next four years, largely agonizing over our club's failure to build upon the strong 1961 season. Cox and his family spent a sabbatical year in Florence in 1966, and he wrote us a marvelous letter about the Arno's massive flood that year, which swamped the city, the river extracting its revenge on Twain (the man of the mighty Mississippi) for his belittling remarks on its puny path in Innocents Abroad. Twain could not resist calling the Arno "a great historical creek" which "would be a very plausible river if they would pump some water in it." Twain got his limp jest; the Twain scholar got the rampaging water.

The Tigers came within a game of the World Series in 1967. The next summer they were determined not to let another solid season crumble in the last days of September. I listened to Ernie Harwell's butter-pecan ice cream voice melting each evening into the hot muggy Bloomington nights and bringing me the late innings of the games in the explosive and tragic spring and summer of 1968.

I had imagined that I would have to survive the 1968 season on my own without a fellow fan to share the daily triumphs and failures with. Miranda and Sam were three and one, not yet ready to be drafted into Tiger fandom. But the baseball (and literature) gods work in odd and sometimes wondrous ways, for in the summer of '68 Jim Cox had been invited back to Indiana to teach in the School of Letters, the program that had originally lured him to the university as a student.

By 1968 Susan and I had finished our coursework, passed our comprehensive PhD exams, and were at work on our dissertations while I had a full-time tenure-track position at Indiana University's campus in Indianapolis. It was too late for me to turn back the clock and take Cox's class (though Susan and I sat in on several), but more importantly, I had him for a companion as the Tigers rolled towards their first pennant since 1945. We found time most days to hash over the previous night's game. Denny McLain's dominating performance throughout the summer, when he became the last pitcher to win 30 or more games in a season, drew our particular attention. We knew that his crazy off-field antics, organ-playing engagements wrapped around quick trips to Las Vegas, might well blow up in his face under the glare of the World Series spotlight. Cox kept insisting that we needed to keep our attention equally fixed on the quirky, potbellied Mickey Lolich (the Tigers' number-two starter, a smooth-throwing left-hander), and in this, as well as in many other things, he proved to be prophetic.

THE 1968 WORLD SERIES

Nineteen sixty-eight was a tragic year for America and Americans. For me, for Cox, for Detroit, and all for Tiger fans, the year was saved by Detroit's return to the World Series after twenty-three years and their triumph over the reigning champs, the St. Louis Cardinals. The '68 Series was the last one where the champions of each league faced off against one another before the institution of the playoffs. The Tigers became the first team in World Series history to come back to win after being down three games to one and having to win the last two games on the road.

The Series was worth the long wait. The Cardinals had beaten the Red Sox in 1967 and were considered the dominant National League club of the sixties. They were led by Bob Gibson, who pitched with a cold fury and had compiled a 1.12 ERA in 1968—a feat as remarkable as McLain's winning 31 games. The series opened in the new Busch Stadium in St. Louis. The all-purpose cookie-cutter stadiums built in the 1960s were antiseptic geometric designs without any distinctive flavor, charm, or history. In contrast, Tiger Stadium, along with Fenway Park, was the oldest surviving major league ballpark, with interesting nooks and crannies, including the deepest center field (440 feet) in the majors, with a flagpole that was in play, and the most inviting right field line (325 feet but for a lofted fly only 315 because of the upper-deck overhang) and history dripping from every pigeon-infested rafter. Gibson dominated McClain in game 1, winning 4–0 and striking out a World Series record seventeen Tigers. The Tigers found their bats in game 2 as Lolich coasted to an 8–1 victory over Nellie Briles and hit the only home run of his career.

Even that early in the series the baseball gods (and Jim Cox) were dropping prophetic hints about what was to come. Cox had worried all summer about Kaline, the Tiger's star right fielder, who broke his arm at midseason. Jim Northrup replaced him in right and finished out the year with a strong performance in the field and at the plate, where he had a knack for hitting grand slams. Deep into July, Cox would tilt his head, screw up his face as if in profound thought, and insist that if Kaline was healthy, he needed to be in the lineup. He deserved it. He was the greatest Tiger since Greenberg and Gehringer, a certain Hall of Famer. A World Series victory without Kaline would be hollow. Then, mid-August, Cox returned to Dartmouth and I was left to get the Tigers a world championship and myself a finished dissertation. Susan, distracted by two young children but not the Tigers, was heroically making steady progress on hers.

Kaline did recover by late September, and the Tigers' otherwise unimaginative manager, Mayo Smith, devised a radical solution to the problem of an overstocked outfield. Mickey Stanley, the Tiger center fielder, was regarded by his teammates as the best natural athlete on the team. Mayo somehow noticed it too and proposed that Stanley (who had played some infield in the minors) replace the light-hitting Ray Oyler at short, with Northrup moving to center and Kaline rejoining the lineup in his customary spot in right. Stanley was naturally skeptical that he could play short at the major league level and with the World Series hanging in the balance as well, but he agreed to the experiment because of his respect for Kaline. He played short the last two weeks of the season and was there when the Series opened. He was still there, having fielded the position almost flawlessly, when the Series ended, and Northrup and Kaline proved to be two of the hitting stars for the Tigers.

The series then moved to Detroit for game 3, where the Tigers jumped out to a 2–0 lead via a Kaline home run in the third, but the Cards came back to score four in the fifth and three more in the seventh to win 7–3. Game 4 was a mess, delayed almost two hours by a downpour and then played in a light rain. McLain did not last through three innings and Gibson once again dominated as the Cardinals rolled 10–1. The Tigers were down 3–1. Only two other teams had ever rallied from such a deficit, and neither had done so by having to win the final two games on the road.

Game 5 proved to be the turning point, and the crucial play is still argued about by Cardinal fans forty years later. The Cards got three runs off Lolich in the first on an Orlando Cepeda homer but could not deliver the knockout punch. In the fourth the Tigers got two back on key hits by Mickey Stanley, Willie Horton, and Jim Northrup. In the top of the fifth Lou Brock—who had killed the Tigers with his timely hits and stolen bases—doubled with one out. Then Julian Javier singled to left, and it seemed certain that the fleet Brock would score easily from second base. But Javier's single got to left fielder Willie Horton quickly and he fired a strike to Bill Freehan blocking the plate. Brock, convinced that he would score easily, came in standing up and Freehan tagged him just as his lead foot reached the edge of the plate.

The umpire, Doug Harvey, did not hesitate in calling him out. Brock argued but to no avail. He insisted that his foot had touched the plate before Freehan's tag, but replays have shown that Freehan's own left foot had blocked Brock from touching home. The Cards still led 3–2, but the play gave the Tigers new life. Lolich, suddenly a hitter as well as pitcher, singled to right, Dick McAuliffe followed with another single, and Mickey Stanley walked. Up came the

Tigers' sixteen-year veteran and Mister Tiger, Al Kaline. Here was the moment Jim Cox and Mayo Smith were waiting for. Now Kaline, known simply as "6" by his teammates, vindicated his long career (and his manager) by singling and driving in Lolich and McAuliffe. Cash then drove in Stanley and the Tigers led 5–3. Lolich, who had not given up a run since the first, set the Cards down in the eighth and ninth for his second complete-game victory. The Tigers were still alive, and the series was headed back to St. Louis.

McLain redeemed himself by finally winning a game made a breeze by the Tigers scoring ten runs in the third inning. I watched the game on our tiny eleven-inch black-and-white television with our ten-month-old son Sam bouncing in my lap. He was not always attentive (or happy), but the blowout allowed me to indulge his whims rather than having them seriously distract from the action. I date our lifelong bond as Tiger fans from this moment when I did not have to choose between fandom and fatherhood. And it was also my twenty-eighth birthday. What a sweet present, and an even better one was on the horizon.

Game 7. Gibson versus Lolich. Lolich was pitching on just two days' rest. When Smith asked him if he thought he could pitch, Lolich told him he'd give him what he had but not to count on more than three or four innings at the most. The angry chiseled right-hander and the bemused portly lefty went at it, and in the bottom of the sixth the score was 0–0. Brock singled, but Lolich promptly caught him leaning and Brock was thrown out at second in a rundown. With two out Curt Flood singled and again Lolich negated the St. Louis running game by picking him off first. Those may have been the two most important tosses Mickey made all day.

I was a young assistant professor in my second year of teaching at Indiana's Indianapolis campus. The game was on a teaching day for me, and I am embarrassed to confess that even the seventh game of a Tiger World Series was not enough to keep me from my appointed rounds, in this instance not with Shakespeare, but with Homer and the

Odyssey. Odysseus never phones it in; how could I? The game began just as my 2 p.m. World Literature class started. When we took a class break about 3:15 (our classes met once a week for two and a half hours), I was delighted to discover that the game was still tied 0–0 going into the seventh. The first two Tigers went down. Lolich miraculously was still on the mound for the Tigers, and Gibson was still throwing darts. And I had to return to the wine-dark sea.

Just as my class began to unpack Odysseus's confrontation with the Cyclops, I later learned, with two outs in the top of the seventh Cash bounced a single to right and Horton followed with a grounder to left. Up came Jim Northrup. He hammered a Gibson fastball on a line into the left-center field gap. Curt Flood took an instinctive first step in, common on a ball hit directly at even an experienced outfielder, and then turned to retreat. He slipped for just a second on the wet field, and then raced back as the ball went over his head for a two-run triple. Flood is convinced that had he not taken that first step in and then slipped he would have made the catch. Watching endless replays later, I doubt it. Northrup powdered the ball and it screamed into the gap. Not even Willie Mays would have run it down.

Gibson, for the first time in the Series, was rattled. He gave up a double to Freehan and the Tigers led 3–0. When the class finished at 4:30 I emerged to see my good friend John Riteris, who taught philosophy, waiting for me with a huge grin on his face. "They did it. They won 4–1," he announced, and off we went to consume as many martinis as possible before we taught again at 5:30. At the bar some sad Cardinal fans (Indianapolis is a National League city) filled me in on the details of Northrup's heroics and that Lolich in fact did the rest, only giving up a harmless two-out home run to Mike Shannon in the bottom of the ninth. Lolich had outpitched Gibson on two days' rest, and the Tigers were the world champions.

Lolich crafted three complete-game Series victories, becoming the only left-hander in World Series history to do so, outshone the number-one starter and 31-game winner on his own team, and outpitched the best right-hander of his generation. A pitching feat not well enough honored as among the most remarkable in World Series history. I went to my evening class as full of high spirits as the celebrating Tigers. I often have wondered what my students thought of my performance that evening.

A post-Series note. A decade later, when I was early in my career at Ohio University, the university hired a new president, Charles Ping. Ping's presidency lasted for nineteen years (a rarity in these days of university president burnout, when the average term is five to seven years) and brought Ohio University from some troubled times to its highest national prominence. He was a success at almost everything he touched: General Education reform, increased research funding, fundraising and endowment building, international outreach, encouraging faculty to capitalize on their patents, and increased enrollment and retention rates. Everything but football. Only one or two teams in his years had winning records. This was something of a paradox because unlike most college and university presidents he had played college football and loved the game. He had been an offensive tackle, and he watched our games with a set of binoculars hanging around his neck so he could catch the line play while everyone else was watching the quarterback.

When Ping completed his PhD at Duke (in philosophy), his first job was at Alma, a small liberal arts college in Michigan. When the team's coach learned of his football-playing past, he wondered if Ping would like to be his line coach. Ping was delighted to accept and probably remains the only college philosophy professor ever to double as the line coach of the football team. Alma had a good team led by an outstanding quarterback who still holds most of the team's records for passing yardage and touchdowns.

Here comes this curious digression rounding third and heading for home. The quarterback was Jim Northrup. When Ping told me this story I was, of course, delighted but immediately wanted to know if Northrup was as fierce and feisty as an undergraduate as he was as a Tiger. "Probably more so," replied Ping with a broad smile. "He had great talent and he knew it and was certain he was always right. The coach gave him his head and Northrup responded with a fine season. But he was a pain." Mayo Smith persuades Mickey Stanley to move to shortstop so he can play both Al Kaline and Jim Northrup in the outfield in the '68 World Series. And Northrup responds with the big hit off Bob Gibson to win game 7 and the World Series for the Tigers. Most Tigers fans of my generation can still see Northrup's line drive screaming over Curt Flood's head into deep left-center field. If such a man is a pain, let us have more of them. Charlie Ping became a valued friend, amused by my attachment to the Tigers but always ready to listen to my Tiger tales and became an eager reader of the Tiger Letters.

The series and its thrilling conclusion (one of those days when baseball did not break my heart) marked the end of the long first phase of my passion for the Tigers. The second, with some detours, was about to begin.

Part 3

The 1970s

In 1970, dissertations at last finished and defended (on the same day), Susan and I joined the English Department at Ohio University in Athens, Ohio. The department was large (sixty full-time faculty) and lively, distinguished by several major scholars and critics, including Neville Rogers (Shelley), Roma King (Browning), Paul Murray Kendall (Shakespeare), Calvin Thayer (Ben Jonson), and Ray Fitch (Ruskin). Most unusually (for 1970), the department featured a significant group of creative writers, including the novelists Walter Tevis, Dan Keyes, and Jack Matthews, and the poets Hollis Summers, Wayne Dodd, and Stanley Plumly. Plumly joined the faculty with us and became a cherished friend. Another close pal, Ed Quattrocki (a fellow Shakespearean and Thomas More scholar), asked me to join the faculty poker group, and soon I was spending every other Friday evening playing cards with Dan Keyes and Walter Tevis, among others. When I was at Hamilton, my friends and I were all fans of Robert Rossen's movie of Tevis's *The Hustler* and were equally impressed with the novel when we read it soon after. And now this novice Shakespearean was occasionally winning pots from its author, an author who is still vitally alive in American popular culture fifty years

"Yes," replied Joe.

"Then tell the white-haired guy that you want to bat second."

Those Reds had it all: power, speed, and baseball smarts. They owned the West Division of the National League from 1970 to 1979, finishing first five times and lower than second only once. We caught one or two Saturday afternoon games each summer, but as good as those Reds were, I yearned for my Tigers and Tiger Stadium. I tried to pick up Ernie Harwell each evening. Some nights he came in clear and strong, but on most I just had to check in every few innings to see if I could pick up the score through the static.

The Tigers sustained some life after the 1968 season, finishing second twice in the new Eastern Division and sneaking by the Red Sox to win it under Billy Martin's tempestuous prodding in 1972. They extended Reggie Jackson and the mighty Oakland A's to five games before losing the Championship Series. The A's advanced to play and defeat the Reds in the World Series, depriving us of a rematch of the 1940 Series. The Reds quickly recovered, while the Tigers spun to the bottom, finishing no higher than fourth from 1974 to 1979. The only good things that happened to the Tigers in those years were Kaline reaching three thousand hits, the exciting years of '76–'77, when Mark "the Bird" Fidrych captured baseball's imagination with his brilliant pitching and eccentric habits of talking to the ball and manicuring the mound down on his hands and knees, the call-up of Alan Trammell and Lou Whitaker in September of '77, and Sparky Anderson's arrival as manager two years later.

SHAKESPEARE AND BASEBALL IV

Shakespeare was responsible for finally getting the family foursome to Tiger Stadium. The mid-seventies were packed with Shakespeare for our family. We took the kids to Stratford in 1972 for their first Shakespeare experience, Carole Shelley as Rosalind in *As You Like It*. Miranda was just six, but I knew the play was working its magic when, after Rosalind's encounter with Orlando in act 4, she leaned over and whispered in my ear, "Daddy, when's she going to tell him?" The Ohio University students selected me as a University Professor in '74–'75, and an important part of the honor was the ability to devise and teach two new courses. The university did not have a London program, so I decided to create a mini one in the London theater. The class met once a week in the winter term, when I briefed them on London's day treasures (museums, churches, historical sights, and pubs) and we read and discussed several of the plays I knew we would be seeing. We departed with a few days left in the quarter, thus adding exam week to the university's spring break, and had fifteen full days to feast on London during the day and the theater in the evenings. Of course, Miranda and Sam came along (my parents too when they got wind of the mad idea), and the experience quickly was dubbed fifteen plays in fifteen days.

We lucked into fifteen remarkable March days in terms of theatrical experiences. We saw plays by Shakespeare, Shaw, Ibsen, Frayn, Beckett, and Alan Ayckbourn, among others, and an entire range of English actors from Olivier's generation to Tom Courtenay's: Peggy Ashcroft, Wendy Hiller, Ralph Richardson, Alec Guinness, Billie Whitelaw, Felicity Kendall, Michael Gambon, Nicol Williamson, Helen Mirren, and Courtenay himself. Miranda and Sam loved it because they weren't being dragged off to the theater each evening by their parents but with a bevy of twenty undergraduates who generously took them under their collective wings. A program Susan and I concocted as an imaginative leap of faith worked. We repeated it in '76, '77, and '82, with our kids, who were coming of age in the London theater, again included. And then again in '86, when Miranda and Sam were both in college but spending their respective winter terms in London on programs sponsored by Hamilton and Lawrence.

Through these and related experiences I got to know John Russell Brown, a noted Shakespearean critic who once taught as a visiting professor at Ohio University and was now serving as Peter Hall's literary manager at the National Theatre, and Maurice Daniels, who was Trevor Nunn's director of educational programs for the Royal Shakespeare Company. They both brought me close to the fascinating action of Shakespeare in production at England's two most famous repertory theaters. In 1979–80 I had my first sabbatical and spent, thanks to Maurice Daniels, the winter and spring in London and Stratford on an Observership with the RSC, invited to sit in on all the rehearsals of Ron Daniels's (no relation) production of *Romeo and Juliet*, from the first read-through in February in London in a cold rehearsal room on Floral Street in Covent Garden to opening night in April in Stratford. Such experiences were unusual for theater professionals and a rarity for an English prof.

As if we didn't get enough Shakespeare in London, Ontario's Stratford also beckoned. The family made annual summer trips from '75 to '78, and Miranda and I went alone in '79 and '80. These were the Robin Phillips years as artistic director and were noted for his own highly intelligent productions and the influx of a few noted English actors, a part of the Stratford experience from Alec Guinness's participation in its inaugural season, including Maggie Smith, Brian Bedford, Keith Baxter, and Peter Ustinov. Smith was the greatest English comic actress of her generation, but her Hollywood triumphs and subsequent Academy Awards had blinded some English directors (and theater critics) to her full range as an actor. Phillips was quite clear-sighted about her talents. In her multiple Stratford seasons, she created the best Rosalind I have ever seen, as well as memorable versions of Beatrice, Millamant, Masha, Arkadina, and Virginia Woolf (in a one-woman show). And she proved her chops as a tragedian with a stunning Lady Macbeth and an ironically wicked Cleopatra. Shakespeare, like baseball, loomed large in our developing family romance.

I incorporated this experience into my work with Shakespeare in the classroom, where I insisted that even as students of literature, we had to understand that Shakespeare wrote his plays to be seen and heard, not to be read. That he turned out also to be the greatest English poet was a by-product of his involvement in the commercial theater, which was perfectly suited to the nature of his theatrical imagination and artistic genius.

When, from the time I started teaching, my students have asked me if I thought Shakespeare would still be central to the English literary tradition a hundred years hence, I responded affirmatively. The last four hundred years have confirmed that his contemporary and rival Ben Jonson got it right: he was not for an age but for all time. I argued that even if we professors questioned his uncanny universal appeal (or tried to oust him from the school and college curriculum), the actors would save him. I am rarely prophetic, but in this instance, like Ben, I nailed it. Now, fifty years later, while the academy debates Shakespeare's continued relevance, actors of all races and genders still relish the opportunity to perform his plays. Race-blind casting, begun years ago by Joseph Papp at the New York Public Shakespeare Festival to mount productions with actors who looked like the city's citizens, has been expanded to include gender as well and has now become the norm in many leading Shakespeare theaters. This practice has been adopted most predominantly at London's Globe Theatre and the all-female Shakespeare company led by Harriet Walter and Phyllida Lloyd, but it has spread to theaters on both sides of the Atlantic, where in recent seasons we have had, for example, several female Falstaffs, two Black female Hamlets (Ruth Negga and Cush Jumbo), a Black female Henry V, a Black Macbeth and Shylock, and a male Rosalind and Helena with entire casts being composed of a blithe and bonny gender scramble, partially mirroring if not quite imitating Shakespeare's own transvestite theatrical company.

As Detroit is two-thirds of the way between Athens and Stratford, Ontario, it became a natural stopping point on the Shakespeare expeditions. We stopped for the night and attended games in '76 and in '77. I hadn't been back in Tiger Stadium since the summer of '62 and it was the first for the family. Finally, Miranda and Sam were introduced to baseball where it was meant to be played, in one of the game's great old temples. At our first game in '76 the Tigers lost to the Red Sox 5–4, but the kids got to see aging Tiger greats from the 1960s Willie Horton and Bill Freehan each get a couple of hits. They also got to see the Red Sox mixture of youth and age (and two future Hall of Famers) hitting 3, 4, and 5 in the lineup: Freddie Lynn, Carl Yastrzemski, and Jim Rice.

Our scorecard indicates that Rice and Freehan hit homers and that Ron LeFlore, the Tigers speedy center fielder who was recruited out of a Michigan prison, stole his 40th base. And Sam and Miranda agreed that Tiger Stadium was "the real thing," even if, in a misguided recent refurbishment, the once-dark "canoe" green (remember it is a *park*) seats had been repainted in blue and the upper-deck box seats painted in orange. Over time I grew fond of the two-toned look, perhaps because I now see it every day as I have a shot on my screen saver of the old stadium looking down the first base line and out to the three decks in right field.

In 1977, as I floated home on the comic energy and intelligence of Maggie Smith's transcendent Rosalind at Stratford, the Tigers beat the Angels 7–6 for us as journeyman catcher Milt May hit two home runs, the last coming in the bottom of the eighth to win it. May had been hired to mentor the Tiger catcher of the future, Lance Parrish, who became one of the crucial components of the great Tiger teams in the 1980s. Barry Bonds's father, Bobby, and Don Baylor were in the Angels lineup, and the carrot-topped Rusty Staub (acquired from the Mets in the offseason) and Jason Thompson led the Tigers. Thompson, one of the many left-handed pull-hitters made for Tiger Stadium, hit his 25th homer deep into the upper deck in right. He was preceded as a power-hitting lefty by Goose Goslin, Vic Wertz, and Norm Cash and followed by Kirk Gibson, Darrell Evans, Mickey Tettleton, and Tony Clark, all of whom took aim at clearing the roof on the third deck and most of whom accomplished it. For the record, Cash cleared it four times; Mickey Mantle and Kirk Gibson three; Thompson, Tettleton, and Tony

Clark twice; and several others, including Ted Williams (who hit the first), Boog Powell, Jim Northrup, Reggie Jackson, George Brett, Carlos Delgado, Bobby Bonilla, and Lou Whitaker once each.

That third deck out in right field was one of the many eccentricities of the park that immediately appealed to the kids, though we never saw one of the twenty-three games in which its roof was cleared. However, Sam and I saw Robert Fick almost do it in the eighth inning of the final game played at Tiger Stadium. He hit a monster shot that hit the roof of the third deck and then ricocheted back onto the field as the full house roared its nostalgic approval. It always struck me as an odd paradox that while Tiger Stadium was made for left-handed power hitters, most of the great Tiger home run hitters were right-handed: Hank Greenberg, Rudy York, Al Kaline, Willie Horton, Rocky Colavito, Bill Freehan, Lance Parrish, Cecil Fielder, and now Miguel Cabrera. The only lefties included in the top-ten Tigers home run hitters are Norm Cash, Lou Whitaker (I bet that name on that list comes as a surprise), and Kirk Gibson.

The kids quickly saw how much closer to the action we were, particularly sitting in the first few rows of the upper deck, than we ever were in Riverfront. And they were amazed at the huge center field bleachers (where you could still sit for two dollars in the 1980s) often filled with beer-guzzling students from Michigan and Michigan State happy to amuse themselves with chanting ("Less Filling . . . Tastes Great"), bouncing beach balls back and forth in the air, and eventually starting up the wave when the action on the field lulled. They were equally impressed to realize how many of the greats had played here: Ruth, Walter Johnson, Grover Cleveland Alexander, Cy Young, DiMaggio, Berra, Mantle, Williams, Feller, Satchel Paige, Dizzy Dean, Jimmie Foxx, Al Simmons, Bob Gibson, Whitey Ford, Bob Lemon, Nellie Fox, Hank Aaron, and of course all the legendary Tigers from Cobb to Kaline.

Since the nineteenth century, Shakespeare has been celebrated as a festive and festival playwright. Though David

Garrick created the first Shakespeare Jubilee in Stratford in 1769, it was a one-time celebration and featured no performances of his plays. Frank Benson was the first actor-manager to create a summer season for performing Shakespeare in Stratford in 1886. In America, Shakespeare went west with the country as though he was a natural part of our landscape and culture. He is found, and brilliantly parodied, smack in the center of the classic American novel, *Huckleberry Finn*, in the thespian antics of the King and the Duke. Shakespeare, to adopt and adapt Rap Brown's famous 1960s formulation, was as American as baseball, apple pie, and violence. Festival Shakespeare exploded after World War II in city parks and small towns across the country sharing the summer months with baseball. Our family feasted, or perhaps more accurately, picnicked on both.

Part 4

The 1980s

The 1980s was a great decade for baseball, the Tigers, and our family. When we returned from London and Stratford in June of 1980, I discovered that my revised essay on Orson Welles's *Chimes at Midnight* had been accepted for publication by the *Shakespeare Quarterly*. Susan became one of the two tutors in the English Department's innovative Honors Tutorial Program, based on the Oxbridge system of education, and produced a major work of scholarship. She and her colleague Roma King edited volumes 7, 8, and 9 of the Ohio-Baylor definitive edition of the *Complete Works of Robert Browning*, the volumes devoted to Browning's epic poem *The Ring and the Book*.

In 1981, I became a dean, with the responsibility of implementing a new comprehensive set of general education requirements for all Ohio University undergraduates—a program I had helped to imagine and draft as a faculty member and guide through the Faculty Senate in my last year as chair of that university governing body. Soon thereafter the kids went off to college, Miranda to Hamilton and Sam to Lawrence. When they graduated, they headed out into the world, Miranda to Botswana in the Peace Corps and Sam to Japan in the JET Program. The family closed the decade with reunions in Africa and Japan. And the Tigers had their greatest extended period of dominance since the years between 1934 and 1945.

THE PERFECT GAME

Our baseball in the eighties did not begin in Tiger Stadium or even with the Tigers, but in Cleveland's cavernous Municipal Stadium on a chilly, misty May evening. Those of you who know all the arcane dates of baseball history (or are Cleveland Indians, now Guardians, fans) will recognize May 15, 1981, as the date Lenny Barker pitched what was, at that time, just the tenth perfect game in baseball history. And history is what led Sam and me and his friend Mike Thompson to Cleveland on that May evening. Mike and Sam and two other eighth-grade pals had won the top prize in a regional Ohio History Day competition with an exhibit about the Millfield mine disaster in 1930, the worst mine disaster in Ohio history, in which eighty-two miners were killed.

Millfield is about ten miles from Athens and was the center of a rich coal vein that had been deep-mined when southeastern Ohio was the center of the Ohio coal industry. The boys had researched the disaster and made the traditional poster-sized story boards of their findings, but the unique part of their report consisted of their videotaped oral history interviews with the last surviving miners of the disaster. As regional winners they were invited to participate in the state finals of the competition, to be held at Case Western Reserve University in Cleveland on May 16, 1981.

Sam invited all four of the team to drive up to Cleveland with us on Friday with the idea that we would catch the Indians–Toronto Blue Jays game that night in Municipal Stadium. Only Mike Thompson was free to accompany us. I had not been to a game in Cleveland since the late fifties. I had forgotten how massive old Municipal Stadium was, seating something like 80,000 for the football Browns and 72,000 for the Indians. This May night was cool (a note on our scorecard indicates that the game-time temperature was

49) with something between a light rain and a Scottish mist blowing in off Lake Erie.

The great hulk of a stadium resembled a haunted house, as the announced attendance was 7,290 but I doubt there were more than 5,000 of us in the stands. As we headed to our infield box seats ten rows or so behind the Indians' dugout a voice called out, "Professor Crowl," and I turned to be greeted by Tony Grossi, a former student, who graduated in 1979 from the School of Journalism at Ohio University. He had landed a coveted job covering sports for the state's largest newspaper, the *Cleveland Plain Dealer.* He was a rookie writer assigned largely to small-college and high school sports, but the Indians were coming off a ten-day, three-city road trip and the regular reporter wanted a night off, so Tony was given an early chance to cover an Indians game. He was obviously pleased and a bit amazed to see his old Shakespeare prof in the crowd.

The Indians got two in the first on a hit by Rick Manning and a two-base throwing error on a ball hit by Mike Hargrove, which put runners on second and third. A sacrifice fly by Andre Thornton and a single by Ron Hassey brought them home. Two of those players have become a permanent part of the Indians family. Manning still does the commentary on the television broadcasts of the Indians games; Hargrove was the Indians manager in the glory years of the 1990s and remains an adviser to the club. Barker breezed through the Blue Jays batting order in the first three innings on six infield grounders and three fly balls but no strikeouts. That changed in the fourth when he struck out two and then maintained that pattern for the next five innings. Sandwiched between two strikeouts in the fifth he got a nice play by third baseman Toby Harrah, who leaned into the seats to catch a foul pop. The Toronto leadoff hitters in both the sixth and seventh (Bosetti and Griffin) hit tough balls to second baseman Duane Kuiper, who made nice plays on each and threw them out at first. Barker was in complete command. He was known for being a hard-throwing right-hander, but on this night it was his curveball that was exceptional. He was also known for being a bit wild, but Hassey said he put every pitch right where he called for it and only shook him off four or five times.

Sam and Mike and I first commented that he had a no-hitter going at the end of the fourth. By the sixth the tiny crowd realized what was up as well. Because we were keeping score, we realized that not only did he have a no-hitter working but also a perfect game. Barker was in such a groove that he struck out eleven of the last seventeen batters he faced. Our scorecard indicates that every one of those eleven hitters went down swinging. Jorge Orta hit a home run for the Indians in the eighth to build the lead to 3–0 (Luis Leal had pitched a solid game for Toronto as well but on the wrong night). In the eighth and ninth, the small, chilly, damp crowd was on its feet, roaring, urging Barker on as Jay after Jay waved at the curve or took it and found that it had hit the strike zone anyway. With two down in the ninth Ernie Whitt, the left-handed-hitting Toronto catcher, came up to pinch-hit and hit a 1–2 pitch on a lazy little fly ball to Manning in center, who waved off the backpedaling shortstop to gather it in.

Bedlam. Or as much bedlam as was possible from a small crowd on a cold night in a big house. We had been high-fiving each other on nearly every pitch and on all the outs since the seventh. What was left? Some big hugs and a loud plea for Barker to come back out for a final bow—which he did, with his long blond hair already totally mussed up by his excited and proud teammates. All we could keep repeating was "Perfect game . . . perfect game . . . oh my God, perfect game." And then, as what we had witnessed began to sink in, "Hey, we are a part of history," said Sam, and that refrain would be echoed on the next day by all the speakers at the History Day competition: "Cleveland made history last night . . . Barker is a part of baseball history . . . History is now as well as then," and we sat in the auditorium with little grins plastered on our faces like the baseball-loving kids we all were because we had been there; we not only lived history, we helped to make it.

Barker was ours. The Indians were ours. And perfection, at least for the moment, was ours. And part of the reason it was ours was that we had written it down. We had the score-card. We had not only observed, and rooted, we had recorded. And that scorecard sits in front of me now as I relive that night and some of its details, like Harrah's catch and Kui-per's two good plays at second, noted in the margins. And we also had Tony Grossi, who had just gotten the biggest break a young sportswriter could imagine—a front-page story. When we got back to Athens, I sent him the scorecard and he graciously got Len Barker to sign it, as well as Gros-si's own *Plain Dealer* story. Grossi's account filled in some good details. Barker had thrown 103 pitches, 84 of them for strikes. A remarkable ratio when two to one is considered a solid performance. He did not go to a single full count on any hitter and never threw more than five pitches called balls in an inning. The recorded attendance of 7,290 was the second smallest for a perfect game, more than only the 6,298 that saw Catfish Hunter's in 1968, making our presence even more special as it was shared with so few.

In the eighties the Tigers caught fire too and had their best decade since the 1940s. In the American League East Division, they finished first twice, second twice, and third three times. They did it with young talent they had drafted and nurtured in the minors, including Alan Trammell, Lou Whitaker, Kirk Gibson, Lance Parrish, Jack Morris, and Dan Petry. They added to that mix veterans like Chet Lemon, Larry Herndon, Darrell Evans, and Milt Wilcox, and finally two powerful late-inning arms, Aurelio López and Willie Hernandez. They were the winningest American League team in the decade. Even though our lives were increas-ingly busy and scattered, some of us managed to get to a few games every summer except for 1985 and 1989, and between Comiskey Park in Chicago and Tiger Stadium we managed to see eleven games in 1984 (no surprise).

For a complicated set of personal and professional rea-sons, we did not return to Tiger Stadium until the summer of 1983, when it was clear that the Tigers revival, under Sparky

Anderson, was reaching maturity. Anderson had been unceremoniously dumped by new Reds general manager Dick Wagner after the 1978 season and was quickly hired by the Tigers. Trammell and Whitaker had been teamed together in the minors for two impressive seasons and made their debut appearance in a doubleheader at Fenway Park in September of 1977. Games seen by my old Tiger pal, Jim Cox, who drove down from Dartmouth to see the future in action. He immediately reported that they were "for real." Jack Morris, Dan Petry, Lance Parrish, and Kirk Gibson had all also come up through the Tigers farm system and were in place by 1983. And in 1982 the Tigers GM, Bill Lajoie, made an astute trade, getting Chet Lemon from the White Sox for Steve Kemp, which brought the team a player who could hit for average and some power and cover Tiger Stadium's vast center field.

We made several trips to Detroit for games in 1983, the best being a three-game series with the Blue Jays in August. Sam and I headed north in our yellow '67 Mustang convertible named Hotspur. The Blue Jays were an expansion team who were on their way to building a club that would eventually win the World Series twice in the early 1990s. Detroit was a natural rival because of Canada's proximity, and on this weekend plenty of Blue Jay fans had come in for the series. The Jays had power at third and first in Rance Mulliniks and Willie Upshaw; power and speed in the outfield with Lloyd Moseby, Jesse Barfield, and Dave Collins; a solid catcher in Ernie Whitt; defensive strength up the middle with shortstop Damaso Garcia and second baseman Garth Iorg; and some good young pitchers in Dave Stieb, Jim Gott, and Luis Leal. When George Bell and Joe Carter joined the ranks several years later, they became contenders.

The Tigers too were building a winner and were just a bit closer to that realization in 1983, when they finished second in the division, than were the Jays. The Tigers core of Trammell, Whitaker, Gibson, Parrish, Lemon, and Herndon was in place, plus the strong starting pitching of Morris and Petry. In 1984 they would add the final pieces to the puzzle by signing their first free agent, Darrell Evans, as well as trading, during spring training, their promising outfielder Glenn Wilson to the Phillies for Willie Hernandez and Dave Bergman. This series with the Jays revealed the potential that would be fulfilled in 1984.

The games drew big crowds: 46,000 plus on Friday night, 39,000 on Saturday night, and 38,000 plus on Sunday afternoon. The games were well played, well pitched (except for a Tigers bullpen lapse on Saturday), tight, and emotionally satisfying. In the opener, Dan Petry and Jim Gott hooked up in a nifty pitcher's duel. Toronto got two in the third on a double, groundout, and single. Trammell drove in Whitaker in the bottom half to cut the margin to one. Ernie Whitt hit a homer in the top of the fifth to restore the two-run advantage, but with Lemon on first Glenn Wilson returned the favor in the bottom half with a drive into the upper deck in left for a 3–3 tie.

Sparky lifted Petry after eight innings and brought in Aurelio López (Señor Smoke), who pitched a scoreless ninth and tenth. The late August evening was hot and steamy, which made the cold beer taste even sweeter and go down even faster. The big crowd was getting restless and the kids in the bleachers were entertaining one another as one side shouted, "Tastes great," while the other responded, "Less filling," mocking a current Miller Lite beer commercial. The Jays stuck with Gott, and in the bottom of the tenth Trammell stroked a sharp line drive into the lower deck in left for a Tiger walk-off homer and a 4–3 victory. The huge crowd rose at the crack of his bat and their joy intensified as Tram rounded the bases and met the greeting party at home plate. It was just his eleventh dinger of the year, but he was developing the knack of hitting them when they counted. The crowd continued its roar until he popped back up out of the dugout for a quick wave before disappearing again. Father and son headed out to a postgame snack and a happy rehash of the night's action.

Saturday's game went the other way. The Tigers, behind Glenn Abbott, led 4–2 after seven. He had thrown 110 pitches, so Sparky went to López again in the eighth. Tonight he didn't have it and promptly gave up a two-run shot to Mulliniks and a solo blast to Moseby. The Tigers got two back in the bottom of the eighth, one on another home run by Trammell, but a rarely used reliever, Howard Bailey, came on and allowed the Jays two more in the ninth, and that was the game. The Jays fans sitting around us were as happy—perhaps even happier—than we had been the night before with the sudden late strike from their team.

Sunday's game was a glimpse into the way the Tigers would win in 1984. Jack Morris, the Tigers' surly ace, went up against Luis Leal (remember him from Barker's perfect game?), and they treated us to an even closer duel than Petry and Gott had on Friday. The Jays got two in the third and might have had more except Chet Lemon cut Mulliniks down at the plate on Moseby's potential sacrifice fly. Mulliniks rammed into Parrish and knocked him down (a feat in itself), but Lance held onto the ball for the final out. The Tigers got one back in the fourth on singles from Herndon, Parrish, and Rick Leach (I saw his name on the back of a Tigers jersey exiting Comerica in June of 2013, reminding us that Tiger fans have long memories, even for those whose playing days were modest in number).

The game remained tight until the ninth. Morris escaped trouble in the fifth when, with two out and two on, Marty Castillo made a nice play charging a topped grounder to throw Upshaw out by a whisker. The play at first was so close Bobby Cox came out to argue and was eventually tossed, to the home crowd's great delight. In the eighth Glenn Wilson made a great leaping catch in right (shades of Al Kaline), robbing Moseby of a homer. Leal was lifted in the seventh after a Lemon single, but Morris, as was his wont, went nine innings, giving up two runs on five hits and striking out eight. Vintage Jack. The Tigers went to the bottom of the ninth trailing 2–1. We were sitting between home and first, fifteen rows up behind the Jays dugout, and were surrounded by Toronto fans who thought they had the series in hand.

Herndon flied out to center; Parrish walked; Wilson flied out to left. Now the Jays fans were certain it was their day and weekend. Then Leach singled Parrish to third and the Jays brought in a right-handed reliever, Joey McLaughlin, to face Lemon. Chet took a ball and then clobbered the next pitch into the upper deck in left for his 19th homer of the year and the second Tiger walk-off home run in the series. Morris was the first out of the dugout, waving a white towel over his head. He raced up the third base line to greet Lemon as he rounded the bag and came on home with Jack trotting along beside him swinging that towel as a sweet sign of victory, not surrender. Great stuff. Sam and I did a little dancing in our seats and then a little dancing in the streets as we headed smiling to the car and the long drive back to Athens.

On the way we talked about how nicely balanced the club was with Whitaker and Trammell at the top, who could hit both for average and with power (at the time Whitaker was hitting .321 and Tram .326; Whitaker had 18 homers, Tram 12, counting the 2 he hit during this series); Parrish and Herndon in the middle (both hitting in the .280s); and Wilson and Lemon providing a threat in the bottom half of the order. Third base was unsettled, as it had almost always been for the Tigers between George Kell and Miguel Cabrera (excepting the Ray Boone and Travis Fryman years). And the other corner, manned over the years by Greenberg, Rudy York, Norm Cash, and Justin Thompson, was momentarily without a permanent occupant. While Rick Leach had several key hits over the weekend, he was not made in the mode of the traditional Tigers left-handed power-hitting first baseman. The outfield of Herndon, Lemon, and Wilson seemed settled, with Kirk Gibson waiting anxiously in the wings. For the starting staff Morris and Petry made a strong number one and number two, followed by Milt Wilcox, Juan Berenguer, and Dave Rozema. Aurelio López anchored a weak bullpen filled with several of Sparky's old Reds, including Doug Bair. This team did not have a Rose or a Bench or a Morgan, but it was strong up the middle, had a better starting staff than the Reds did in the seventies, and the greatest keystone combination in baseball history, Alan Trammell and Lou Whitaker. We were excited not only about the club we had just seen but about its future as well. And how often is one treated to two walk-off home runs in a single series?

As much fun as those 1970s trips to Cincinnati were, and as good as those Reds teams were, and as much true father-son and father-daughter pleasure they provided, I never became a Reds fan. The club never got under my skin and into my consciousness the way that the Tigers had. Miranda loved them because her grandmother did and because they were such a diverse and varied bunch. But once she ended up sharing a Woodward Avenue address with the Tigers, she happily returned to the fold. Over the years I became accustomed to listening to Marty Brennaman, the Reds' longtime announcer. Evidently, according to several friends (including our dentist!) who were listening, Marty once mentioned me on one of his broadcasts. Two of his children went to Ohio University, and he heard a welcoming speech I gave as dean during our summer Precollege orientation program about the university's distinguished history, reaching back to the Northwest Ordinance of 1787, and was impressed. In a slow moment in the game, he decided to share what he had learned with his partner, Joe Nuxhall, so for a moment Ohio University's history slipped into the baseball conversation. America's natural gregariousness at work.

I also quoted Shakespeare in the speech, but it would have been too fortuitous for this account if that too had miraculously found its way into Brennaman's banter. But even that flattering attention did not relocate my baseball loyalty. I think I could, with honor, have ditched the Tigers for the Reds—the losers for the winners, the Ohio team from my region of the state for the distant Michiganders—but it did not happen, and it rarely does. Once a fan's bond is cemented with a team, they tend to mate for life. Orioles or Redbirds or Blue Jays may flap into view with winning ways, but once a Cubs or Red Sox or Tigers fan . . .

The fan's bond is like being infected with a virus that lingers in the system forever, temporarily becoming more virulent in accordance with the team's place in the standings. I can confess that in the preinternet age, even during mediocre seasons, I have searched for the Tiger scores in places as far remote as Lamu (Kenya), Myajima (Japan), and Bodrum (Turkey) or as cosmopolitan as Paris, London, and Madrid. And in the modern era of instant internet communication, I have booted up a computer at 5 a.m. in St. Petersburg (in a flat once lived in by Turgenev) to see what the Tigers did (they lost) as they moved towards the playoffs in September of 2006. It is as if the new day cannot begin without the knowledge of what the Tigers did the night before. A win quickens the step; a loss momentarily diminishes the world's radiance until the mind moves on to the next day's game. And then the cycle begins again. Baseball is not a game for melancholy brooders. The football fan has a week to wallow in a loss; a baseball fan less than twenty-four hours.

Baseball is unique among games in the way in which it combines action and statistics. Its history is written in numbers as well as personalities. A reference to Michael Jordan is never preceded by his lifetime scoring average; Joe Namath is never defined by his quarterback rating, or Pelé by his goals scored. But Cobb is defined by his .366 lifetime batting average, DiMaggio by his 56-game hitting streak, Ryan by his 5,714 strikeouts, Rose by his 4,256 hits, Cy Young by his 511 games won. These numbers are a part of the language of the game and the conversation that surrounds it carried on by the average fan, not just the sabermetric pros like Bill James. For baseball, unlike football or basketball or soccer, is not just a game but a continuous conversation fans have about the game, both as it unfolds on the field and as it lingers in the memory. Baseball's leisurely pace, which irritates some attuned to the rapid tempo of our high-tech-driven world, is also its beauty. As many have observed, it is the only major team sport played without a clock.

"There's no clock in the forest," Orlando observes in Shakespeare's *As You Like It*. And he is right. The forest is a holiday rather than a working-day world. Work runs by the clock; play unfolds in timelessness. A game is organized play, but the best games have the fewest rules. Baseball is a game that can be scored; the results of each at-bat can be recorded on a scorecard, and many of the game's individual details can be reconstructed from a rereading of that written record. No such instrument exists for football or soccer, and while basketball has a scorecard, all it records are baskets and free throws made by each player—no assists, no rebounds, no blocked shots; no distinction in the kinds of baskets made (dunks, drives, jumpers, hook shots, bank shots, pick-and-rolls, etc.). Baseball's pace makes the scorecard possible just as it makes the conversation about the game possible. There is time (because there is no clock) to record the action just as there is time to comment upon it and even link it to previous moments in other games in other seasons. The scorecard links the keeper with the history of the game and all those other fans who have kept the game alive not only in memory but on paper. I learned to keep score from my mother, who in her later life even kept score of the Reds games she listened to over the radio. I passed the practice on to Miranda and Sam, and now their children continue the tradition.

When I was recounting the Tigers–Blue Jays games we saw in August of 1983, I could have gotten all the basic information (the sort contained in the box scores still printed in the sports section of some newspapers) rather quickly from the internet. But those box scores would not have given me the details of Lemon's throw home (and Parrish being upended) to cut down Mulliniks, or Wilson's great catch to rob Moseby, or most dramatic and telling of all, Jack Morris bouncing out of the Tigers dugout—as Lemon's home run disappeared into the stands in left—swirling that towel over his head in giddy triumph as his teammate rounded third and headed for home. Those are the details that define the game as it gets retold and relived. Those are the details that remind one of Lemon's essential contributions (on defense as well as at the plate) to the making of the 1984 Tigers and help to challenge the image of Morris as a sullen, cantankerous teammate.

Keeping score is becoming a lost art, though I am often impressed that there are always one or two others doing so in my immediate vicinity at Comerica Park, maintaining the practice into baseball's third century. They are reliable extra eyes when one has missed an at-bat or even part of an inning fetching a grilled Polish sausage with onions and green peppers (this is Detroit, remember) and a cold Labatt Blue. Now the conversation extends beyond the immediate family and into the neighborhood as little communities of Tiger fans are formed section by section around the ballpark. On rare occasions you discover a fellow fan whose history with the team reaches as deep as yours, and the game suddenly has an added dimension as names from the past are conjured up and bounced around as if they were still a part of the action. Walt Dropo and Frank Bolling popped up recently. In most instances watching a baseball game is a civilized and civilizing experience. Yes, the crowd becomes full-throated when a great hitter comes to the plate, or a rally builds, or a closer nails down a tight win in the ninth, but those raucous moments are the exception rather than the rule.

SHAKESPEARE AND BASEBALL V

I readily admit that linking the Bard and baseball seems an old Shakespeare professor's giddy leap of the imagination. The territory I have been exploring is, I hope, rich with suggestions about such resonances. But we should not ignore the ways Shakespeare does use various sports and games, in fact and metaphor, in his plays. Shakespeare is distinguished as an artist by the myriad ways his mind absorbs small, telling details, from life and his sources, and then how his imagination transforms and universalizes them. Shakespeare's comedies are rich in their evocation of seasonal communal activities, from May games to Morris dancing to the Lord of Misrule presiding over carnival, but his plays, especially the tragedies, are also filled with instances of specific sports.

Hamlet is an obvious example, as it concludes with the most famous and lethal fencing match in dramatic literature. Shakespeare devotes detailed attention to setting up the competition by having Claudius recount Lamond's (a skilled Norman horseman) high estimation of Laertes's skill with a rapier. Claudius goes on to inform Laertes that Hamlet so envied the report that "he could nothing do but wish and beg / Your sudden coming o'er, to play with him." Later, when the match and the odds are proposed to the prince, Horatio counsels, "You will lose this wager, my lord," and Hamlet immediately replies: "I do not think so; since he [Laertes] went into France, I have been in continual practice; I shall win at the odds." When Hamlet apologizes to Laertes before the match about his connection with the deaths of Polonius and Ophelia, he does so with a metaphor from archery, lamenting, "I have shot my arrow o'er the house / And hurt my brother."

Shakespeare knows the competitive nature of young men and the sports that they play. The duel between Hamlet and Laertes recalls the example of another young Frenchman (the Dauphin) and his mocking gift of tennis balls (a "ton of treasure") to his rival and newly crowned King of England, our old friend, Prince Hal. The young king's vigorous response reveals his feisty spirit, his knowledge of tennis, and his use of language as a powerful game changer:

> When we have match'd our rackets to these balls,
> We will, in France, by God's grace, play a set
> Shall strike his father's crown into the hazard.
> Tell him he hath made a match with such a wrangler
> That all the courts of France will be disturb'd
> With chaces.

Here "set," "hazard," "courts," and "chaces" all do double duty as tennis terms transformed into puns on the language of war and politics.

Another example of the language of sport used as an aggressive gesture is revealed when Kent (disguised as Caius) trips up Goneril's surly servant, Oswald—who has ignored Lear's requests—as he calls him (to the old king's delight) a "base foot-ball player." The early game of football (soccer) was associated with the town's thugs, a reputation in today's England preserved less by the game's players than by its fans. But the sport most evenly matched with theater for entertainment was also the cruelest: bear baiting. The bear-baiting pits existed in the Liberties side by side with the theaters. In a daring move, Shakespeare has Macbeth, as Malcolm and the English army close in on Dunsinane, imagine himself as the bear hounded by the dogs: "They have tied me to a stake: I cannot fly, / But bear-like, I must fight the course."

In a moment that touched me as particularly Shakespearean, when I first encountered *Love's Labours Lost*, a gentler form of sport is evoked. At the end of the play, the local community who surround the aristocrats at the center of the romantic comedy includes a curate (Sir Nathaniel), a schoolmaster (Holofernes), a constable (Dull), a fantastical Spaniard (Don Armado), his clever page (Moth), and a clown (Costard). To supplement the revels surrounding the various wooing games among the aristocrats, the locals decide to present a pageant involving the Nine Worthies. This presages, of course, Shakespeare's more brilliant use of a similar device at the conclusion of *A Midsummer Night's Dream*, where Bottom and the rude mechanicals put on their version of "Pyramus and Thisbe."

Sir Nathaniel is to represent Alexander the Great but has trouble remembering his lines and is mocked by the aristocrats, who themselves have just been made fools of in another context. Costard immediately comes to Sir Nathaniel's defense by reminding his detractors that he is "a marvellous good neighbor, faith, and a very good bowler," even if he has been, as Alexander, "a little o'erparted." Shakespeare uses the small detail of bowling to remind us of the simple pleasures sport provides in making a community of "good neighbors," while simultaneously exposing the limp wit of the nobles. Sport in Shakespeare's world, as in ours, is a source of social cohesion as well as aggression.

Baseball's origins were in New York City, but from the beginning it needed lots of space, green space. The original players found it by moving across the Hudson River to a picnic area in New Jersey called the Elysian Fields. As it quickly spread across the country carried by young men following the gold rush or fighting in the Civil War, it became the game of village greens, farm pastures, and college campuses. The commercial sport settled on cities, while America's game was rural. It recalls the deep past in the festive present. Both Shakespearean games and American baseball revive the spirit of primal fun. Rooted in ritual, these games push up into the sunlit afternoon air of pit and park, whether Globe Theatre or sports arena. Baseball parks, old and new, evoke their origins in their names: Fenway Park, Wrigley Field, Coors Field, Comerica Park.

Baseball began as an exclusively day game and kept that holiday spirit alive in the city. Slipping off from work to join a midweek afternoon crowd at the ballpark intensifies the release that the pleasure of play is meant to bring to the cycle of living. Shakespeare's Prince Hal has a strong handle on this relationship, which he neatly manipulates to acknowledge his reputation as the wild and unruly prince:

> If all the year were playing holidays,
> To sport would be as tedious as to work;
> But when they seldom come, they wish'd for come,
> And nothing pleases but rare accidents.

Most of us wish for holiday as a respite from the world of getting and spending. Hal, on the other hand, seems overly committed to holiday, so he reassures his audience that he does understand the balance that must be struck between work and play to achieve a healthy life and that he will make his reformation glitter over his faults. He will make his play, work.

Sport, play, and holiday were originally built into the rhythm of the pagan celebration of the seasons, which eventually was incorporated into the Christian calendar. Their spirit now survives as religious ritual in our own age only in the exaggerated New Orleans version of Mardi Gras and the Dickensian excesses of Christmas. Holiday derives from Holy Day, as Bart Giamatti reminds us in his lucid little book on the place of sport in the modern world, *Take Time for Paradise*. Holiday is the release from the everyday grind of the world of work, but it is a meaningful social ritual, not anarchy, and in its incarnation as sport it has its own internal logic and set of rules.

Shakespeare in his great romantic comedies created distinct landscapes for the world of work and the world of play. He associated work with the city (or court) and holiday with nature, with what a famous literary critic, Northrop Frye, dubbed "the green world." But the green world is less a specific landscape than a state of mind where imagination and play are valued over rules and responsibility. Falstaff's Boar's Head Tavern is as much a green world as is Rosalind's Forest of Arden, for both are playgrounds where the imagination can flourish. In *Henry V*, Shakespeare provides Mistress Quickly with a nostalgic account of Falstaff's death. Agreeing with Pistol that in his final moments he cried out for sack and for women, she also insists that she saw him "fumble with the sheets, and play with flowers, and smile upon his fingers' ends," and she heard him "babble of green fields."

How dazzling that Shakespeare's great champion of holiday should die crying out for sack and women and babbling of green fields. Falstaff is Shakespeare's greatest democratic comic creation. He waddles into Shakespeare's version of English history straight out of the playwright's imagination, not out of the historical chronicles Shakespeare used as his sources detailing the lives of the nobility. Falstaff struck such an immediate chord with the audience because they shared a subversive love of holiday. Falstaff, thinking back on the pleasures of a rural, merry old England, dies by prophetically babbling about those green fields that morph, in this account, into the nineteenth-century village greens where baseball worked its way into the holiday fabric of American life and then eventually into the urban baseball diamonds of our world. At the ballpark, barber shop, local tavern, and now internet blog we baseball fans spend our winters babbling of those green fields where the greats roam and play.

The evocation of holiday and carnival and its relationship to Falstaff and the Boar's Head Tavern provides another wild link between Shakespeare and baseball: beer. Beer is as essential to the experience of the game as hotdogs and Cracker Jacks. Since the game's beginnings, American brewery owners have been attracted to owning and sponsoring teams. Two of the most successful were Jacob Ruppert, whose New York brewery was famous for its Knickerbocker Beer, and August "Gussie" Busch of the Anheuser-Busch brewery, the maker of Budweiser, whose family still owns the St. Louis Cardinals. Ruppert was the man largely responsible for transforming the Yankees into baseball's most potent franchise by hiring Miller Huggins as manager in 1918, acquiring Babe Ruth from the Boston Red Sox in 1919, and building Yankee Stadium in 1923. In 1953, Jerold Hoffberger, owner of the National Brewing Company, bought the floundering St. Louis Browns, moved them to Baltimore, and rechristened them the Orioles. No surprise that the Orioles' games were sponsored by National Bohemian Beer ("Natty Boh"). As birds and beer and baseball seem improbably to nest together, when Canada's Labatt Brewery won the rights to create a major league team in Toronto, they named it the Blue Jays.

Though the Cards remain the only team still associated with an old brewing family, beer has remained a consistent sponsor of radio and television baseball broadcasts. As I mentioned earlier, Stroh's was long a sponsor of the Tigers, while Hamm's sponsored the Twins, Iron City the Pirates, Miller's the Brewers (no surprise), and Schaefer's the Dodgers in their Brooklyn days. What's the connection with

Shakespeare? Beer is the people's drink; Shakespeare is the people's playwright (what other almost five-hundred-year-old writer maintains such a universal appeal, with summer festivals or permanent theaters in his name spread across the United States, Europe, and Asia). Both have their origins in popular culture, as does Shakespeare's greatest comic creation, Falstaff. No surprise that his name graced a leading American brewery from 1903 until 2005. Though Falstaff's preferred drink is sherris-sack (to which he delivers an inventive ode), his young sidekick, Prince Hal, is a beer man. His rival Hotspur mocks him by saying "he could be poisoned with a pot of ale," while Hal boasts of his ability to "drink with any tinker in his own language." That language includes his ability to triumph in beer-drinking games, which remain the sport of the young. Hal reports that all the good lads of Eastcheap who hang out at the Boar's Head Tavern call "drinking deep, dyeing scarlet, and when you breathe in your watering, they cry 'Hem!' and bid you play it off." This is what we called "chug-a-lugging" in my college days and today is an element in the game of beer pong played at campuses across the country.

Spirits, high and low, flow through Shakespeare's works, from Jack Cade's rebellious promise to ban "small [weak] beer" and make the "pissing-conduit [to] run nothing but claret wine" in the early Henry VI, Part Two, to Stephano's "celestial liquor" in his penultimate play, The Tempest. In Richard III, Richard's older brother Clarence is murdered and dumped into a butt of malmsey, and Iago entices cautious Cassio into a drunken revel in his plot to displace him in Othello's command. Claudius celebrates his coronation and marriage by keeping wassail as he "drains his draughts of Rhenish down," to Hamlet's bitter disgust. Sir Toby, Sir Andrew, Feste, and Maria hold their own wassail in Olivia's house of mourning, and, in perhaps the sweetest drinking scene Shakespeare ever wrote, Falstaff, Shallow, Silence, Davy, and Bardolph get tipsy-mellow in Shallow's Gloucestershire orchard in Henry IV, Part Two as they pass the jug around and sing, "A cup of wine that's brisk and fine, / And drink unto the leman mine, / And merry heart lives long-a."

In his great festive tragedy *Antony and Cleopatra*, Shakespeare reprises this moment in a much more dangerous environment, where the tipplers are the triple pillars of the Roman world (Lepidus, Caesar, and Antony). They punish the grape on their rival Pompey's galley. Lepidus gets smashed, Caesar confesses he would "rather fast from all four days / Than drink so much in one," and only Antony, his mind always circling back to Egypt and Cleopatra, celebrates that their bacchanal "ripens towards . . . an Alexandrian feast." Led by Antony, they all carry on in forced festivity, dancing and singing, "Cup us till the world go round." Shakespeare, with his intended or unintended felicities of depth and resonance, then reprises this archetypal scene with Stephano and Trinculo and their newfound admirer, Caliban, in *The Tempest*. As this clownish trio share Stephano's seemingly inexhaustible supply of wine, Trinculo has the jester's wisdom to observe, "They say there's but five of us upon this island; if th'other two be brained like us, the state totters."

The state of Shakespeare has rarely tottered, but when it did in the Victorian age, beer came to its rescue. There were big ideas to celebrate Shakespeare's tercentenary in London and Stratford in 1864. There were plans for memorials to be erected in both locations, special performances of his plays, grand banquets. Almost nothing of lasting consequence resulted. The leader of the Stratford celebration was the town's mayor and leading businessman, Edward Flower, who founded the Flowers Brewery in 1831. He donated several acres of land along the Avon River for the plans that never fully materialized, including the construction of a permanent theater where Shakespeare's plays could be performed.

What father envisioned, his son, Charles, accomplished years later when he successfully took up the challenge of creating a theater devoted to performing Shakespeare's plays on those acres along the banks of the Avon donated by his father. The Shakespeare Memorial Theater became the first permanent theater in England to be devoted to performing

Shakespeare's plays and became the future home, almost a century later, of the Royal Shakespeare Company. Members of the Flowers family continued to guide the theater through its long history and repeatedly bailed it out when it ran into trouble.

When the construction of the original theater faced funding delays, it was the Flowers family who repeatedly came up with the cash. The project was repeatedly mocked by locals and by national newspapers. But Shakespeare won even if Stratfordians referred to the finished product as "the theater built on beer." In 1926 the theater was destroyed by a massive fire and once again the Flowers family, this time in the person of Sir Archibald Flower (Charles's nephew), came to its rescue and led the funding drive to build a new playhouse. When Flowers had trouble raising funds for the new theater in England, he turned to America. He and his wife sailed to New York, where they wined and dined leading bankers and industrialists and hit the mother lode when John D. Rockefeller and others donated more than half of the £250,000 fundraising goal. Shakespeare would have survived in Stratford as its most famous native son but not as a vital, living playwright, if not for beer and America.

Stratford, in Shakespeare's day, was a thriving market town. Today it continues to thrive, but on the Shakespeare tourist trade, which reaches back at least to the eighteenth century. When Thomas Jefferson and John Adams visited in 1786, they were urged to buy a sapling from a mulberry tree they were assured Shakespeare himself had planted (sprigs of mulberry from that True Bush were still, in 1927, being distributed by the Flowers as gifts to the American contributors to the fund for the new theater). Thanks to the Flowers family, many of those tourists now are lured as much by the reputation of the Royal Shakespeare Company as by the opportunity to buy a contemporary version of that mulberry sapling!

If you are lucky to be in Stratford on a warm Sunday afternoon in July, you might be treated to an impromptu cricket match (a distant cousin of America's game) in the garden behind the Swan Theatre by members of the company (much as Broadway actors often gather in Central Park for softball games). In the 1960s and '70s Judi Dench was likely to be one of the players. I recommend you enjoy the experience with a can of Flowers Original Bitter with Shakespeare's image on the label. The Flowers Brewery no longer exists but is a part of the gigantic international beer conglomerate called, as we once again round third and dash for home, Anheuser-Busch InBev. American baseball's most famous brewing family is now united with Shakespeare's.

Beer is the elixir of baseball. It is a crucial component of the festive summer atmosphere surrounding a trip to the park. A cold brew enhances the experience of being in an urban garden rooting for the home team. If, as I have suggested, baseball brings the country to the city, so it also brings something of the spirit of the seasonal country agricultural revel to an industrial age. Beer keeps Falstaff's carnival spirit alive in pub and park, enriches the experience of the game, and reinforces our pleasure in the festive atmosphere baseball evokes.

THE 1984 WORLD SERIES

For Tiger fans, there was never a better season for baseball and beer than 1984. Contrary to Orwell, it was a utopian year for all who rooted for the Detroit side, including a couple of Athenians. Sam was in his senior year of high school and was now my baseball peer rather than protégé. The remarkable start the club made took the pressure off; we did not have to grind out the season and experience the September agony of a tight pennant race. The Tigers led wire to wire, sharing this feat only with the 1927 Yankees. The season was essentially about the first forty games and the last eight. The Tigers started 35–5 and finished up 7–1, sweeping the Royals in the playoffs and defeating the Padres 4–1 in the World Series. Those first forty games were a precious gift to the parched Tiger fan as the club got off to the greatest start in the history of the game and quickly mastered the art of winning.

Here is the breakdown of 35–5: They started 9–0, then lost their first game; then they ripped off seven straight before losing again; then they won three and lost two; then they reversed the starting numbers by going 7–1 and then 9–0. They scored five runs or more in twenty-five of those games while allowing two runs or fewer in nineteen. They came from behind in the seventh inning or later to win in seven games, with the game-winning hits coming from Parrish (3), Whitaker (2), Bergman (1), and Trammell (1)—a grand slam in the seventh versus the Royals. Morris went 9–1 with a no-hitter on national television against the White Sox in early April; Petry 7–1; Wilcox 6–0; Juan Berenguer 3–2; and Aurelio López won four in relief. Willie Hernandez had seven saves, López six. In eighteen games the Tigers scored in the first inning. The first quarter of the season was over, and they were eight and a half games up.

The Tigers won number thirty-five in Anaheim versus the Angels. The next morning Anderson was sitting with his wife in the hotel coffee shop having breakfast when a stranger came over and said, "Sparky Anderson. I'm from Dayton. When you managed Cincinnati, I was a big fan of yours, and I just want to thank you for all the happy times you gave us fans." Sparky thanked the man, who then continued by asking, "By the way, what are you doing now?" Sparky was on top of the world, but that remark brought him back to earth, as did the rest of the season, where the Tigers won-loss percentage was far more prosaic. They clinched on September 18 with a record of 97–54, thirteen games up on the Blue Jays, and finished the season 104–58.

Our personal experience of the '84 season was not as giddy until the World Series. We saw more games, eight, and in more locations, three, than usual, but the results did not mirror the regular season, as the Tigers lost five of the eight games we saw, including a Fourth of July weekend sweep by the White Sox in old Comiskey Park when we were visiting friends in Evanston. Sam and I saw them beat the Brewers on a Friday night in mid-June, 7–2, but we could not stay for the rest of the series because of an event we had to attend in Maumee, Ohio.

Later I saw them play a rare day-night doubleheader with the Twins. They lost the first game, but the second spoke to the season they were having. Gibson hit a two-run homer in the first to get them off to a typically strong start, and they picked up two more in the second, but Milt Wilcox couldn't hold the Twins, who scored runs in the fourth, fifth, and sixth to go up 5–4. The Tigers tied it in the seventh and then won it in the ninth when Gibson hit another two-run shot into the upper deck in right. That evening they demonstrated how they could win early and win late *in the same game*. Such was the pattern during much of the season; a pattern which held in the World Series as well.

In August, Miranda and I stopped for a game with the A's on our way to Stratford for a weekend of Shakespeare (where we would have the treat of seeing Douglas Campbell play Falstaff again almost thirty years after I had first seen him in the part in 1958) and were treated to a 14–1 blowout as Morris coasted to his sixteenth win. It was the last time Miranda and I took in a game by ourselves in Tiger Stadium, but we did get to see the Tigers play the Orioles in the penultimate game in Baltimore's old Memorial Stadium when she and Bill were living in Ellicott City, Maryland. The earlier game had the added pleasure of once again reuniting Detroit and Stratford, baseball and Shakespeare. And then, by pure serendipity, I had a conference to attend in the East in late September, so I caught their last game of the season, in Yankee Stadium, where Sparky rested many of the regulars and the Yanks won 9–2. The only notable item of the game was that Don Mattingly went 4 for 5, edging out his teammate Dave Winfield for the batting crown, .343–.340. It was the first time I had been back in the Bronx for a game since September of 1961, but this time we were finishing the season seventeen games up on the Yanks. So, there was no sting in the defeat, but only a subtle reminder of that fateful Labor Day weekend series back in 1961. And now Yogi Berra was the Yankee manager. The long, lovely 1984 campaign was finally over, and the Tigers were headed to the postseason for the first time since 1972.

Starting with the 1969 season each league was divided into an Eastern and Western Division. We had won the American League East while the Royals had won the West. In the National League the Cubs had finally made it to the postseason by winning the East while the Padres were the surprise winners in the West. The baseball world was rooting for a repeat of the Cubs–Tigers 1945 World Series. The Tigers did their job by sweeping their series with the Royals, displaying all facets of their brand of baseball: power, pitching, solid defense, timely hitting, and important contributions from the bench and bullpen.

Game 1 featured both power and pitching as Morris coasted to an 8–1 win with a strong seven innings and Herndon, Parrish, and Trammell all hit home runs. In game 2 the Tigers jumped out to a 3–0 lead on Brett Saberhagen thanks to a homer by Gibson, but Petry and Hernandez could not hold it and the game went into extra innings tied 3–3. In the eleventh Parrish singled off ace Royals reliever Dan Quisenberry, Evans attempted to sacrifice but was safe on an error, and John Grubb (getting a rare start) finished the job with a two-run double and a 5–3 win, sealed by three shutout innings of relief by Aurelio López. Game 3 was a brilliant 1–0 pitcher's duel between Milt Wilcox (the sole link with Sparky's 1970s Cincinnati teams) and Charlie Leibrandt. Wilcox got a single run in the second inning on a groundout by Marty Castillo and made it stand up as he threw a two-hit masterpiece with Willie Hernandez closing it out in the ninth.

With the '75 and '76 Reds, Sparky had gone with a settled daily lineup (who wouldn't with that group?), but with the '84 Tigers he began early in the season to use bench players as starters several times a week. Certain positions in the lineup were fixed, with Parrish behind the plate, Trammell and Whitaker at short and second, Lemon in center, and Gibson in right, but after that there was great fluctuation at third base, left field, DH, and first base. In the batting order, 1 through 4 were almost always Whitaker, Trammell, Gibson, and Parrish, but Sparky shuffled the bottom half like a deck of cards with Barbaro Garbey (remember him?), Darrell Evans, Larry Herndon, Ruppert Jones, John Grubb, Dave Bergman, Rusty Kuntz, Tom Brookens, Marty Castillo, and Howard Johnson all playing in seventy games or more and all appearing at least once in the postseason. While everyone remembers the colossal upper-deck three-run shot Kirk Gibson hit off Goose Gossage in the bottom of the seventh to salt game 5 and the World Series away, who remembers that it was Rusty Kuntz (later a longtime first base coach for the Kansas City Royals) who drove in the run that put the Tigers ahead for good (4–3) in the bottom of the fifth? And that it was only Kuntz's second plate appearance in the Series?

Sparky, known as Captain Hook for the rapidity with which he pulled his starters when managing the Reds, now did something similar with his position players. Over the course of the '84 season Sparky got game-winning hits from almost everyone on his bench, including Jones and Grubb and Garbey and Kuntz and most memorably from Dave Bergman in an at-bat that came to symbolize the Tigers season. The game was on a Monday night in early June at Tiger Stadium against the Blue Jays and their ace, Dave Stieb. Stieb, who dominated the Tigers, had them shut out 3–0 through six. In the seventh rookie Howard Johnson hit a two-out three-run homer to tie it. The game remained tied until the bottom of the tenth. The Tigers had two on with two out with Bergman coming to the plate.

Bergman was a lanky slick-fielding left-hander who shared first base through most of the season with Darrell Evans and Barbaro Garbey. He had come over to the Tigers in the last days of spring training in the great trade that had sent our fine right fielder Glenn Wilson and reserve catcher John Wockenfuss to the Phillies for Bergman and Willie Hernandez. At the time Jim Cox thought Bergman was the steal in the deal. As it turned out, they both were.

Wilson was expendable as he prevented Gibson, a natural right fielder, from getting into the starting lineup. This was the trade that many believed made the '84 team, primarily because of the exquisite year Hernandez had as our closer.

But Bergman also provided more than the Tigers front office, but not Cox, had bargained for. The Jays solid reliever Roy Lee Jackson and Bergman battled to a full count and then the confrontation became epic. Bergman managed to foul off seven straight pitches, several of which sure looked like ball 4 to me. Then he went down and golfed Jackson's thirteenth offering deep into the upper deck in right for the 6–3 win. The game was the first to be broadcast that season as part of ABC's Monday Night Baseball package, and Sam and I watched it all miraculously unfold sitting in beanbag chairs in front of our TV. Sparky spoke for many when he commented after the game, "Tonight I saw the greatest at-bat in my life." That game has so lodged itself into the great memory bank of Tiger games that when Dave Bergman died, all his obituaries made mention of that defining moment in his baseball career.

Though little noted, Sparky's use of Marty Castillo in the postseason was emblematic of his insistence on using his bench as an integral part of his team's dynamics. During the season he played five different players at third base: Howard Johnson, Tom Brookens, Barbaro Garbey, Darrell Evans, and Marty Castillo. Johnson, a promising rookie who would go on to have a fine major league career but with the Mets rather than the Tigers, got the most starts, but he was almost always replaced for defensive purposes by Tom Brookens in the late innings. Evans was a former third baseman in the process of converting in his later years to first, where he got most of his starts that year. Garbey, seemingly, could play anywhere and in 1984 had starts at third, first, left, and DH. But who remembers Marty Castillo?

Castillo was a third baseman and reserve catcher. He had been drafted by the Tigers in 1978 and had made brief September appearances with the team in '81 and '82, where he had a combined seven plate appearances. Over the next three seasons, which concluded his major league career, he had a combined total of 344 at bats. His lifetime batting average was .190. Sparky didn't play him in 1984 until the eleventh game and only sporadically thereafter, generally spelling Parrish, who was the strongest Tiger (Mike Schmidt said he was the strongest baseball player he ever met) and who never wanted to be out of the lineup. In the regular season Castillo appeared in seventy games and hit .234 with four home runs and 17 runs batted, the weakest numbers for any of the third basemen. Yet there was Castillo in the starting lineup for the first game of the playoffs, where he banged out two hits and drove in a run. Evans got the start in game 2, but Castillo was back out there for game 3, where, as mentioned, he drove in the only run of the game in the duel between Charlie Leibrandt and Milt Wilcox, in which each team only managed to get three hits.

What did Sparky know that everyone else in baseball, including Castillo, failed to anticipate? Whatever it was, it worked. He repeated the pattern in the World Series, with Castillo starting games 1, 3, and 5, going 3 for 9 and hitting a two-run upper-deck homer to left in the second inning of game 3 to put the Tigers in the lead in a game they won 5–2. In the game 5 clincher he went 2 for 3 and scored on Gibson's mighty eighth-inning blast. The kid had the greatest series of his life, and in the World Series! Mayo Smith's decision to move Mickey Stanley from center field to shortstop in the 1968 World Series to get Kaline into the lineup is a fixture of Tigers lore, but no one mentions Sparky's surprising use of Marty Castillo in 1984. They should. And he also played errorless ball at third.

The Tigers swept the Royals, but they had to wait for the Cubs. And are still waiting. The Cubs went to five games with the Padres and then missed their rendezvous with the Tigers in Wrigley when, after winning the first two at home, they lost three in a row, and the Series, in San Diego. The crucial game was the fifth. The Cubs led 3–2 in the bottom of the seventh when, with one out and a runner on second, a tame little groundball and sure second out squirted through

Leon Durham's legs and into right field to tie the game and then the valiant Rick Sutcliffe, who had gone 16–1 since the Cubs acquired him in midseason, suddenly lost it and gave up a single to Alan Wiggins, a double to Tony Gwynn, and a single to Steve Garvey for a 6–3 lead and the game and the NL championship as Goose Gossage came in and shut the Cubs down in the eighth and ninth.

It is a familiar phenomenon that professors become attached to the colleges and universities where they teach and inevitably begin to see their institutions as the center of the world. I was amused by this as an undergraduate at Hamilton College observing some of my professors' certainties about the college's place in the universe, but now I find myself often guilty of the same romantic perspective. Ohio University is an old university. With roots in a provision in the Northwest Ordinance of 1787, it was founded in 1804 and is the oldest public university west of the Alleghenies, but if you listened to me, you might think it was as ancient as Harvard and as distinguished as our much younger cousin Michigan, not founded until 1837. We have produced our share of outstanding graduates, including a Nobel Prize winner now teaching at Cambridge University, former senators, governors, and statesmen, and, for the purposes of this account, Mike Schmidt, Bob Brenly, and Steve Swisher.

So how was Ohio University going to get me tickets to the World Series? One of our most successful alums was John Galbraith. Mr. Galbraith was a builder and developer who was a part owner, along with Bing Crosby among others, of the Pittsburgh Pirates. He also owned the finest racing stable in Ohio, Darby Dan Farms, which had bred and trained the 1963 Derby winner Chateaugay. His daughter, Jodi Phillips, followed her father to Ohio University, and when I began teaching there she was on our Board of Trustees. She was a warm, naturally generous woman who loved her university and was quick to appreciate faculty who were able to share their subject matter with alumni groups. Shakespeare is unbelievably handy for such occasions, and she and I quickly became mutual admirers.

Nineteen eighty-four was long before StubHub; I didn't know anyone in Detroit; I knew a Shakespeare prof at Michigan but didn't figure him to move in sports circles; where the hell was I going to get my hands on World Series tickets? Because the Series was set to open in the National League city that year, it was perfectly set up for Sam and me as the three middle games would be played on the weekend in Detroit. I figured that we could always just go and trust that we could find some tickets from the scalpers we dealt with on normal trips to Tiger Stadium. But at what cost? And because it was the World Series would the cops be less likely to look the other way and let the underground market do its work?

And then that cartoon light bulb went off in my head: Jodi Phillips. I knew all the major league teams got tickets. Would the Pirates want to use all of theirs? Perhaps not, went the dream reasoning. I called Jodi and explained the situation. She listened politely and then said, "I think I can be of help. Let me have your phone number and I'll have the clubhouse manager of the Pirates give you a call."

Within an hour I got a call from Pittsburgh: "How many do you want?" says a gruff, whiskey voice.

"Two for each of the games in Detroit," says I.

"Are you sure that's enough?" comes the reply.

I was so excited about scoring two that it never occurred to me to get my hands on as many as possible. "No. Two would be swell, and what do I owe you?"

"Twenty-five bucks a ticket." And that was it. And wasn't Sam going to be ever so pleased with his father? We were in. And years later (in 2006) he would return the favor. And not for $25 a ticket. The ones we bought for the most recent Tigers World Series in 2012 had a face value of $250. And sadly, no Jodi Phillips to help us get them for that!

The World Series began on my birthday, October 9, in Jack Murphy Stadium. It opened as the season and the playoffs had with a Morris gem. The offense started early as Whitaker led off with a double and Trammell promptly singled him home. That should be enough for Jack, we thought.

But Morris was unaccountably nervous in the bottom half of the first and gave up two runs, and we were suddenly worried. What happens if our ace doesn't have it? But he did. The jitters over, he shut them down the rest of the way and got the win when quiet, unassuming Mr. Clutch, Larry Herndon, hit a two-run homer off Mark Thurmond in the top of the fifth. That was all Morris needed: 3–2 Tigers.

The next night looked like a repeat when the Tigers jumped on Ed Whitson for five hits and three runs in the first with Whitaker and Trammell setting the table for Gibson, Parrish, and Evans. Dick Williams pulled Whitson immediately and went to his pen. I wondered if that was a World Series first, a starter pulled in the first inning. Remarkably, Hawkins and then Lefferts held the Tigers scoreless for the next 8⅓ innings. The Padres chipped away at Dan Petry's lead, and in the fifth Kurt Bevacqua—who would turn out to be something of the series clown, including blowing kisses to the crowd as he rounded the bases—hit a three-run homer and that was it: Padres 5–3. Perhaps we would have a real series after all.

The teams moved from the new America to the old, from sunny, prosperous Southern California to gloomy, gritty Motown. It was gray and spitting rain when I picked up Sam at noon from Athens High School and we sprinted the four-and-a-half-hour trip in Hotspur, our bruised and weather-beaten 1967 yellow Mustang convertible, making the last road trip of its frolicsome life. "The Eye of the Tiger," "What's Love Got to Do with It," Huey Lewis and the News and Stevie Wonder were our radio companions until we hit Bowling Green and could pick up WJR and baseball talk. We checked in at the Holiday Inn in Taylor about fifteen miles south of Detroit and were mingling with the big crowd at the corner of Michigan and Trumbull by 6:30. Not many Padres fans in evidence and nothing seemed to distinguish this crowd in any way from the large ones we mingled in on a normal Friday night.

A Bud at Hoot Robinson's just across Trumbull from the stadium and a lingering glance, for legacy and luck, at

the old Tigers whose pictures filled the walls: Cobb and Cochrane, Kell and Kaline, Newhouser and Lolich, Greenberg
and Gehringer, Horton and Cash, the Bird and Hoot Evers.
Father and son were both excited but were trying hard to
play it cool. We were worried about Wilcox. He had an unexpectedly exceptional year, winning 17 as the third starter
and getting his worn-out right arm through the season on
guts and cortisone. On the plus side, he was pitching on a
full week's rest after his masterful 1–0 AL pennant clincher
versus the Royals, and Sparky had his fine bullpen in good
shape should Wilcox falter. On the other hand, Tony Gwynn,
Terry Kennedy, Alan Wiggins, Steve Garvey, Graig Nettles,
and Garry Templeton had all begun to hit in game 2, and if
Nettles and Kennedy got hot the Padres could be formida-
ble, as the Cubs had learned.

We headed to our seats in section 232, about ten rows
up from the field down the right field line parallel with and
just up from the Padres' bullpen. Our row was just ahead of
the massive steel girders that held up the upper deck and
allowed it to lean out far over the lower deck—a unique
feature of Tiger Stadium. The old girl was dressed up in
the typical red, white, and blue bunting, proud to be the
oldest park to host a World Series game at the time, only
later surpassed by Fenway (they were both built in 1912)
when the Red Sox made it to the Series in 2004. Roger
Angell, in his report for the *New Yorker* on the '84 World
Series, described Tiger Stadium's atmosphere of antiquity
and the way it and older baseball fields like it, tucked into
dense urban landscapes, "seem to hold and intensify the
sounds and hopes and intimate oneness of their crowds,
and when you're inside, watching your team (in its old
brilliant home whites, with the same famous, old-timey
gothic initial) violently at play, it's possible to wonder for
a moment which decade you are in and which wonderful,
hero-strewn lineup is on view down there, in the instant
of its passing from action to history."[5] Sam and I found
ourselves, as we had been with Len Barker's perfect game,
trapped in that instant.

We could tell from the conversations swirling around us that we were among players from other clubs or Tiger fans who had gotten their tickets from them. The light rain had stopped, and the temps were in the high fifties—not what you would call ideal baseball weather—as the pregame activities got underway and Vice President Bush threw out the first pitch. The country was about to reelect Reagan in a landslide, but I don't recall that Bush, an old first baseman, got a particularly warm or energetic welcome: we're here for the game, the large crowd seemed to say, get on with it. And we did.

Milt Wilcox versus Tim Lollar, and after a scoreless first the Tigers once again jumped out to the lead. They scored four in the bottom of the second on a two-run homer by Sparky's lad Marty Castillo, a Trammell double, and a Herndon walk with the bases loaded. And, as in game 1, the Padres starting pitching imploded as Lollar gave up four walks as well as four hits and the four runs, and Williams pulled him in the second. And, again as in game 1, the Padres pen was as strong as its starting pitching was weak, pitching 5⅔ innings and giving up only one more run. The huge crowd kept waiting for the Tiger hitters to explode so it could also, but it wasn't to be. The Tigers left fourteen runners on base, usually a recipe for disaster, but Wilcox gave his club six solid innings, yielding seven hits but only a single run. Bill Scherrer and Willie Hernandez worked the final three giving up a run and the Tigers held on for a 5–2 win.

Our scorecard indicates that the crucial point in the game came in the seventh when, with one run in and a runner on third, Terry Kennedy hit a smash into deep right center. Lemon raced back, glanced up once over his shoulder, turned on the jets, and made a basket catch just as he reached the warning track for the last out of the inning. The big crowd was on its feet cheering for its own Willie Mays and continued to roar its approval until Lemon, greeted robustly by his teammates and doffing his cap, disappeared into the Tigers dugout. Tiger Stadium's center field was the deepest in the majors at 440 feet. Kennedy's smash would have been a home run in San Diego.

The game wasn't pretty, but then the Tigers had shown during the season that they could win the ugly ones as well. We headed back to Eureka Road and a late-night sandwich, beer, and recap at Schwartzmann's Deli. We went to bed in good spirits. We were up two games to one with Morris going tomorrow. Saturday's game was at 4, so we slept in and headed out about 10 for a fast eighteen holes at the nearby Riverview Highlands golf course. Weather much like the day before. Gray, overcast, misting, but mild in the low sixties. The golf handicap is one of man's greatest inventions as it can create genuine competition between two golfers of widely separated skills. I am a duffer, but Sam had made himself into a much more accomplished player, winning several letters on his high school golf team and many more later in college. He usually must give me five strokes a side and still wins, though once in a great while the old man pulls a surprise. I didn't on this day, but I was still in the match until the seventeenth hole—a par 3 with the green guarded by a small pond. I put two into the water and limped home. Back to the room for a cold beer and off to the game.

We cut it a little closer that day, so we headed right to our seats with a couple of the Tiger Stadium specialties: grilled Polish sausages with onions and green peppers. We settled down to a quintessential Morris masterpiece. Jack Morris is the greatest pitcher I have had the joy of watching in person on multiple occasions over almost two decades. He was the best right-handed pitcher of the 1980s, squeezed in between Tom Seaver and Roger Clemens. He is unlike them (and other greats) in that he tended to pitch not to dominate the game but just to win. He could and did win games by 1–0 and 2–0 scores, including one of the greatest concluding World Series games of all time, when the Twins beat the Braves 1–0 in ten innings in 1991. Morris refused the attempt of his manager (Tom Kelly) to lift him after nine and went the distance for the win. Morris had Bob Gibson's fierce competitive spirit, but all he wanted to do was to beat you, and if that took winning 1–0 or 5–3 or 7–4, fine. Like many power pitchers, he was given to moments of petulance as he struts and frets his hour upon the mound. He was fortunate that for most of his career he had Lance Parrish as his catcher. Parrish was a figure of natural authority and did not shy from confronting Jack on the mound when he showed his dissatisfaction with an ump's call or a teammate's error. Parrish (and Sparky) made Morris channel his anger to his own purposes rather than dissipating it in petty tantrums.

Game 4 turned out to be the Morris-and-Trammell show. Trammell joined Morris as the two most deserving players made to wait far too long to get their Hall of Fame invitations. Most baseball fans know Trammell as a steady solid shortstop whose major claim to fame is playing nineteen seasons with the same second base partner, Lou Whitaker. But he made all the plays at short, and when the Tigers needed offense from his bat, he provided it. In the first, Whitaker was safe on Wiggins's error and Trammell followed with a line shot into the lower deck in left. In the third, after one out Whitaker singled and Trammell promptly hit an Eric Show changeup on a high arc into the upper deck in left. That was all Morris needed. He gave up a home run to Kennedy in the second and then a double to Bevacqua and was so burned that he struck out the next hitter, Carmelo Martínez, on three pitches, looking. He gave up a double to Garvey in the ninth with one out. Garvey moved up to third on a bounce out and came home when Morris threw a splitter in the dirt that got past Parrish. Bevacqua then lined to Gibson in right and that was the game: 4–2.

Morris went the distance, only faced five hitters over the minimum, got eleven groundball outs and three popups to the right side, and threw only 102 pitches. He didn't walk a batter and set the Padres down in order in the first, fourth, fifth, sixth, and seventh innings. The game was over in two hours and twenty minutes. Morris did not make it look as easy as Tom Seaver, for instance, did. He had a herky-jerky motion to the plate which seemed to expend lots of energy, but he had season after season of 220-plus innings, was known for pitching complete games, and was never on the disabled list. Sam and I had just seen him at his best, but he had done the same thing in the first games of the playoffs and World Series. In three pressure games he had pitched twenty-five innings and given up just five runs. And one knew that if the Padres somehow rallied from being down 3–1 to extend the Series to its limit, Morris would be there with a similar performance in game 7. Sam and I realized we were watching a player working at the top of his art and craft and getting all the help he needed from his steady-fielding power-hitting shortstop. We lingered in our seats for ten or fifteen minutes going back over the scorecard, marveling at just how dominant Morris had been. And man did we feel good about our team and our good fortune.

Back to the motel we went for a quick change and then out in search of large steak and a good California cab. We found it in the Detroit suburb of Framingham at the Chicago Road Steakhouse and had the added treat of discovering that Steve Trout, the son of the old Tiger hurler from the 1940s Dizzy Trout, was having dinner there too. He had had a solid season with the Cubs (13–7) and was another reminder that this should have been a World Series featuring the Cubs and the Tigers. His dad pitched for the Tigers in the 1940s and was still with the club when I first visited Tiger Stadium in 1950. The sentimental reminder of the 1950s, fathers and sons, coupled with this historic moment with the Tigers on the verge of winning just their fourth World Series title, was rich and only increased by a martini, a Heitz cab, and a New York strip, "burned rare" as my father used to order his.

A 5 p.m. start. The last World Series game to begin in daylight. We slept very late, played just nine holes, returned to pack up and check out, and had a little lunch. We were at the Corner by 4. Another gray, misting day. Very little scalping action on the street. Nobody in Detroit wanted to miss this: the Tigers' first chance to win the Series at home since 1935. A Bud at Hoots and conversation with some Padres fans who couldn't believe how tawdry Detroit and Corktown were. I've never been to San Diego, but I imagine there can't be two more varied major cities in the country: the Rust Belt and River Rouge versus Surfer City and Coronado Island. They also couldn't believe (along with the rest of the baseball world) how poorly the San Diego starters had performed in the Series. In four games they had pitched a total of ten innings; Morris alone had pitched eighteen in two. I tried to steer the conversation to the different ways in which each team was built. The Tigers shaped their club almost exclusively from the inside with a few crucial additions from free agency and trades: Wilcox, Evans, Hernandez; while the Padres were largely a collection—many in their last playing days—of pickups from other clubs: Garvey from the Dodgers, Nettles and Gossage from the Yanks, Templeton and Kennedy from the Cards, with the great Tony Gwynn the only major player produced by the Padres' farm system.

I suggested that most of these Tigers had been playing together for four or five years and had become a team, something more than just a collection of former All-Stars. My argument was ignored, as the San Diego fans continued to flog one long-dead horse: starting pitching, starting pitching, starting pitching. Game time. Sam and I made our way one last time through gate 12 into the concourse and then up the short ramp to look out over the green expanse as we proceeded down the walkway just a few feet to our aisle. If you entered Tiger Stadium from the corner of Michigan and Trumbull, you were in right field. The few but charmed balls hit out over the third deck of the stadium landed on Trumbull, or in the case of a famous Ruth shot, into the lumber yard on the other side of the street (just down from Hoots), where, rumor has it, the ball is still rolling.

Dan Petry versus Mark Thurmond. Morris, Petry, and Wilcox were a solid trio, winning 19, 18, and 17 games during the season. Morris and Wilcox had already shown their stuff in the postseason, but Petry had scuffled in game 2 in San Diego. The Padres wanted to get off to an aggressive start as the Tigers had been doing. Wiggins obliged by singling and stealing second and moving to third on a bad throw. But Petry fanned Gwynn—who, sad to say, was having a

middling series for a great hitter who had led the National
League with a .351 average—and Wiggins tried to score on
a Garvey grounder to second, but Lou threw him out on
a close, very close, play at home. Dick Williams came out
to protest and kicked some dirt while the crowd got into
it with all the old bromides. Nettles grounded out. So the
Padres had had a chance to grab the lead and failed. Now it
was the Tigers' turn.

They did not disappoint. Whitaker singled; Trammell
forced him at second but beat the double-play throw from
Wiggins; Gibson, grabbing the spotlight from Trammell,
homered; Parrish singled; Herndon singled; Lemon singled,
scoring Parrish, but then Herndon was out trying to steal
third. Garbey then popped to second, but the damage was
done. Tigers 3–0. But Petry wasn't sharp. He gave up a single
run in the third and two more in the fourth, when Sparky
had seen enough and sent the lefty Bill Sherrer in to get the
last out. The Battle of the Bullpens was on. Sherrer got two
outs in the fifth and then gave way to Aurelio López (Señor
Smoke), who was on fire and retired the next seven hitters,
including three strikeouts. In 2⅓ innings he threw twenty-
one strikes, including his last fourteen pitches. He brought
the crowd to life, who began to roar with his every whiff.

With the game tied 3–3 in the bottom of the fifth, Gibson singled, Parrish flied out, Herndon and Lemon walked,
and Sparky sent Rusty Kuntz (Rusty who?) up to pinch-hit.
He hit Craig Lefferts's first pitch and lifted a lazy fly into
short right. It should have been Gwynn's ball, as he would
then be better positioned to throw home rather than the
backpedaling Wiggins. But in one of the many little mistakes that can influence a Series, Wiggins waved him off and
then made a weak throw home off his back foot that badly
missed the speedy Gibson, tagging up: 4–3. A good tight
ballgame. Things remained that way until the seventh when
with one out Lance Parrish hit a fastball from Goose Gossage (who had just entered the game) into the lower deck
in left. "Goose-buster," the big crowd chanted as Parrish
rounded the bases.

Willie Hernandez came in to pitch the eighth. "Game over," we said, as it had been in thirty-four of his thirty-five appearances as the closer during the season. But the Padres were not done yet, as after a popup and a lineout to Whitaker, the crowd responding with its melodious "Louuuuuuuu . . . Louuuuuuuu . . . Louuuuuuuu," Mr. Razzle-Dazzle, Kurt Bevacqua, hit a two-out homer to left to tighten things up. The crowd suddenly went quiet as the next hitter, Martínez, singled and Williams sent in Luis Salazar to pinch run. Hernandez threw four straight pitches to Templeton without once going over to first. On the sixth Salazar took off before Willie went to the plate, and Willie picked him off, 1-3-4. Tiger Stadium let out an audible sigh of relief and to the bottom of the eighth we went. Had Sparky intercepted the Padres steal sign, we wondered, or did Salazar, in breaking for second too soon, make another of those small mistakes that were now adding up?

And then the climax of the long weekend's brilliant Tiger baseball began. Goose was still on the mound. Castillo (remember him?) worked a walk after Goose got two quick strikes on him. Whitaker laid down a bunt to Nettles at third, who fielded it quickly and made the throw to second to try and catch the lead runner. But Templeton, sure that Nettles would go to first, was standing in front of the bag, not on it, and Castillo slid in safely. Another San Diego mental error. Now with the best hitter of the Series coming to the plate with a runner in scoring position, Anderson played National League ball. In a move that surprised all of us, he had Trammell lay down a perfect sacrifice bunt, moving the runners up. Then came the beautiful defining moment of this World Series. Castillo on third. Whitaker on second. One out. First base open. Gibson to the plate and Williams to the mound. From the dugout Sparky was holding up four fingers to Gibson, saying, "He's going to walk you." Well of course he is. And that's why Williams is on the mound. To tell Goose to walk him. More "Goose-busters" booming in from the center field bleachers packed with Wolverines and Spartans. But Goose is telling Williams, "I own him. I've fanned him before, and I will again." Turns out Gibson did face Gossage several years ago in his first major league at-bat and Goose struck him out on three pitches.

Williams acquiesces and makes the slow walk back to the dugout, and we can see that he is shaking his head, unconvinced, but he is going to let him do it. A light rain begins to fall. Is Hemingway in the house? Goose rears back and that huge body, with arms and legs flying off in all directions, lets one rip that Gibson takes low and in. Ball 1. Here comes another zinger but this one is up in the zone. Gibson's Thunder Boy meets it perfectly in the sweet spot and sends it like a rocket deep into the upper deck in right. Everyone leaps to their feet. Ecstasy and pandemonium.

The Tigers, all gathered on the upper steps of the dugout, race to greet him at the plate as Gibson prances around the bases, pumping his right arm in the air, then both arms are over his head as he rounds third, then he loses his helmet in the wild melee when he reaches home and turns towards the dugout and the fans behind it with both arms again in the air and his blond hair bouncing to the music of the night. An awful scene to endure if you are a Padres fan but heaven if you have been waiting to be present at such an iconic moment for what amounts to all your life.

I am trying to high-five Sam. The guy behind me has me locked in a bear hug. And I am trying to wrestle free to accept a sweeter hug from the woman seated in front of me, who has turned to join our celebration. For an educated man and a college professor I have a salty mouth, and I gave it free rein in the bloody joy of the moment. Now those choice expletives erupt from the simple overwhelming amazement that my club's most charismatic player has delivered a mythic blow against a mighty foe named Goose in the fifth and final game of the World Series. The crowd drowns out my exclamations with a reprise of "Goose-buster" and then a rousing version of "Na na na na, na na na na, hey hey-ey, good-bye." And then a roaring version of the primordial Detroit chant: "Let's go, Ti-gers, let's go."

The damage done, Goose promptly struck out Parrish and Herndon and we went to the ninth. Willie got Templeton on a bounce out, gave up a harmless single to the pinch-hitter Bruce Bochy (yes, that Bruce Bochy), popped Wiggins up to Parrish, and then got Gwynn to lift a lazy fly to left that Herndon chased down near the line, and it was over. Willie at 6′2″ and Parrish at 6′3″ had a hard time trying to jump into each other's arms. They never quite made it as their teammates mobbed them and made the traditional happy pile of mingled bodies on the mound.

The rain intensified but did not keep the fans seated near the field from vaulting over the railing and running out into right field, including Sam, gone before I could say, "Not a good idea." But what did I know? I thought for a moment that he was violating sacred ground by doing his dance on turf belonging exclusively to Gibson and Kaline and Ruth and Robinson and Wahoo Sam Crawford and Harry Heilmann and all the other great right-fielders who had played there and that he might incur the wrath of the baseball gods. But he was celebrating at the shrine, urged on by Dionysus and Falstaff. Sam stuffed his pockets with turf, which he brought home and replanted in our side yard. Without success. Spartan turf (thank you, Mr. Gibson) won't grow in Athens. I walked down the ten or so rows to stand in the rain on the edge of the field as more youngsters invaded the now-muddy outfield. And once again Shakespeare popped into my head, reminding me that medieval English Morris dancers performed in groups of nine:

> The nine men's morris is fill'd up with mud
> And the quaint mazes in the wanton green
> For lack of tread are indistinguishable.

These lines from *A Midsummer Night's Dream* describe the dislocations in the natural world caused by a quarrel between two powerful supernatural figures. Oberon and Titania. Their quarrel has interrupted the normal Morris dances celebrating midsummer festivity. The "wanton green" has turned to mud. But here at the corner of Michigan and Trumbull, the wanton green of Tiger baseball since 1912, the mud (as it turns out to be in Shakespeare's *Dream* as well) was not an obstacle but a release, crucial to the festive moment.

I was drained and drenched and full of bliss and beer and, like Bottom, in need of a nice cold bottle of hay. Sam rejoined me and we made our way around the stadium on the inside saying a long farewell to the looming hulk and exited down the left field line to our lot across I-75, which ran behind the stadium. We walked over the footbridge and crawled into Hotspur and were pleased to note that much of the crowd had already departed. I located a cold Bud at the bottom of the cooler, and as Sam eased us out onto I-75 South we were struck by the fact that there were as many cars streaming into the Corner as there were those like us, leaving. I gave it no further thought and enjoyed my beer as we turned on WRJ and headed south to Bowling Green, where we had planned to spend the night.

By the time we were out on I-75 we had missed all the presentations but quickly learned that Trammell had been named the Series MVP, and deservedly so. Sparky was chirping with Ernie Harwell and spinning out the usual clichés that he, like Stengel before him, could almost make sound like wisdom. "These are a fine group of men." "They are professionals, and they play like it." "I was glad the fans finally got to see some fireworks tonight. We showed 'em we can with win with power as well as pitching." "Alan Trammell is the finest young man I've had the pleasure of managing and Kirk Gibson's future is unlimited . . . unlimited." Then he said something I thought was out of place, as rather than enjoying this day and this great victory he was already beginning to manage for the next season. "I'm so proud of these men for all they have accomplished, but winning one isn't enough. The mark of a great team is winning them back-to-back." This did not seem the appropriate moment to jump forward to next year and to hold up his '75 and '76 Reds as the model. I wished Harwell had asked him about Trammell's sacrifice bunt in the eighth. Those are the little details one wants to savor and turn over and wonder where his thinking came from when flashing the bunt sign or if Trammell had acted unselfishly on his own.

Sam had been keeping a running composite of Series batting averages, and while some were obvious, like Trammell's .450 and Gibby's .333 and Whitaker's solid .278, others managed to escape the attention they deserved, starting with Larry Herndon, who was 5 for 15, and Lemon, who was almost as good at 5 for 17, and Parrish, who was 5 for 18. The surprises were at first base where we got nothing from Evans and Bergman, who were a combined 1 for 20, and DH, where Barbaro Garbey was 0 for 12. And of course, Marty Castillo hit .333 and Rusty Kuntz drove in what came to be the winner of the final game (eclipsed in memory by Gibson's blast) with his second at-bat in the Series.

On the other side, it was the Padres' big hitters Garvey, Nettles, and Kennedy who let them down, going a sad 11 for 51, while the table setters like Wiggins and Templeton were a solid 14 for 41. Gwynn was a respectable .263, but that was almost one hundred points lower than his season' s average. Only Bevacqua played over his grade level, hitting .412 with two home runs and four RBIs—the best on the team. And the San Diego starters were, of course, atrocious. For the baseball world this was not a great Series, but for Tigers fans our greats were great. Morris and Trammell and Gibson and Sparky made it indelible. And finally, for those brown-and-orange Padres uniforms, I am with King Lear, who says to Poor Tom about his tattered rags, "I do not like the fashion of your garments. You'll say they are Persian; but let them be changed."

When we got to Bowling Green and turned on the television, we were amazed to see the postgame carnage out on Michigan and Trumbull as the celebrants streaming into the city quickly got out of hand, turned over several cars, including a police vehicle, and set them on fire. It wasn't a riot (what was there to riot about? Winning the World Series?), and it did not spread out of Corktown, but it was boorish behavior and another sad black eye for Detroit. I have been in small college town versions of such moments. They are over by 3 or 4 a.m. and the mess cleaned up by dawn so that anyone driving by the next morning would have wondered what all the fuss was about. But of course, in this instance, the several hours of mindless hooliganism was broadcast to the nation and the youth of Detroit managed to tip the celebration of liberty into the chaos of license.

We were up and on the road by 8; I dropped Sam at the high school before noon; came home, showered, and was in the office by 1 to be greeted by the silent treatment from the staff. Where have you been? Nice weekend, was it? When I went to teach my class the next morning at 11, I had a last sweet surprise. On the desk was a baseball wedged into a holder with three gold prongs signed by most of the members of my freshman writing seminar on Shakespeare. And as monikers they had used the grammatical errors they were known for. Thus: James "Comma Splice" Smith or Lorin "Dangling Participle" Green or Keith "Run-on Sentence" Ross or Sherri "Frag" Ruttan. At the bottom, the plaque read, "Detroit Tigers 1984 World Series." That ball is still on my desk, many of the signatures now faded, but it remains the most treasured autographed baseball in my collection.

Sparky's lobbying for two in a row did not come to pass, and the Tigers did not return to the World Series under his leadership, which stretched from 1979 through the 1995 season, but he remains the longest-serving and most successful (in terms of victories) Tiger manager. His Tigers had the best record of any American League team in in the 1980s, with nine straight winning seasons, but only made it back to the postseason once. And that was in dramatic fashion. As our kids grew up and headed to college and their parents found their professional lives more tied to administrative duties with heavy summer responsibilities for me, we were pulled in many different directions, none of which pointed north to Detroit. Miranda went to Hamilton in the fall of '83, spent her junior year in Paris, and by '87 had graduated and was off for two years in the Peace Corps in Botswana. Sam headed to Lawrence in the fall of '85 and by '89 had graduated and was off for two years in Japan. He and I got back to Tiger Stadium in '86 to see the Red Sox win three of four and then again in '88, when we won three out of four from the Angels and Mariners. Perhaps all the excitement and satisfaction of '84 had filled our baseball tank after such a long drought. Nineteen eighty-seven turned out to be the last great season for the Anderson-led Tigers as soon free agency would lure away some of its core: Morris, Parrish, and Gibson. Only Trammell and Whitaker stayed on as the great bargain duo, playing for six figures when their former mates were cashing in for seven.

I only got to Detroit once in the summer of '87, and that was a solo journey to see them play two against the Twins in mid-August. They showed me they were happy to have me back in the house by rolling to 7–1 and 8–0 wins. The Tigers were in a tight race with the Blue Jays all the way deep into September, and the season came down to the last ten games, seven of which would be played head-to-head—four in Toronto, and then, after each played a series against another club, three games in Detroit to finish the year. Those final seven Tiger-Jay games remain among the greatest of season-enders in baseball history. All were decided by one run; in six of them the losing team scored first; four of them were decided in the ninth inning, one in the twelfth, and one in the thirteenth; starting pitching, in all but one game, was effective, with the games being decided by low scores: 4–3, 3–2, 3–2, 4–3, 3–2, 1–0, but the bullpens were crucial in both saves and losses. When the series in Toronto began, the Jays had a half-game lead, and they promptly won the first game, beating Morris 4–3 with four runs in the third. In the second they entered the ninth trailing 2–0 but scored three off Willie Hernandez and Mike Henneman for the win. In the third (with both starters departing in the third inning) they trailed 9–7 in the ninth and scored three to win 10–9 when Henneman couldn't hold the lead. Toronto was up three and a half and the Tigers were on the ropes.

The '87 Toronto series reminds me that, except for '84, the Tigers have long had bullpen woes and here they were happening not at midseason but at crunch time. Game 4 in Toronto, in retrospect, was crucial. If the Tigers lost, they would be down four and a half with six to play; if they won, they would be two and a half back and still hanging on. Doyle Alexander (the great late-season pickup but at the price of John Smoltz) versus Jim Clancy. Alexander gave up one in the first, and that remained the game's only run when we reached the ninth. The Jays' relief ace Tom Henke was on the mound with Kirk Gibson leading off. The game was nationally televised, and I was hoping for a little fifth game of the World Series magic from Gibson, who loves the limelight. And he delivered again with a magnificent shot over the fence in right: 1–1. The game went to extra innings. Darrell Evans hit one out in the eleventh and we were up one, but the Jays got it back on a rare Trammell error and a single by Jesse Barfield. In the thirteenth Gibson did it again, only more modestly this time. Jim Walewander (how's that for a name? One of Sparky's favorites) walked, was sacrificed to second by Sweet Lou, and came home on Gibson's single up the middle. The Tiger pen finally closed one out, the Tigers had a 3–2 win, and we were still in the race.

Toronto was stunned and promptly lost three in a row to the Brewers while the Tigers split four with the Orioles, and it was down to the Jays and Tigers on final weekend of the season. In a repeat of the home team pattern established in Toronto, the Tigers won the first two games 4–3 and 3–2 (this one in twelve innings with a single from Trammell driving in the game winner) after initially trailing in each. Game 162. Frank Tanana versus Jimmy Key, two crafty left-handers. If the Tigers lose, the two teams are tied with a playoff game scheduled for Monday; if they win, they clinch. Again, the game was on national television, and again I was glued to the set. Both pitchers were remarkable, but Tanana, being my guy, was never better. He had been a flamethrower in his youth, blew his arm out, and reinvented himself as a junk man. And his junk was a thing of beauty on this Sunday afternoon. He had the Jays power hitters off stride all day with one teasing toss after another. Larry Herndon hit a second-inning home run, Tanana made it stand up, and the Tigers were the Eastern Division champs again.

The Tigers went 5–1 in their final six, while the Jays lost them all and once again had to limp back home to Toronto, but they would eventually get their revenge by maturing into the dominant American League power in the early 1990s, capped by two World Series victories. We remember the season for the way it ended, but need to be reminded of the remarkable year Alan Trammell had. Trammell over his career was the prototypical number-two hitter. He was a master of the hit-and-run, could put down a bunt when required, move runners over, and reach the gaps as a doubles hitter. He also had a little power, as evidenced by his performance in the '84 World Series, and rightly was included with the new wave of shortstops like Cal Ripken Jr., Robin Yount, Dave Concepción, and Barry Larkin, who were known as much for their bats as their gloves. After the 1986 season the Tigers lost Lance Parrish via free agency and Sparky turned to Trammell to fill his hole as the number four hitter, the cleanup man. And Trammell responded with a season in which he hit .343, blasted 28 home runs, and drove in 105. Those are Ernie Banks numbers. Modest, unassuming Trammell was asked, and he delivered. But he was not rewarded, as the Blue Jays' George Bell, who hit 47 homers and had a strong season, won the MVP award. After the season's last game Lou Whitaker pulled up the second base bag, put a message on it, and delivered it to his partner in the locker room. The message read: Alan Trammell 1987 MVP.

The Twins won the Wild Card in '87 with 85 victories while the Tigers won the East with 98, but in baseball's convoluted ways, the opening of the postseason rotated from year to year, and it was the West's turn to host in '87. That meant that the Tigers had to open the series in the Metrodome, not a tough place to play during the year, when it was usually half full, but a clamorous madhouse when jammed. And jammed it was for the two opening games of the series. The Tigers, though a veteran team, let the noise and the Twins get to them. They collapsed, and it did not get any better when the series, with the Twins up 2–0, switched to Tiger Stadium. The Tigers managed a Saturday afternoon victory thanks to a Pat Sheridan home run, but the Twins won on Friday and Sunday and what had been a sweet triumph a mere week ago had now turned to ignominy. The good news was that the Wild Card Twins went on to win the World Series, and even though Kirk Gibson followed Parrish out the free agency door in the offseason, the Anderson Tigers would make one last run at the Eastern Division championship the following year in a race in which the top four teams, at season's end, were separated by only two games.

SHAKESPEARE AND BASEBALL VI

Nineteen eighty-eight was a landmark year; the powerful Tigers of the 1980s had their last hurrah and a final run at the pennant. In the following year they completely collapsed and fell to 59 and 103—the first time in the decade they had not won at least 83 games and the first time they finished dead last. Nineteen eighty-eight was also the year I wrote the first of the Baseball Letters. The Shakespeare Association of America traditionally holds its annual conference on Easter weekend. Since this is a time most conventions avoid, the association can negotiate lower rates at the more elegant hotels where the Shakespeareans, a classy bunch, prefer to gather. The 1988 meeting was in Boston at the Copley Plaza. I had become friends with an Ohio University alum, Sandy Elsass, who lived in Boston. Sandy had an enormous appetite for the good things in life. He had come to Ohio to play baseball but had torn up a knee as a sophomore and thus missed out on playing on the greatest team in university history, headed by Mike Schmidt, which finished fourth in the College World Series in 1970.

When I noticed that opening day in 1988 was the Monday after Easter and that the Tigers were playing the Red Sox at Fenway, I called Sandy and said, "Any chance you can find a couple of tickets for us?"

He laughed and said, "You always make the easy ask. I'll see what I can do but I can't join you because I've got to be in New York on business that day. Have you ever been to a Celtics game?"

"No."

"My company has season tickets, and they play in the Garden on Friday night. Can you join me?"

"Absolutely."

"In the meantime, I'll see what I can do about opening day."

Pro basketball never got under my skin the way the college game has. Perhaps because, unlike my early bonding with the Tigers, I never had a steady team to root for in my part of the world. I admired the Bill Russell Celtics, but they belonged to Boston, not Waterville. In college at Hamilton, I followed the Knicks because many of my friends did, and several years later in graduate school I enjoyed their great 1970 season and NBA championship achieved on Willis Reed's gimpy knees and the unselfish play of Walt Frazier, Earl Monroe, Dave DeBusschere, and the remarkable Bill Bradley.

I have seen very few NBA games live. The first was also one of the best as a group of us drove over from Hamilton in 1959 or '60 to Syracuse to see Oscar Robertson and his Cincinnati Royals play the Nats. The Big O did not give us a triple double on that night, but he did score in the high thirties and made several dazzling passes that seemed effortless in their efficiency and grace. Sometime in the eighties, when in Chicago for a dean's conference, I slipped out to the old Chicago Stadium to see Jordan and his Bulls. They won easily, but it was Scotty Pippen's night, not Michael's, who seemed content to play second banana as there was nothing on the line. Years later Sam took me to Cleveland to see Jordan in his final season with the Wizards take on the Cavaliers, but the bounce had gone out of those great legs and the joy out of his game. I caught a Wizards game in Washington and a Bulls game in Chicago with my grandsons Charlie and Theo Pistner. In Chicago, the Bulls played the Lakers and Kobe scored 40-plus, including a balletic midcourt breakaway that finished with a 360 rotation and a slam. My eyes kept drifting to the play of the Bulls rookie guard Derrick Rose. Even the casual fan could tell that he was a player.

The Celtics-Pistons game on Good Friday 1988 in the Boston Garden topped them all. Sandy's seats were on the second level in the corner, so you saw the action rushing towards you and then reversing and swooping off in the other direction. Have three big men ever run the floor as well as Bird, Parish, and McHale? Whenever the Pistons missed a shot and one of the bigs grabbed the rebound and made the outlet pass to DJ, the crowd began to murmur its excitement as those three large men spread out and headed down the floor. The murmur grew louder as DJ passed to Ainge, who hit Bird on the run in the corner, and when his body rose for the jumper the murmur became a shout, and when the ball ripped through the net it became a roar. Or the pass went the other way to McHale, who on the run and without a dribble fired a perfect lead to Parish, who had beaten Bill Laimbeer by three paces and then elevated for the slam finish as once again the crowd let out an explosion of pure delight.

That Celtic fast break was a thing of beauty and a thrill to watch unfold either pounding towards your end of the floor or sweeping away in the other direction. Isiah Thomas and Joe Dumars kept the Pistons in the game by executing with Laimbeer one fine pick-and-roll after another, but on this night the Celtics literally ran them into the ground and emerged with a 121–110 victory. The Pistons would have their revenge, though, as this was the first season in which they dethroned the Celtics as the Eastern Conference champs, though they went on to lose the championship itself to the Lakers four games to three. If I had had more opportunity to see games like this in the flesh, I might have become an NBA fan. As it is, I follow the season more in the sports pages of the New York Times than on the tube until we reach the second round of the playoffs or the finals. I watch, generally rooting for the team that shares the ball and plays defense, but am not emotionally involved except to admire astonishing performances.

Sandy dropped me off at the Copley after the game and said he was still working on tickets for Monday. If he was successful, they would be delivered to me at the hotel. I told him I had arranged for a late Monday flight home and would head to Fenway even without a ticket in the hopes of finding something I could afford from a scalper. And I thanked him for a great evening, which had begun with drinks and a steak somewhere near the Garden.

The conference went well. I contributed a paper on Orson Welles's film of *Othello* that eventually became a chapter in my first book, *Shakespeare Observed*, but the image of Bird and Parish and McHale streaking down the iconic Celtic parquet floor kept intruding on my Shakespearean thoughts. On Sunday afternoon I went to a matinee performance of *Macbeth* starring Glenda Jackson and Christopher Plummer previewing in Boston before heading to New York. Jackson and Plummer and Shakespeare managed finally to erase the Celtics front line from my imagination, now filled with scorpions, steeped in blood, and fallen into the sere and yellow leaf. I was also busy trying to reconcile two very different acting styles the production featured. Jackson did some ferocious kinetic body work, while Plummer stood center stage like a tortured statue and went for Macbeth's poetry at the expense of his torment. It was good to see two old pros strutting their Shakespearean stuff, but the production, directed by the former leader at Stratford Robin Phillips, never reconciled the opposing directions in which its two stars were pulling it. When I got back to my hotel room and opened the door, there was an envelope with tickets for tomorrow's game. Way to go, Sandy. Shakespeare and baseball linked again.

When I opened the envelope, I was startled to see two tickets, not one. My Shakespearean pals, including one who taught at Bowdoin and was a passionate Red Sox fan, had all headed home. Miranda was in Africa and Sam was in northern Wisconsin with no chance of reaching Boston by game time tomorrow. A gift thrives on being shared, but where were my secret sharers? I slept late, packed and checked out, and then checked my bags with the young bellman managing the Copley luggage room. He looked to be in his early twenties, with a mop of red hair. I explained to him that I was headed to the game and would return to collect my bags in the late afternoon. "Red Sox fan?" I asked.

"All my life," he shot back.

"When do you get off work?"

"Three."

"Would you like a ticket to the game? I have an extra."

"Yes, sir," he said. I think he thought I was jerking him around, but when I produced the ticket and handed it over, he beamed.

And he showed up in the top of the fourth. "I got to leave a little early," he said with a smile as he slipped into the seat beside me.

"I'm Sam, and you?"

"Mike. Mike Keogh." And Mike became my quiet red-headed Irish piece of the luck for the rest of the afternoon.

In the several hours I was at Fenway before Mike arrived, I amused myself by scribbling some notes on my scorecard of how this opening day was unfolding. When the game turned out so magnificently for Tiger fans, I knew I had to share it with Sam and Miranda and Sandy and so, using those notes and the scorecard itself, I wrote them a letter trying to capture the flavor of the afternoon. This impulse created the tradition of writing a baseball letter after each of the Tiger games I have seen, alone or with others, over the past thirty years. Most of those games were played in Detroit, at the Corner or Comerica, but some took place on the road as well, most often at the Indians' new park, known first as Jacobs Field (or the Jake) and now as Progressive Field. I saw no games in the sad season of 1989, so the idea of the baseball letter was revived in 1990 when Sam was in Japan and Miranda, back from the Peace Corps in Botswana, was working in Washington, and I began to head north once or twice a summer on my own.

The letters have lasted ever since, though now their core audience has grown with the arrival over the past eighteen years of six grandchildren, all of whom are baseball fans, though varying in their passion for the game (and the Tigers) from 3 to 9 on a scale of 1 to 10. And now a baseball letter is written even if the whole lot of us has been at the game—the scorecard translated into narrative. The letters have remained letters even in the age of email, and all are posted and delivered by US Mail. Now the game is not over until the letter has been written and dispatched. And it is often not over then, as my readers often come back with important details I had gotten wrong or just plain overlooked. Baseball prompts writing, and with the birth of the letters, I had finally joined the club.

The game was baseball at its best, made even more so for me as I moved from presenting a paper on Orson Welles's stunning film of *Othello* at the Shakespeare conference, to Glenda Jackson and Christopher Plummer as the Macbeths, to Roger Clemens versus Jack Morris, the two best right-handed pitchers in the American League, on opening day at Fenway. Here is my report and the first of the Tiger Letters.

TIGER LETTER #1

3 April 1988

Dear Sam, Miranda, (and Sandy),

It was raining as I left the Copley Plaza Hotel and walked to the T station for the ride to Fenway Park. I was traversing between two venerable institutions both built in 1912: it must have been a very good year. The transit car was loaded with fans sporting blue caps with a big red B and I was pleased that I had decided to leave my Detroit cap with my bags and to wear only my tie sprinkled with tiny gothic Ds. This was a true baseball crowd who did not look to a man's tie to discover his loyalty; in fact, this crowd didn't wear ties.

I was surprised, once again, how anxious I was for the new season to begin. Those last seven games of 1987 with Toronto (and then the collapse against the Twins in the playoffs) had left me and obviously the Tigers as well, depleted, exhausted, fulfilled, and disappointed. But here I was a scant six months later ready for more.

The sweet smell of grilled onions and green peppers and hotdogs filled the air as I made my way up from the Kenmore stop to Yawkey Blvd and the entrance to the park, which looks like a normal Boston three-storied brick building from the exterior. Sandy Elsass, a Boston Medici, had managed tickets in the eighth row of the field boxes half-way between home plate and the Red Sox dugout. I grabbed a beer and headed around to the Tigers' dugout as the rain halted and the skies appeared to brighten. Here is a brief account of the next five beautiful hours.

I arrive early, 11:15, to absorb as much of the Opening Day atmosphere as possible. As I settle into an empty seat behind the Tigers dugout, ten or twelve Tigers are running in the outfield—no batting practice or infield practice be-cause of the rain—and Tom Brookens and Alan Trammell are playing catch with Darrell Evans and Pat Sheridan in front of the dugout.

A fan calls out "How are you guys?"

Brookens: "Same old crew"

Fan: "Minus Gibson and Parrish"

Brookens: "We're weeding out the deadwood."

Morris emerges with warm-up jacket on and half swaggers / half saunters into short left field to banter with Jim Morri-son before beginning his exercises. Soon he is running sprints with Trammell. This is his ninth consecutive opening day start for the Tigers. He is 6 and 2 over that span. The first Red Sox emerge across the park and after the first wave a solitary figure comes up the steps and the fans on that side raise a cheer and from behind me comes a chorus of "Go Rocket." Clemens is an imposing physical presence even a hundred plus yards away. He is followed by a tall, lithe figure who glides by him in right field as a voice shouts out, "Hey, it's the Can." Oil Can Boyd has arrived.

Sparky crosses from the television interview area on the first base side of home plate. He sports a great Lakeland spring training tan, and his wonderfully expressive eyebrows are as white as his famous thatch. He blows kisses and waves to someone leaning over the top of the Tiger's dugout and proceeds to carry on an animated conversation with her as kids roll balls and push scorecards out for him to sign. He is full of high spirits and grace as he presides as baseball's most winning active manager.

Brady Anderson, the hot-hitting rookie who will open for the Red Sox in centerfield because of an injury to Ellis Burks (last year's phenom), begins to field balls being lined off the left center portion of the Green Monster. He's never seen Fenway Park before, and this is his first opportunity to accommodate himself to the intricacies of the famous wall. As he takes the measure of the wall, Mike Greenwell, Chet Lemon, and John McNamara are all being interviewed for television as the field gradually empties. A motley grounds crew, what looks to be to be a collection of local college students, appears and begins to remove the infield tarp, only to have the rain return. I go up for shelter and a hotdog. By 12:30 the rain has stopped, and the tarp comes off.

The teams begin reappearing and the players pair off to play catch. In a touch which would have caught Norman Rockwell's eye, Jim Rice, the great veteran, exchanges lobs and zips with the rookie, Brady Anderson. Clemens pops out of the dugout and begins the long walk to the right field bullpen to warm-up eliciting the biggest cheer yet from the ever-increasing crowd. John Kiley peals the organ into action with a rousing chorus of "Everything's Coming Up Roses." The new season inches closer on a wave of Sondheim song and great expectations.

Morris begins his long cross to the bullpen area and stops to exchange banter, hand slaps, and strategy with his catcher Mike Heath. I had forgotten how good looking many of these players are with Heath and Jim Morrison and Ray Knight along with the rookie, Billy Beane, radiating a male handsomeness. The less photogenic mugs of Evans and Nokes bring me back to a more equitable understanding of the distribution of nature's gifts.

The opening day line-ups are announced, and the players are all introduced and head to line-up along the third
and first base foul lines. Sparky is given a warm cheer by
these good fans. A cheer unmixed with the smattering of
boos which greet the Red Sox manager, John McNamara,
when he is introduced. The Red Sox failure to hold off the
Mets two years ago still hurts too deeply to be ignored even
with opening day's optimism. The longest and loudest cheer
("Lee . . . Lee . . . Lee") greets the last player to be introduced,
#48, Lee Smith. Smith, the Cubs' commanding closer over
the past six seasons, was traded to the Red Sox last December
and the general feeling is that the Red Sox got a steal and may
have stolen the American League East division crown as well.
Smith gave up only four hits and one run while striking out
17 in spring training adding to Beantown's anticipation of his
contribution to this year's team, particularly after what Jeff
Reardon's presence did for the Twins last year.

The National Anthem is sung by Craig Shulman who
is starring as Jean Valjean in the Boston Company of Les
Misérables—a production which began its life with the Royal
Shakespeare Company and Trevor Nunn, thus providing
another link between my passion for play in many forms and
baseball and Shakespeare in particular. Clemens has had an
awesome spring and looks even more imposing perched on
the mound less than thirty yards away from me. He takes care
of the Tigers in the first on fourteen pitches which include
a walk to Whitaker and a whiff of Evans. He follows that up
by striking out the side in the second (on eleven pitches) as
the crowd increases its roar of approval and appreciation with
each subsequent strike.

Morris also breezes through the first two, striking out
three but giving up a wicked line-drive double off the scoreboard on the wall by Wade Boggs, the first hit of the game.
And, as it turns out of the season as the other games have
not started yet. Rice followed by fanning on a slow curve
bringing the immediate ire of a fan just to my right, "You
million-dollar bum. You ought to pay us." Rice is a proud man
with great talent and impressive career numbers, but he has

never won the devotion of the Red Sox faithful and will not
be enshrined next to the kid and Yaz in their hearts (though
perhaps the Hall of Fame) when he leaves the game.

The Tigers score first. In the 3rd, after Clemens struck
out Heath for his fourth in a row, he came unglued a bit by
walking the Tigers' ninth hitter, Tom Brookens. He was clearly
angry with himself and with several of home-plate umpire
Jim Brinkman's calls. On his second pitch to Gary Pettis he
balked, sending Brookens to second. He got Pettis on a routine fly to left but then Lou Whitaker hung tough and after
fouling off two heaters got a curve he could handle and sent
it back through the box for a run-producing single. In the
top of the 4th the Tigers got another when Clemens walked
Sheridan, another light hitter, after two were out and Lemon
followed with a line drive double down in the right field
corner sending Sheridan home all the way from 1st. Clemens
only walked three in the entire game, but two of them cost
him. Morris only walked Greenwell in the 2nd, but he was
erased by Heath trying to steal.

In the bottom of the 4th the Red Sox break loose. Boggs
leads off with another vicious double off the wall in left. Rice
pops up eliciting more nasty remarks which are not allowed
to build as Greenwell immediately lines a single to right scoring Boggs. Then on the first pitch Evans hits a screamer to
right center that Pettis can't reach before it bangs off the wall,
but Morgan, the third base coach, holds the runners to the
crowd's great displeasure. Morris seems to have lost it. Boggs,
Greenwell, and Evans have all ripped him. Now he goes to
work on Big Sam Horn and becomes a pitcher again mixing
in the change with the forkball, but Horn gets a piece of a
change and taps it to the right side where it scoots just out a
Whitaker's reach into right for two runs. Somehow Morris re-
covers and fans Gedman and gets Owen on a soft fly to right.
Clemens has been given the lead, and Morris is on the ropes.
Even worse, as we open the 5th it begins to rain again and
when Clemens gets through the inning with the only damage
a single by Brookens, I sense that the sky will open and send
the Sox home an early winner. Morris opens the bottom half

by striking out Rice on three hard ones and appears to have
regained his form, giving up only a harmless single to Greenwell. The rain eases to a light drizzle and then stops.

Nokes takes a Clemens fastball 400 ft plus landing ten rows
back in deep right center and the Tigers are back in it. In the
second when Clemens struck Nokes out on a curve which
bounced a foot in front of the plate, a fan had remarked "This
turkey's going to have a monumental sophomore slump."
I must confess that such a thought had crossed my mind
too and quickly disappeared as I watched his homer lift off
towards the Hancock building. Both pitchers took command
with the old master Morris having regained his composure
setting down nine of the next ten batters in a row including
striking out the side in the 9th—a "So There" to Clemens's
work back in the 2nd. Clemens did not have such smooth
sailing, giving up a double to Brookens to open the 7th; but
he died at third as Whitaker and Evans couldn't bring him in
after Pettis had bunted him over. Clemens struck Brookens
out to end the 9th. His eleventh and last of the day. He had
thrown 136 pitches, enough for Fish [Bill Fisher, the Boston
pitching coach] and Mac. Opening Day. Fenway Park. Tie
Game. Extra Innings. Love Supreme.

Big #48 walks in from the bullpen to pitch the 10th and
the crowd regains its mid-game voice. I wonder why Mc-
Namara wants to use his main man now in a tie game. Isn't it
better to save him until he has a lead to protect? The first hitter, Pettis, rolls a weak grounder to Owen's left which he lets
play him for an error. Owen only made 13 errors all last season. I wonder if not having had infield practice and the wet
field contribute to this unlikely break for the Tigers. Whitaker moves him along and Dwight Evans comes up and hits
Smith's first pitch 380 feet to Greenwell backed up against the
fence in right. A drive that would have been a homer in Tiger
Stadium. Pettis takes third after the catch.

Trammell is 0 for 4 and has not been up with a runner in
scoring position. In fact, he led off the 4th, 6th, and 8th with
routine flyballs and a weak groundout. But he is the guy we
want up there with the game on the line. He hits Smith's

fourth pitch on the nose and up on a line into the screen
about ten feet above the Green Monster. I leap to my feet
giving my loyalty away as I sneak a glance at all those little
gothic Ds dancing on my tie. The Red Sox fans, again, have
been had. "I knew he had to be on drugs," comes the grouse
from behind me about Lee Smith as we settle back into our
seats. Henneman comes in to pitch the 10th and throws
strikes. He gets Owen to line to right on an 0–2 pitch and
Anderson—who has gone 3 for 4 but got picked off first by
Morris in the 5th—hits a first pitch hard liner which Trammell spears at his waist. The crowd begins to file out as Barrett
hits a slow roller to Whitaker which dribbles right through
his legs and my heart, thumping right along since Trammell's
shot, skips a beat and sinks. The exit stops. Boggs is up. He
takes a strike and then hits a hard grounder just to Trammell's
left which he scoops up and gently tosses to his old partner
and order is restored in Tigerland. Morris, having gone the
distance and finished strong, is now 7 and 2 in opening games
in the decade he has dominated as a pitcher without ever
having won the Cy Young Award. Maybe this year.

I spring up and out and happily weave my way through the
dejected hometown fans, glad that baseball is back and wish-
ing only that you all could have been here with me to add
this to our list of mutual pleasures the Tigers have afforded
us over the years. This letter is my way of sharing the day and
this great game with you.

Love,
Dad

The 1980s Tigers made one last competitive push in '88. At
the All-Star Game they led the Yankees by three games with
the Red Sox back in fourth, but the second half of the season belonged to Boston as they started a 19–1 run right after
the All-Star break to take command. By mid-September
they were six games up, and only a last-minute stumble allowed the Tigers to narrow the lead. It was the last hurrah
for the core group of Tigers who had anchored the team in

the eighties. But now they were drifting off into free agency or declining talents. Parrish had left after 1986, and Gibson bolted to the Dodgers in 1988 and led them to a World Series victory with another iconic home run. Jack Morris would be the next to go. Only Trammell and Whitaker remained to play out their remarkable careers side by side in Detroit.

My decade as a dean was winding down as my major focus had been on implementing our new comprehensive set of general education requirements. The toughest challenge of this task was creating more than one hundred new multidisciplinary courses at the senior level to satisfy the plan's "synthesis" requirement, and baseball, happily, came to my aid. I have mentioned that Mike Schmidt played ball at and graduated from Ohio University. I only met him twice. The first was in the late 1970s when I was in Chicago and went out to Wrigley to see the Cubs play the Phillies. I arrived early and went down to the field as the Phillies were warming up. When they finished and headed to the dugout I called out, "Bob Wren." Schmidt stopped, looked at the caller, and immediately made his way to where I was standing.

Bob Wren was our baseball coach and one of Mike's mentors. I greeted him and we shook hands as I explained who I was and passed on greetings from Wren. Schmidt, on his way to being the greatest third baseman ever to play the game, was not a natural diplomat. He had some of Ted Williams's arrogance and pride, but he was perfectly gracious to me. Wren's name was the magic. Several years later, when I became dean, I was left with a wonderful gift by my predecessor, Don Flournoy. He had written a successful grant to FIPSE (the Fund for Post-Secondary Education, sponsored by the Department of Education) providing funds to help the university underwrite summer faculty seminars to create some of the needed Gen Ed capstone "synthesis" courses. The FIPSE program officer understandably was troubled at our change of leadership just as the grant was beginning. Flournoy assured him that I had been an active participant in the creation of the new program and would be the right faculty member, now the new dean, to see it through to full implementation. The program officer remained skeptical.

When I met him several months later at a FIPSE conference for new grant directors, we discovered we were both baseball nuts. He was a Phillies fan still basking in their recent (1980) World Series triumph. I said nothing then, but when I returned to campus, I went to see Bob Wren. I asked him when he might next be seeing Mike Schmidt. "Next month at spring training," he replied. I had not known that for many years Bob had joined the Phillies at spring training helping to coach in their minor league camp. I made my request, and when Bob returned to campus, he was sporting an 8 × 10 color photo of Schmidt signed by Mike with a personal greeting to my FIPSE man. I had it framed and presented it to him at our next meeting and explained the story. He was stunned, our relationship was cemented, and any changes down the road I wanted to make in our grant's plan or budget were immediately approved. When I saw Mike several years later when he was back on campus, I reminded him of this story. Understandably, he had no memory of the courtesy, and seemed a bit puzzled at my account, but nevertheless, thanks, Mike. Those senior "synthesis" courses got created and became a unique feature of the university's core requirements for twenty-five years, and the full General Education program was selected for a Program Excellence Award given by the Ohio Board of Regents in 1990—the only such program ever so honored by the state.

Part 5

The 1990s

I did not make my first book until I was fifty. I worked on it off and on during my years as dean as a way of preserving "a space to move in" during my administrative life. I also knew that my colleagues in the English Department would be happier to welcome me back to the academic trenches if I came armed with a new book. *Shakespeare Observed* examined the relationship between stage and film productions of the plays. This was unexplored territory in Shakespeare studies. The book was given an unexpected boost by Kenneth Branagh. His highly regarded film of *Henry V*, based upon Adrian Noble's 1984 Royal Shakespeare Company stage production starring the brash young Branagh, was released in 1989. The film was a winner and an excellent example of the stage-to-film pattern I had been tracing, and it became the fitting focus of my book's final chapter. Branagh's film made *Shakespeare Observed* timely, and the book sold surprisingly well for an academic monograph published by a university press.

When I stepped down as dean, Susan and I both had sabbaticals for the 1992–93 year. We spent the fall in France at the University of Toulouse, where Susan was a visiting professor. In December we left for seven months in London just in time to be greeted by Adrian Noble's RSC production of Hamlet, starring—guess who—Kenneth Branagh. I dropped an inscribed copy of Shakespeare Observed off for him at the Barbican Theatre and soon received a gracious reply about my work. We began a brief exchange of notes culminating in his agreement to be interviewed about the current stage Hamlet and his tentative plans to film the play. Even though separated in age by twenty years, we established an immediate rapport as we chatted in his dressing room at Stratford's Memorial Theater, where the production had moved in the spring. It was a lovely English April afternoon.

His window was open, letting the sweet sounds drift up from the gardens and the Avon below, including kids kicking a soccer ball and swans flapping their mighty wings. Talking with him about Shakespeare was like having a conversation with your fantasy graduate student. He was courteous, smart, well-read, engaging, and, of course, knew the play by heart. His work and the work of his film contemporaries became the focus of my next book, Shakespeare at the Cineplex, as one Shakespeare film after another began to appear in the 1990s, which became the most prolific decade in the history of the genre, and thanks to Branagh I was in on the action from the beginning. He was gracious enough to allow me several more interviews over the decade as his Shakespeare-on-film work proliferated, and I remain impressed by the range of his work, from Shakespeare to Hollywood blockbusters like Thor to small black-and-white gems like Belfast. He has also become the only artist to be nominated for an Academy Award in six different categories: Best Actor, Best Supporting Actor, Best Director, Best Picture, Best Adapted Screenplay, Best Original Screenplay. He finally won in the last category for Belfast.

Sparky Anderson did not have my Shakespeare luck in finding his next group of baseball stars. One of his few blind spots as a manager was in identifying, developing, and retaining young talent. He can deservedly take credit for nurturing Trammell and Whitaker and Gibson and Morris, but little else. For years the Tigers had had a glaring hole at third base, and in 1984 the club promoted Howard Johnson from the minors to share the spot with Tom Brookens. Johnson was a switch-hitter, always a valuable commodity, and he hit with power. His defense was weak, but that came largely from being young and lacking confidence in his abilities. Sparky repeatedly undermined that confidence by frequently replacing him with Brookens in the late innings, rather than letting the kid play through his defensive struggles as a means of surmounting them. Though I have touted Anderson's playing of Marty Castillo in the '84 World Series it had the downside of putting Johnson on the bench. He got to bat but once. After the '85 season the Tigers traded Johnson to the Mets for Walt Terrell. Terrell was a solid number three or four starter and did have several strong seasons with the Tigers, but Johnson became an All-Star third baseman with the Mets.

In 1987, when the Tigers were in the great race with the Jays for the Eastern Division title, they went looking in late July for more starting pitching. In August they made a deal with the Atlanta Braves, which brought them the aging (thirty-six) but still effective Doyle Alexander to boost the rotation. And Alexander did the job, going 9–0 for the Tigers down the stretch. But the price was the Tigers top minor league pitching prospect, John Smoltz. Smoltz became part of one of the game's great rotations, along with Tom Glavine and Greg Maddux, and now all three of them are in the Hall of Fame.

In the late eighties the Tigers had a couple of young infielders, Chris Pittaro and Torey Lovullo, who had promise, but Sparky, perhaps thinking of what he had not done for Howard Johnson's self-confidence, overpraised them and created expectations that neither could live up to at the plate or the in the field. The Tigers kept thinking that one of them would suddenly blossom and provide much-needed homegrown youthful talent, but it never happened. The only such talent to arrive on the scene in the early nineties was a lanky shortstop, Travis Fryman, whom the Tigers converted into a third baseman and who was a young fixture in

the Tiger infield in Trammell and Whitaker's last years. Fryman was solid rather than flashy but managed every season
to hit 20–30 home runs, drive in 80–90, and hit .275. And
he went to school to Trammell and became a fine defensive fielder and someone who bought into the Tiger ethos
as represented by Anderson. But the Tigers needed five or
six such players, including an outfielder or two and several
pitchers. They were not to be found in the farm system.

As a result, the Tigers tried to rebuild with experience
rather than youth—something much harder to do unless you're a George Steinbrenner willing and able to pay
for two or three high-priced free agents every year. In the
early nineties the Tigers went after a slew of older power
hitters, including Lloyd Moseby, Rob Deer, Mickey Tettleton (whose son Tyler was years later a record-setting quarterback on the Frank Solich–led Ohio University football
team), Pete Incaviglia, Larry Sheets, and best of all Cecil
Fielder. But except for Bill Gullickson, who won 20 games
for them in 1991, they had less success with adding pitching
to replace the retirements of Petry, Alexander, and Tanana
and the departure of Jack Morris to the Twins. What had
been a balanced offense with solid pitching became a group
of slow-footed thumpers with mediocre pitching. The one
superb acquisition was Tony Phillips from the Oakland A's.
Phillips quickly became my favorite, along with Bobby Higginson, of the 1990s Tigers because of his versatility. He was
a switch-hitter with some power from the left side, and he
could play second or short and all the outfield positions. He
played the game with a savvy mixture of passion and élan.

But the man who brought the fans back to Tiger Stadium was Cecil Fielder. Not since Hank Greenberg had the
Tigers had a great power hitter. He was recruited by Bill Lajoie, the Tigers general manager, from Osaka and the Han-
shin Tigers (a happy transnational coincidence), where he
had migrated after several less than sensational years with
the Blue Jays. The family missed seeing him play in Japan by
a single summer. Sam's teaching duties for the JET program
were in Osaka, and Susan, Miranda, and I visited him there

in the summer of 1990. Cecil's photos still adorned every yakitori restaurant where players and fans ate and hung out before and after games. We went out to the stadium for a game to honor the spot where Fielder had re-created himself and earned a return ticket to the big leagues.

In Japan, the home and away teams have rooting sections in either left or right field equipped with large flags, loud horns, and chanting fans, dressed in their teams' colors. These fans carry on nonstop when their team is at bat, with coordinated chants and cheers. Those in the central stands around the all-dirt diamond are more modest in their cheering but show their unique engagement by eating bento boxes of sushi as the action unfolded. The game was an exaggerated version of National League ball, with an emphasis on moving runners over with the bunt, with most hitters following the Ichiro fashion of hitting down on the ball, driving it into the hard infield dirt, with the left-handers launching themselves towards first base as they swung. Some of the pitchers threw in the low nineties, but most were off-speed magicians who relied on keeping the hitters off balance with a variety of slow curves, sliders, and changeups. But even though the game was played as Japanese small ball, on the night we went it was won the American way with the Tigers winning on a "sayonara" (walk-off) home run in the bottom of the tenth.

Fielder was perfect for Detroit, a large Black man who talked softly and carried a big stick. He had soft gentle eyes, a shy smile, and could hit a baseball a long way. He became only the fourth man ever to hit a ball out of Tiger Stadium over the upper deck in left (the right field roof was more easily cleared) by connecting with a Dave Stewart fastball. He joined Harmon Killebrew, Frank Howard, and Mark McGwire as members of the "Over the Roof in Left" club. Going into the last week of the season, Fielder had hit 49 home runs but the magical 50 eluded him until the very last day. He ended the season with a bang, not a whimper, hitting two at Yankee Stadium and becoming the first player since George Foster in 1977 (Sparky's last year with the

Reds) to hit 50 or more home runs in a season. The nineties proved to be the mirror opposite of the eighties, with the Tigers managing only two winning seasons (in '91 and '93) and never making a serious run for the playoffs. The decade proved as problematic for baseball as it was for the Tigers, calling to mind the destructive fissures in Shakespeare's tragedies rather than the festive surprises of Shakespeare's comedies.

SHAKESPEARE AND BASEBALL VII

My earlier entries have intentionally focused on the game it- self, the endless fascination of what can happen on any given afternoon or evening between (and sometimes just outside) those white lines. Much of what I have tried to provide is called "thick description" by the cultural anthropologists, trying to let the game speak for itself through the details of its unfolding in the communal rituals of work and play. My love is for the game and not for all the agitation that often surrounds it. But in the nineties elements that surrounded the game—the reserve clause, Marvin Miller and the players' union, free agency, strikes, lockouts, expansion, retraction, drugs, betting, the move to new stadiums—were like the light towers at Tiger Stadium, which cast large shadows over the mound and the batter's box. Suddenly we could not es- cape baseball's dark side. Traditionally, baseball owners were neither seen nor heard except for mavericks like Bill Veeck, George Steinbrenner, Charlie Finley, and Marge Schott. Now, because of the reserve clause, free agency, the resultant con- flicts with the players' union, and the move to build new sta- diums, the owners became a big part of the story.

I have linked baseball with elements in Shakespeare's comedies that celebrate the garden over the city, play over work, holiday over every day. Now the generous easy grace of the comedies gave way, in the world of professional base- ball, to the sound and fury of Shakespeare's tragedies and the power politics of his histories. In the histories and trag- edies, Shakespeare is fascinated with the clash of powerful egos defining and being defined by larger political and historical forces they seek to contain, dominate, or transcend. Macbeth and Lady Macbeth are prime examples. Shakespeare constructs dramatic worlds which put such strong personalities under enormous psychological, social, moral, and political stress. The plays are pressure cookers ready to explode. Shakespeare's imagination is preoccupied with dramatizing power under pressure. Grace is a quality associated with his comedies, power with his tragedies. How much can the strong, but psychologically damaged or vulnerable, endure before cracking? And what happens when the fissure appears? How does the tragic figure struggle to confront, assimilate, transform, or become destroyed by such huge personal and social challenges?

Hamlet is, for many, the representative Shakespearean tragic figure. His story is the ultimate tale of the unmaking and then remaking of a precarious young male identity as it struggles to coalesce in the intertwined worlds of the individual, the family, and the state. In a manner of months, Hamlet's stable world of prince and student and lover is destroyed by his father's death, his mother's remarriage (to his uncle), and his lover's seeming betrayal. In baseball lingo, he has lost his fastball and been given his unconditional release. And before he is shipped to the minors to reimagine himself, he discovers, with the Ghost's appearance, that he is not a free agent after all, but is still bound by the reserve clause. Rather than being free, he is now bound between two powerful fathers, one commanding him to kill the other. Beginning with the organization of the players' union under its brilliant labor leader Marvin Miller in the 1960s, the players and the owners began their inexorable march to confrontation, clash, and seeming inevitable tragedy as the game itself became threatened every time the basic agreement (or contract) was due to expire. Like the Ghost and Claudius, the owners wanted control. The players, like Hamlet, wanted independence.

The 1990s was baseball's worst decade. The decade began on August 24, 1989, when Pete Rose accepted a deal with commissioner Bart Giamatti in which he was suspended from baseball for life (with future appeals possible) without having to admit that he had bet on baseball, including on his own team. Rose, perhaps even more so than Mays or Aaron or Ripken, was in the last half of the twentieth century the embodiment of the game itself. Rose squeezed more out of his modest physical talents than any other player in the history of the game. He was a throwback, a man cut in Ty Cobb's mold, a ferocious dirtbag, Charlie Hustle, Charlie Hustler. He played the game with a passion that was all-consuming, yet he was universally admired by his teammates. He played hard and never complained. He was even forgiven by his fellow players on other clubs for perhaps his most reckless moment, when he ran over and injured catcher Ray Fosse blocking home plate in the 1970 All-Star Game. The All-Star Game!

Mike Schmidt credited Rose with turning the Phillies into world champions. When Mike was inducted into baseball's Hall of Fame, he wore a red rose with the number 14 woven in it in his lapel to honor his former teammate. If the baseball gods were looking to craft the perfect player to finally surpass Ty Cobb's all-time hit total of 4,191, they certainly did it in creating Pete Rose. Rose carried baseball's rural rawboned past into the modern era. He came from the Midwest, he came from Ohio River farm stock, he turned "headfirst" from an adjective into a noun. Baseball flirted with tragedy throughout the nineties, and the conflict between Rose and Giamatti, the player and the professor, had ripe Shakespearean resonances.

"I never dreamed of being president of anything but the American League," quipped the noted renaissance literature scholar Bart Giamatti when he was named the nineteenth president of Yale. Giamatti's appointment came as much of a surprise to the Yale community as it did to the rest of academia. In an age where future university administrators are singled out early in their professorial careers (often in the law school), promoted up the line from department chair to dean to provost, sent off to Harvard's famous summer program in Educational Management, and then crowned with a presidency, Giamatti, like Rose in his profession, seemed a throwback to the days when a well-liked and well-respected faculty member was plucked from his department and given the keys to the campus without any spring training or minor league experience. Giamatti's quip quickly made him famous well beyond Yale, but it also made the Renaissance scholar seem like one of the boys. An Italian American from the small college town of South Hadley, Massachusetts, becomes the president of a Yankee Brahmin university whose history is filled with Endicotts, Cabots, Peabodys, Lodges, and Brewsters and proclaims his love for the Red Sox. Move over, Dom and Rico and Tony, there is a new Italian prince in the Fenway.

But Giamatti's jaunty ease in straddling the worlds of Yale and the Red Sox would only end up contributing to his tragedy. And while Giamatti knew that rooting passionately for a baseball team, especially the Red Sox, was a tragic experience doomed to end each October in defeat, he could not see what was coming when his quip turned out to have unexpected consequences. In the summer before he became Yale's president, at the tender age of forty, he was already in an elegiac mood, daydreaming about baseball and the "green fields of the mind." In one of the most lyrical passages ever inspired by the game, Giamatti, in response to the Red Sox losing to the Orioles 8–7 on the next-to-last day of the 1978 season and being eliminated from the race, wrote:

> It breaks your heart. It is designed to break your heart. The game begins in the spring when everything else begins again, and it blossoms in the summer, filling the afternoons and evenings, and then as soon as the chill rains come, it stops and leaves you to face the fall alone. You count on it, rely on it to buffer the passage of time, to keep the memory of sunshine and high skies alive, and then just when the days are all twilight, when you need it most, it stops. Today, October 2, a Sunday of rain and broken branches and leaf-clogged

drains and slick streets, it stopped, and summer was gone.[6]

The men who ran baseball pricked up their ears and tucked Giamatti's quip away in their collective memories. Eight years later, after Giamatti had survived a bitter fight with Yale's unions over a new contract, he was beginning to weary of the job and suddenly there was an opening in baseball's hierarchy: president of the National League. Baseball offered him the job. He could not resist, and three years later when the commissioner's job itself became available he was invited to move up a step, and once again he could not resist.

He became commissioner in September of 1988, and less than a year later he had to preside over the deal that effectively banned Pete Rose from baseball for life. Less than a week later, at the age of fifty-one, he was dead from a massive heart attack. There can be little doubt that the Wars of the Rose were a huge contributing factor (cigarettes another) in his collapse. The Shakespearean resonances are rich. The clash between the scruffy baseball immortal and the renaissance prince was Shakespearean material. Giamatti could not escape his Yale past, just as Rose refused to confront his gambling addiction and the lowlife characters, who might have stepped right out of the Boar's Head Tavern, that he had surrounded himself with outside of the game. Rose, lacking Falstaff's wit, reacted like Coriolanus, not only refusing to show his wounds but, against all the evidence, insisting that he did not have any.

Giamatti believed in the rules that make play possible, and the most important rule since the Black Sox scandal of 1919 was, no betting on baseball. But he was also a humanist and wanted to find a means for Rose to graciously accept his punishment, step away from the game, and maintain some of his dignity as a baseball icon. Neither man succeeded. The decision cost Giamatti his life and Rose permanent exile from the game he relished and played with such abandon. For having taken the moral high ground, the only man who could pardon Pete was Bart. And Bart is now himself in exile, locked someplace between the literary paradise he elucidated in his scholarship and the baseball-less autumn world of rain and broken branches and clogged drains and slick streets he evoked in his elegy about the game. Rose and Giamatti are like vivid Shakespearean characters, emblematic of the controversies which would threaten to swamp the game in the 1990s as the players and the owners and the commissioner found themselves in repeated conflict.

In Detroit, in the 1990s, not only did the game decline on the field, but the field itself became a divisive issue. For almost fifty years, from the mid-thirties until the mid-eighties, the Tigers had been owned by just two men: Walter Briggs and John Fetzer. And one man, Jim Campbell (hired by Briggs, promoted by Fetzer), had been responsible for running the club since the fifties. That is called stability, and it was true of many other leading clubs, including the Red Sox, the Dodgers, the Cardinals, and the Pirates. In 1984 John Fetzer sold the Tigers to the Domino's Pizza man, Tom Monaghan. Monaghan founded Domino's when he was in college and turned it into a fast-food giant and himself into a multimillionaire. He had followed the Tigers as a kid, but baseball was not a passion. Monaghan bought the Tigers because he could, not because it fulfilled a life's ambition. He was a serious man, but he was not a sportsman. He preferred collecting Frank Lloyd Wright houses and building a new Catholic college in Florida to presiding over a baseball team.

While he did not intrude upon Jim Campbell's running of the club, he did realize that to produce the revenue generated in the newer stadiums by luxury suites and shopping malls that Tiger Stadium needed to be replaced. He faced a tough sell. The stadium had legions of fans who regarded it as one of baseball's surviving original temples like Fenway Park and Wrigley Field. Detroit was a city in crisis and did not have the revenue, bond ratings, or political will necessary to create the public capital that all the new retro parks (Camden Yards, Jacobs Field, PNC Park, etc.) relied upon for a substantial portion of their financing. Those new parks were also replacing stadiums for which there was little historical interest or fan affection. When Jim Campbell retired, Monaghan made an error of Shakespearean proportions in the man he hired to replace him: the University of Michigan's former football coach and athletic director, Bo Schembechler. This was a tragic mistake of misjudgment, like Duncan's naming Macbeth the Thane of Cawdor.

Schembechler was an icon in Michigan, but he was not a baseball man, and he was not a skilled diplomat or politician. And he was hired primarily to get Monaghan a new stadium. Bo, like his mentor and rival Woody Hayes, was a Patton, not an Eisenhower. Nuance was not in his toolkit. Bo's approach to most things was to be bold, blunt, belligerent, and, if all else failed, a bully. And those were the banners he carried into battle with Detroit, the Michigan State Legislature, and the powerful coalition of fans uniting to oppose the proposed new stadium. Tiger fans were so devoted that they twice organized what they called a Tiger Stadium hug-in, where thousands of fans gathered to surround the stadium, link arms, and give it a hug. Imagine Kaline's old, gray battleship getting a hug! To my knowledge, hugging a stadium was a unique experience in the history of protest movements. Schembechler sealed his fate when he made the colossal blunder of firing the man held by Tiger fans with as much affection as they did the stadium, Ernie Harwell. Harwell was not only the voice of the Tigers for thirty years but their soul as well. Bo later said it was WJR, the radio station that broadcast the Tiger games, that wanted Ernie canned, but he could easily have told them to go to hell. He certainly did it to many others.

Monaghan saw that the writing on the wall for a new stadium was "No," so he fired Bo and sold the team to his rival Detroit pizza mogul Mike Ilitch. Though Ilitch was a former minor league baseball player and devoted to the game and the Tigers, nothing improved on the field. But the move to build a new stadium gained momentum. Ilitch hired John McHale Jr., from an old baseball family, who had guided the Colorado Rockies and Coors Field into existence. He turned out to be the anti-Schembechler as president and spent the next several years putting together a package that would lead to the financing and construction of Comerica Park on the northern fringe of Greektown, just a few blocks from the heart of downtown Detroit and a little over a mile away from the Corner.

As the controversy over a new park reached its climax, the long thirty-year battle between the players and the owners over the reserve clause and free agency came to a head in 1994, just as the great Tiger dynasty of the 1980s was finally crumbling, on the field and in the front office. While Kirk Gibson returned to the team for his final two seasons, Jack Morris departed to the Twins and Lance Parrish to the Phillies. Only Alan Trammell and Lou Whitaker remained, and they were soon to retire. Nineteen ninety-four was the disastrous year that ended with the players' strike that led to the cancellation of the rest of the season and postseason. When the strike was not resolved in the offseason, the owners determined to begin the new season with replacement players. Sparky Anderson, the handsome, white-haired, syntactically challenged poster boy for major league baseball, became the only manager who refused to open spring training as manager of his team of misfits and retreads, saying, "This ain't baseball."

Though the dispute was settled by the end of April and Sparky was back in the Tiger dugout, his days were numbered and he knew it. Sometime during the season he announced it would be his last. Lou Whitaker decided nineteen seasons was enough, and it looked like Alan Trammell would also exit with his longtime partner and the manager who had seen them through so many successful seasons. The Tigers were back to where Anderson had found them in 1979, only the situation was even worse as there were no young future stars like Trammell or Whitaker or Morris or Gibson waiting in the minors, and even Cecil Fielder, the one star to emerge in Sparky's last years, had reached free agency and was off to the Yankees.

"When sorrows come, they come not single spies, / But in whole battalions," Claudius remarks when witnessing the mad Ophelia distribute her wildflowers. When the world begins to unravel, it is hard to ravel it back up again, as all of Shakespeare's tragic heroes come to discover. And so it was with the Tigers. Ilitch got his new stadium but not a new team. The Tigers went more than a decade (1994–2005) without a winning record and hit the club's all-time low by going 43–119 in the 2003 season. The team's loyal fans got sucker-punched twice: by the loss of their beloved historical home for eighty-eight years and by the quality of play on the field. John McHale knew the right buttons to push for the new stadium, but his general manager, Randy Smith, went through a revolving door of managers, and even traded for an established power hitter, Juan González, without coming close to putting a winning team on the field.

With all this bad news, what kept sending me back on the long drive to Detroit each summer as the nineties turned the corner into the new millennium? An old fan's irrational loyalty, the last years of the historic stadium, and the promise of new Tiger fans in the making in the family. Once McHale was in charge and Ilitch agreed to provide a major portion of the funding for a new park, one knew Tiger Stadium's years were numbered. What made its coming demise a terrific and unique baseball story was the way the stadium was embraced (literally and metaphorically) by Tiger fans across the state and region. It became the only baseball stadium with a fan club and the only one for whom that club, as mentioned earlier, organized not one but two massive hug-ins. Unfortunately, love did not triumph. The nineties became a lost decade in many ways for the game itself and turned into one great long goodbye for Tiger fans to the only house they had ever known. Goodbye, goodbye.

Hello, hello. There was also new Tiger fan blood in the family on the way. Miranda married Bill Pistner in the summer of 1993. Bill was a great sports fan who had carried on a long-distance relationship with his team, the Pittsburgh Pirates. His dad was from Pittsburgh and a Pirates fan and passed his loyalty on to his oldest son. Unfortunately, the Pistners lived in Roanoke, Virginia, so Bill saw even less of the Pirates growing up than I did of the Tigers. But the bond was equally strong. The next summer Sam married Terry Kelleher, who had grown up rooting for the Orioles. So suddenly there were some new fans in the family who had to be introduced to the Tigers and Tiger Stadium. The stadium had always been overshadowed by Fenway and Wrigley, but now that it was doomed, and its apparent demise debated in sports pages well beyond Detroit, it joined their exalted status in the popular imagination as one of baseball's last sacred temples.

And as the decade and century grew to a close, the new generation began to tumble into the world: Charlie Pistner in '97; Aidan Crowl in '98; and Theo Pistner in '99, with more brothers and a sister to come in the new millennium. Charlie got to a game in the summer of '99, when he and his parents drove up from Ellicott City, Maryland, to join us all for a week in Harbor Springs in northern Michigan. We sat in the upper deck and saw the Tigers get pounded 13–1. I was glad that Charlie, not yet two, could not grasp just how poorly his grandfather's team played. Aidan also got to several games in '99 riding in a backpack on his father's shoulders, including one great afternoon in September when, after the game had ended, the club let us all out on the field to wander wherever we wanted, provided we stayed on the warning track or the rubber walkways they laid down around the edge of the infield. Here's a report on the first of several visits to say my personal farewells.

TIGER LETTER #2

30 September 96

Dear Tiger Fans:

The all-day pour we got here on Friday and Saturday (and Sam's commitment to finishing the re-do of their upstairs bathroom before their company invades this weekend)

dampened my spirits for a dash to Detroit to say farewell
to Trammell and the worst Tigers team in history [I spoke
too soon]. But when the Weather Channel on Sat evening
declared that the skies had cleared to the north and that
Sunday promised to be bright and sunny, my enthusiasm
returned. So . . . feeling a bit like Lester [my father and an
early riser and avid bird hunter and skeet shooter] up early
on a Sunday morning for a run to the Findlay Skeet Club, I
headed out into fog about 8 am. Sun broke through just south
of Lancaster and while temps in the 50s precluded unhooking
the top, Sweet Lou [our cars have nicknames. This black VW
cabrio was named for Whitaker] and I skimmed through farm
country Ohio on a swell fall day. Pulled up to our regular spot
in front of the National Bank of Detroit's branch office on
Trumbull just two blocks from the stadium at 12:55.

Slipped into my seat and a Bud in Section 215—parallel with
the left side of the infield and the best vantage point for Trammell watching—just as Justin Thompson was zipping a first
strike past the Brewers' Gerald Williams. Thompson was an
added and unexpected treat (I thought he had pitched on Sat
night). He is our young left-hander who had had a fine minor
league career and was brought up in early June, pitched well in
three outings and then strained something in his left shoulder
which put him out of action until September. He hasn't been
impressive in his Sept starts but he showed, in the five innings
he worked, why the organization is high on him.

He's got a good fastball in the low 90s and a wicked soft
curve he can throw for strikes, and did, even when behind in
the count. He wasn't sharp, walking three, but he managed to
get out of bases loaded jams twice and ended up stranding ten
runners while giving up just two runs in his five innings of
work. He left with a 4–2 lead courtesy of Tony Clark's (our 6'7"
rookie switch hitting first baseman who is impressive in size
and talent) two-run homer—a line drive into the lower deck
in left just above the 365 sign—in the second; back to back
two out doubles by Nieves and Raul Casanova in the fourth;
and sweetest of all, a speed-and-Trammell manufactured run
in the fifth when Pride, with one out, walked stole second

and went to third on the catcher's errant throw out into right center, and then came home on Trammell's sacrifice fly to the great delight of all 13,083 of us.

Clark hit another home run—a mammoth shot off the facing of the third deck in right center above the 395 sign—in the 6th and AJ Sager breezed through the 6th and 7th but hit the wall in the 8th. He gave up a lead-off single, then fanned the catcher, but allowed a kid named Banks starting his first Major League game to rip a double into right center which closed the gap to 5–3. Lima came in and resembled a potential closer by working fast and throwing strikes, but sadly he grooved a few too many hard ones. Here he struck out the first man he faced but then gave up a single and double to tie the game before getting the last batter on a pop to first. The hits came on 1–2 and 0–2 fastballs. Not wise to throw fat ones when you are ahead in the count.

The Brewers won it in the 10th where a small mental error by Clark kept the inning alive. The new reliever Cummings loaded the bases with one out with two walks sandwiched around an infield hit. He then got Kelly Stinnett to rap a one hopper to Fryman at third who started the certain DP by coming home but when Casanova looked to fire to first to complete the play Clark was standing four feet off the bag admiring Fryman's work. Ouch. The next hitter drilled a liner into left center which scored two and put the Brewers up 7–5.

We got a little something going in the bottom half when with one out Pride popped a single into left and then Trammell, in his last plate appearance, wrapped a bouncer up the middle (later he would say that his very first major league hit was a liner up the middle off of Reggie Cleveland against Boston in Fenway in Sept of 1977) and Pride raced to third. Here came Fryman—who has put together another steady season .260 with 22 HR and 100 RBI—and memories of the grand slam he nailed to beat the Mariners on my last visit back in early August. But no miracles today as he hit into a 6-4-3 DP on a 3–2 count to end the game, the season, and Tram's career. It had been announced during the game that Trammell would hold a press conference at shortstop twenty minutes after the game ended so most of us hung around to pay our last respects. Here is a recap of his last day, after twenty years.

Nice standing ovations on each of his five plate appearances; each time he stood back from the plate once, took off his batting helmet, waved, stuck the helmet back on and immediately got back in the box and began his steady smooth swings saying, "I'm ready." He bounced out to third in the 1st and 7th, hit one into the hole and off the 3rd baseman's glove for a hit in the 3rd, delivered the sac fly in the 5th, and the final single (and hit #2,365) in the 10th. Buddy Bell took him out then for a pinch runner which allowed us to hail him as a player one last time. Nice. He also started the last of how many 6-4-3 double plays in the 2nd. A typical Trammell day: solid, steady, productive.

His press conference—attended by all the Brewers as well as his teammates—was understated in the manner of a consummate professional. No false sentiment or modesty. "Today was my last day. . . . I feel fortunate that I have been able to do it longer than most. And I'm very proud that I have been able to do it with one ball club. When I first came up, I was a thin, skinny kid and they said if you are solid defensively and can hit .250, you'll be able to play. But I turned out to be part of the group—led first I guess by Davey Concepción and then joined by Robin Yount and Cal Ripken—of middle infielders who also did damage with the bat. I tried to play every day with the same careful preparation and intensity and concentration which is the mark of a professional." Here I think we could hear the future manager already giving a lesson to the younger players who stood at his side. He said "I'll be around. I have an arrangement with the club to be helpful in the future though we haven't yet worked out the details." Then he was given 2nd base. And we all cheered again and again, and he waved his hat one last time before disappearing down the familiar steps into the tiny, ancient third base dugout. Twenty years playing shortstop for the same club. Will have to check what distinguished company that puts him in. He played his career in parallel with Cal's and Ozzie's and for a minor-market club perhaps makes him a long-shot for the

Hall-of-Fame, but I think both Trammell and Whitaker will make it—if not by the baseball writers, then eventually by the Veterans' Committee.

Came out to find the car's left rear tire quite deflated from being left out of the festivities. Fortunately, there's a gas station right across from the stadium on Michigan and they patched up the tire and got me on my way. I was home by 11. Sushi and Sam had just watched the highlights of the game and Trammell's last remarks on the News. Some Sunday. Glad I went but glad too that I don't have to make that roundtrip in a day again—at least anytime soon. Kaline got me from the teenage years through grad school and the beginning of marriage and fatherhood, Trammell and Whitaker have gotten me through the middle years, and now it's up to this kid Clark or the nifty compact outfielder Higginson to take me into grandparenthood and beyond. It sure looks like there will be at least two more seasons in Tiger Stadium so perhaps some grandchildren will get to a game in the great old park even if in swaddling clothes. And Go Tiki [Tiki Barber broke Bill Pistner's Virginia high school record for the long jump and then went on to a fine football career at Bill's Alma Mater, Virginia, and a strong NFL career with the New York Giants. We've always considered him an adopted member of the family].

Love,
Dad

Some of the games we saw in the 1990s had strong baseball moments, but usually for the opposing team, including Sammy Sosa's nineteenth home run in June of 1998, breaking the record for most homers in a month, and then later that year, in August, Ken Griffey's remarkable catch in right center field, so amazing that the Tigers fans gave him a standing ovation when he came in from the field at the end of the inning. But too many were disappointments, with the Tigers, like most losing teams, repeatedly failing to get the two-out hit to bring the runner in from third or second, or the pen failing to hold a one- or two-run lead in the eighth

or ninth. But there were also players to relish, like Bobby
Higginson, who took over right field and for several seasons
made us believe he belonged there as the rightful successor
to Kaline and Gibson, and Tony Clark, the switch-hitting
first baseman and former basketball star at Arizona State,
who joined the long line of lefty first basemen who owned
the upper deck in right and even successfully launched one
monster shot over the third deck and out onto Trumbull.
Tony did not have Norm Cash's short, quick stroke, but he
knew the strike zone and did not give away many at bats.
He was also, for his size, a smooth fielder and demonstrated
even then the leadership skills that would eventually make
him the leader of the players' association.

The 1995 season, which began with the previous year's
strike still raw and the fiasco of spring training with the
replacement players still fresh, had one redeeming feature,
much like Pete Rose's season-long advance on Ty Cobb's
all-time hit record ten years before. Cal Ripken Jr.'s pursuit of Lou Gehrig's consecutive game record of 2,130—long
thought to be, like Joe DiMaggio's 56-game consecutive hit
string—a mark that would never be topped. And certainly
not by one who played one of the most physically demand-
ing positions in the game, shortstop. This narrative now
momentarily shifts to our son Sam, the Tiger fan who married Terry, the Orioles fan. They were living and working in
Washington in 1995. Both marveled at Ripken's achievement
of playing almost fourteen seasons without missing a single
game. Back in April they determined to buy tickets for the
Oriole home games in early September, which seemed the
most likely stretch when Cal would break the record. They
bought the tickets on the day the strike ended, so it was still
uncertain just when the season would begin. To be safe they
purchased tickets for six straight home games from September 1 to 6. I am sure the irony was not lost on them that
Gehrig's streak, as mentioned earlier, had ended against
the Tigers on May 2, 1939, when he took himself out of the
lineup against the Tigers in Detroit in Briggs Stadium. He
never played again.

The last two games, as Ripken approached tying and then breaking the record, were remarkable even for those of us who were not lucky enough to be in Camden Yards and had to catch them on television. Ripken was an authentic baseball hero, like Pete Rose, but without the rough edges and the gambler's itch. His ability, his demeanor, his perseverance, his grace silenced the cynics. As Sam said, "It was like a fairy tale," and the maiden being rescued was baseball. Ripken's wonderful lap around the warning track after breaking the record, personally reaching out to touch and be touched by the fans, was an extraordinary moment in which belief began to be restored between the fans and the game. And Ripken went on to play another 600-plus consecutive games before finally taking a break.

The other element that brought fans back to the game did, however, provide much fodder for the cynics: the remarkable assault on Roger Maris's single-season home run record by Mark McGwire and Sammy Sosa. Their competition was played out at the end of the decade; it was a spectacular show until the steroids scandal exposed their feats as boosted by a fraud. As the cynics have reminded us, major league baseball was happy to turn a blind eye to the steroids issue while the two sluggers matched each other dinger for dinger until McGwire pulled ahead and not only broke the record but obliterated it, only to be topped several years later by Barry Bonds.

The Tigers' only role in the tale was the way in which Cecil Fielder's several 50-plus home run seasons created a renewed appetite for the long ball. In the summer of '98, in the Cubs' first visit to Tiger Stadium since the 1945 World Series, Sammy Sosa broke the record for most home runs in a month (eighteen, set by a Tiger, Rudy York, back in 1937) on a sultry night in late June. Sam and Terry (and Aidan in his mother's womb) and I were there sitting just a few rows away from the Cubs on-deck circle, so we got to see plenty of Sosa up close. Nicely chiseled, we thought. Little did we know who or what the sculptor was. We even joined in the cheers when he led off the seventh with a blast into the upper deck in right field above the 370 sign and was asked back out—by Tiger fans—to take a bow after he returned to the dugout. Happily, Sosa got his record, but the Tigers won the game on Tony Clark's three-run bomb over the 440 sign in dead center in the bottom half of the inning.

Baseball likes pairs: Ruth and Gehrig, Mantle and Maris, Koufax and Drysdale, Spahn and Sain, Bagwell and Biggio, Greenberg and Gehringer, Rose and Morgan, Ford and Berra, Gibson and McCarver, Trammell and Whitaker. So does Shakespeare.

SHAKESPEARE AND BASEBALL VIII

Shakespeare's dramatic imagination focused on pairs: Hal and Hotspur, Helena and Hermia, Beatrice and Benedick, Romeo and Juliet, Othello and Iago, Macbeth and Lady Macbeth, Antony and Cleopatra, Ariel and Caliban. He was more interested in them as complementarities than as binaries. He explored the psychological, social, and political ways in which they each made the other possible. The deaths of Duncan and Desdemona would not have happened if their fates had been left to a single adversary. It is the convoluted mixture of personalities in Macbeth and Lady Macbeth and Othello and Iago that is murderous. The Beatrice and Benedick comedy is created not by their differences but by their similarities. They are subversively working together to make comedy in spite of themselves. Baseball also pivots on crucial pairs: pitcher and catcher, shortstop and second baseman, two great rival hitters. Even when constructed between two radically different personalities and temperaments, their fluid ability to play together (or challenge each other) is essential.

I mentioned early on the ways in which the Tigers provided a parallel stream to the unfolding of my life and world. Certain players came to represent the team in that journey: George Kell and Hoot Evers and Frank Lary in the fifties, Kaline and Cash in the sixties and seventies, and then the Bird to fill the brief gap between Kaline's retirement in '75 and the arrival of Alan Trammell and Lou Whitaker in September of '77. The two of them, the greatest double-play combination in the history of the game, then carried me, and Sam, through the arrival of Sparky in 1979, the great decade of the eighties, and into the team's decline in the nineties. They patrolled the middle of the infield for nineteen years before Lou decided to retire in 1995. Trammell originally planned to leave with him but was persuaded by Sparky Anderson to stay on for another year. A mistake, I think. I would have urged him to go out with his partner as they had arrived together and will always be linked.

They made for an interesting pair. Whitaker was from Virginia, Trammell from California. Whitaker was quiet and shy; Trammell was polite and candid but not voluble. One was White, the other Black, but neither had an ounce of eccentricity in his DNA. They were steady, consummate professionals. They went to work every day, side by side, in the middle of the diamond and for nineteen seasons, unlike the big bashers or showy crowd-pleasers, they created honest measured record-breaking performances. As Whitaker has commented on their learning to play together: "It was work and we continued to work. We were just playing baseball. It wasn't rocket science. We loved it. We were just 18 or 19. Together we got better at what we did. It took years."

They were reliable—to the game, to one another, to their teammates, and to us. They had, as Hemingway liked to call it, "the true gen." Neither was flashy, but I have never seen another second baseman be able so consistently to go to his right, backhand a ball headed up the middle into center, and pivot in the air and make a perfect throw to first. And I have never seen another shortstop elevate so gracefully above second to complete the double play. Whitaker recounts that when they reached their maturity as a pair in the mid-eighties, Tiger fans described them as "poetry in motion . . . but we never took it for granted." They, of course, hold all the records for double plays achieved by the same combination. They were the Keystone Kings. And to top it off, they were good for the game, good for Detroit, and good for the country. Their relationship acknowledged race even as it transcended it. In their own dignified way, they worked together every day as efficient, effective partners; they roomed together on the road; they represented the rarely achieved American dream of racial harmony and partnership and mutual achievement.

Their careers reveal the equality of that achievement. They each played in approximately 2,300 games; Trammell hit .285, Whitaker .276; Trammell had 2,365 hits, Whitaker 2,369; Trammell had 412 doubles, Whitaker 420; Trammell hit 185 home runs, Whitaker 244; Trammell drove in 1,003 runs, Whitaker 1,084; Trammell had an OPS (on-base plus slugging percentage) of .767, Whitaker .789; Trammell has a WAR (wins above replacement) of 70.7, Whitaker 67.7. Even the honors were almost evenly distributed. Tram played in six All-Star Games, Lou in five; Lou was Rookie of the Year in 1978 and the MVP of the 1983 All-Star Game; Trammell was the MVP of the 1984 World Series. Trammell has four Golden Gloves, Whitaker three; Lou has four Silver Slugger awards, Tram three. Observing them at work in the field and at the plate was the longest-running pleasure of my baseball-watching experience.

Trammell's achievement at short has finally been recognized by the Hall of Fame. Now it is Lou's turn. His offensive and defensive statistics and WAR number are equal to or superior to almost all the second basemen in the Hall. Only three second basemen in the history of the game have accumulated at least 2,000 hits, 1,000 RBIs, 1,000 runs scored, 1,000 walks, and 200 home runs. Two of them are Rogers Hornsby and Joe Morgan. The third is Lou Whitaker, whose lifetime numbers place him sixth on the list of all second basemen according to Hall of Stats. The Trammell and Whitaker partnership should end as a comedy, but baseball, which should know better, seems bound to make it tragic by denying Whitaker his rightful place beside his partner in the Hall.

The record shows that I made six visits to Tiger Stadium in 1999. No surprise, for even though the team still struggled it was the last year of the great old park at Michigan and Trumbull and she could still sing her siren call. I was there for opening day and Sam and I were there for the last hurrah on September 27. In between there were the first (and last) trips for Charlie Pistner and Aidan Crowl, and even Sandy Elsass flew in from Boston for a game against the Orioles. Sam and Terry and Aidan and I also caught three games versus the Indians at Jacobs Field in May.

The family did have the opportunity to say a long goodbye to our old haunt, though nothing like Tom Stanton's *The Final Season*, where he attended every home game and wrote a fine book about the experience. These last moments in the corroded peeling fading beauty reached the heights of baseball sentiment. Being in the stands and then down on the field with three generations of family Tiger fans provided a warm, rich experience almost as good as some of the great games we had experienced. Now the thrill was mixed with melancholy that our future Tiger watching would play out in a different landscape, a different space.

The last game, on September 27, was one for the ages. To their great credit the Ilitch team did it right and provided historic pageantry, and the Tigers responded with a winning display of offense, capped by a mighty grand slam by the young catcher Robert Fick in the bottom of the eighth. After the game was over, the great parade of former Tigers, reaching back to Billy Rogell and Elden Auker from the mid-thirties, and including Tigers stars (all in uniform) from each succeeding decade, dashed, strolled, or limped in from deep center field to take the positions where they had played. The Bird was first, Trammell and Whitaker last, and a world of Tigers in between, from Hall of Famers George Kell and Al Kaline to Virgil Trucks and Frank Lary to Willy Horton and Bill Freehan to Chet Lemon and Jack Morris. There were more than sixty of them, and when Trammell and Whitaker emerged as the final duo, the crowd let loose with a mighty roar of "Louuuuu . . . Louuuuu . . . Louuuuu," and Sam and I dissolved in the rapture of Tiger history. I will say no more here of that glorious late afternoon and evening, but this next letter provides a full account.

TIGER LETTER #3

29 September 1999

Dear Charlie and Aidan and Tiger Fans,

The last baseball has been played at Tiger Stadium and it is as if the last Mass has been said at Notre Dame, the last bull has been killed at Ronda, and the last Shakespeare has been spoken at Stratford. One of baseball's great temples now is forever empty and silent but what a grand glorious noisy wake the old ball field was given by 43,639 of us on this past Monday. And what a splendid final experience this struggling generation of young Tigers treated us to as we roared and wept for them, the game, and the place. If the game, like no other, is famed for being passed on within the family from one generation to another, then this experience was one given by son to father as I would not have made this mad dash north fresh (more like stale) off of a 18 hour trip from a Shakespeare conference in Malaga to Madrid to Dulles to Port Columbus unless Sam had insisted that we couldn't miss the LAST GAME. So, he collected me at the airport at 7:30 P.M. and off we went, with the top down, through the warm September night up the familiar route past Delaware and Marion and Findlay and Toledo to nestle into the Ramada on Eureka Road just in time to enjoy a few beers and countless Sports Center replays of Justin Leonard's 45 foot putt, which had won the Ryder Cup six hours earlier.

The next day was worthy of Falstaff: Indian Summer at its finest. Blue sky, easy breeze, temps in the mid-80s. Perfect for baseball, but also for golf so first there was a quick trip to Riverside to squeeze in 15 holes before heading down to the Corner for pre-game festivities and the late afternoon 4:05 start. The place was jammed, much more so I thought than for any of the three World Series games back in '84, but we managed to find one last parking spot down on Bagley next to the DNB branch in Corktown. The fans were mingling all over Michigan and Trumbull and the walks around the Stadium were packed, but we made our way to the Will Call window at Gate 9. There was a long line, but Sam made some enquiries and learned that if our tickets had been arranged by the Tigers to go right to the front, so we did, and Sam quickly had them in hand. Turns out the line was for Kansas City fans whose tickets had not yet been sent down from the office. Thanks again to Dave Glazier (the Tiger's VP for Finance, son-in-law of my friend Alan Geiger, and graduate of Ohio University's Master's Program in Sports Administration) for taking such good care of us. Entry was slow as all the tickets were specifically stamped, and we all were given a plastic holder for them to wear around our necks so the soon to be historic tickets wouldn't get crumpled in one's pocket. Nice Touch.

We worked our way around the narrow inner corridor from left field to home plate and picked up a Big Blue before climbing the ramp to our upper deck beauties just 10 rows up behind home plate. For the record: Section 420, Row C, Seats 14 and 15. We had a perfect view out over the wide expanse of green and orange and blue. The grounds crew had cut the old path from the mound to home plate which is how the diamond was configured when I first saw games here. Ernie Harwell was presiding below, and Kaline was in uniform with the familiar No. 6 on his back broadcasting from in front of the Tigers dugout.

As most of the newspaper accounts have mentioned, the Tigers were wearing the uniform numbers of players who had just been selected to the All-Time Tigers All-Star team by a vote of the fans. So Tony Clark was wearing Greenberg's #5, Dean Palmer Kell's #21. And Deivi Cruz Tram's #3. Gabe Kapler, playing center, wore no number (as there were no numbers in Cobb's era) and in what would prove to be a prophetic touch, Robert Fick—our young rookie DH just up from a short season in the minors after shoulder surgery—was assigned Norm Cash's #25. And in perhaps the biggest mismatch, Luis Polonia—our tiny leadoff hitter 5'8" 160 lbs—was wearing Kirk Gibson's #23. Billy Rogell, the Tiger shortstop

in the 1930s, was carted in from center field to throw out
the first pitch. He threw it a bit wildly, but Ausmus stabbed
it bare-handed, the first sign that all was going to work like
magic for the home club on this day. Rogell's appearance, the
current Tigers wearing the numbers of the past greats, the
stands full of fans like us recalling favorite moments from
our personal histories in the old park, all established the nice
flow of memories as past was repeatedly linked with present throughout the long sweet late afternoon. I saw my first
game here sometime in the summer of 1950; Sam his in the
summer of 1976; Trammell and Whitaker were as fresh in his
memory as Virgil Trucks and Hoot Evers were in mine.

A second sign that this was to be our day was the way
Brian Moehler worked his way out of a bases loaded, one
out jam in the top of the first by striking out Mike Sweeney
and getting Joe Randa to line out to Damion Easley. A third
sign followed quickly in our half as Polonia, after trying (and
failing) to drop a bunt down the 3rd base line, hit a massive
shot deep into the lower deck in deep right center at the 415
marker. Must have gone 425 feet. A blast from the diminu-
tive Polonia worthy of Gibson. Quinn, the Royals rookie just
called up from the minors and who has been on a tear, hit
Moehler's fifth pitch in the 2nd into the upper deck in left
to tie it up. We got one back in the bottom half on an Easley
lead-off double, a Garcia ground out to the right side (smart
hitting) to move Damion to 3rd, and a Fick sacrifice fly to the
warning track in right. The Royals came back to tie in the 3rd
on three hits and a walk but a nifty 5-4-3 double play in the
middle of the activity kept the damage from getting worse.

Lots of hits and baserunners but no more scoring until
the 6th. When Dean Palmer led off with a single, Easley
sacrificed him to 2nd, and Karim Garcia (wearing Kaline's
#6) hit a line drive into the seats in left to give the Tigers
a 4–2 lead. Pandemonium as the place erupted. High fives
all around. Meanwhile Moehler had found his rhythm and
handled the Royals with relative ease in the 4th, 5th, and 6th
and was done for the day. He'd thrown lots of pitches (106 in
6) as he kept going deep in the count and Larry Parrish felt

his bullpen—the strongest most consistent part of the team over the year—would close it out for the win. Well almost. Cordero came on in the 7th and promptly gave up two singles and a walk sandwiched around a strikeout. Parrish went back to the pen to bring in Doug Brocail who, with the bases loaded, got Joe Randa to hit into a sharp 4-6-3 double play and we were out of the inning. Huge cheers for Brocail and the defense.

But the best was yet to come. In the bottom of the 8th we were treated to the final bit of Baseball-at-the-Corner magic. We loaded the bases on a Palmer double, an Easley single to left, and an intentional pass to Garcia. With the infield in, Kapler hit a roller to the mound and Jeff Montgomery got Palmer at the plate. Big groan from the crowd. Up came the rookie Fick who hit the first pitch like a rocket up on the ROOF in right just above the 1968 and 1984 World Series banners. It took a big bounce but had too much backspin which brought it back into the park rather than skipping up over the roof and out on Trumbull. A grand slam roof shot as the final home run in Tiger Stadium! And from a kid wearing Norm Cash's number, the man who hit four out over that roof in 1961 and 1962—the most by any player in the stadium's history.

We were all on our feet stamping and whistling and shouting: "Fick . . . Fick . . . Fick" and the kid came back out of the dugout to receive a hero's welcome. He doffed his cap and re-vealed a shiny shaved head—a tribute we learned on the radio on the way home to his bald dad who passed away last year. Fathers and sons again. The game had begun by Moehler's kneeling out on the mound and scratching his father's initials into the backside of the mound as he does before every game he pitches. The fans, having come more for the past than the present, were treated to a great baseball game. The best 8–2 game I have ever seen (or will ever see) testifying again to the wonderful pleasures of the game itself even when divorced from the nostalgia generated by today's special circumstances. Todd Jones came on in the 9th, and with the fans standing and roaring on every pitch as though it were a no-hitter or the last inning of game seven of the World Series, struck out Pose, got Sánchez on a liner to Easley, and then got the sure rookie-of-the-year Carlos Beltran (a terrific young hitter who had been 3 for 3 in the game) to chase a low change down in the strike zone for the final strikeout. So, the final hit in Tiger Stadium was a home run on the roof in right by a puppy and the final out was a swinging strikeout fashioned by one of the game's cagey vets. Parrish had said some time ago that Jones was the only player who had made a special request to play in the final game at the Corner. He got his wish and he delivered. Great stuff.

Everyone stood and cheered and pounded one another on the back and snapped pictures. The place looked a bit like the National League parks last year with the flashes going off each time McGwire or Sosa stepped to the plate. Sam had his camcorder out taking it all for the grandchildren who may wonder what all the shouting was about when they have a look at the video years hence, but for us it was sweet, overwhelming pleasure at its best.

When the tumult had subsided, we got Ernie Harwell narrating a 20-minute filmed history of the team and the stadium and then the sentimental parade and the tears began. From out under the bleachers in center field came a procession of Tiger greats—one by one and all in uniform—from the last 60 years. They were led by the tall, gangly, mopheaded Bird who sprinted to the mound and got down on his hands and knees to groom and talk to it as he had done in his rookie year back in 1976 when he grabbed the attention of baseball fans everywhere with his playful antics and a brilliant 19 and 9, 2.34 ERA season. Fitting for us as 1976 was the year Sam and Miranda saw their first game at Tiger Stadium when it was still all green. Bird didn't pitch that night but several other Tigers in the line-up then were here now: Ron LeFlore, Steve Kemp, Aurelio Rodríguez, and Jason Thompson (another right roof clearing home run hitter).

From the early days of my Tigers watching came Virgil Trucks (still looking like he had another no-hitter in him), George Kell, Art Houtteman, Charlie "Paw-Paw" Maxwell (many of these names I had already evoked in my last letter when talking about being down on the field itself and now here they all were as if emerging out of that cornfield in *Field of Dreams*), and most emotionally (for me) Ray Boone who took over from Kell at 3rd and who has fathered two more generations of major league players: Bob Boone, the great catcher, and his kids, Bret and Aaron, who are both headed into post-season play this year with the Braves and the Reds. Amazing. By now the tears were streaming down my cheeks and I just gave in to the moment and let them roll.

In a masterstroke the Tigers didn't announce the players as they emerged but let the crowd recognize them as their faces appeared on the big scoreboard screen above the bleachers. And the crowd around us knew their Tigers as with the first glimpse of a player caught on the screen they'd call out "It's Mickey Stanley," or "It's Eddie Yost," or "It's Dick McAuliffe," or "It's Billy Hoeft," and out they continued to stream, all in their home whites with the old English **Ð**, sprinting or strolling in from center to join the others who played third or short or first. Now the infield consisted of clumps of white on the mound and gathered around the bases. The cheers intensified as the heroes of '68 joined the flock, with the loudest roars for the hometown stars: Willie Horton and Bill Freehan and Mickey Lolich (who pitched and won a master-piece against Bob Gibson in game seven of that World Series) and Jim Northrup, the old grey fox who gave him the runs he needed in that final game by hitting a fierce triple over Curt Flood's head.

Then came our guys from '84 with the crowd imme-diately picking up the old familiar chant of "Dare—ell . . . Dare—ell . . . Dare—ell . . ." as Evans appeared and headed to join the men at first and "Ches—ter . . . Ches—ter . . ." as Chet Lemon joined the center fielders. Then here came Gibby, grandstanding as always, sprinting into right and finishing off with a mighty slide and Peaches [Dan Petry] and Milt Wilcox and tough surly old Jack Morris (my pitcher for the one must win game) joining the big throng at the mound where the Bird was still and forever busy greeting all comers, and Lance Parrish to join Freehan at the plate and then Kaline as the noise seemed to reach its crescendo, but no, there was more, as the last two, together for 19 years at the corner of the Corner, Whitaker and Trammell came dancing out and the crowd broke into "LOUUUUUUUUUUUU . . . LOUUUUUUUUUUUU . . . LOUUUUUUUUU" and Whitaker cupped his hands to his ears as if to say at once: enough and more. All 60 of them then formed a single historical continuum from the flagpole in center to home plate. The flag was lowered, folded, and passed, starting with Elden Auker, the old sidewinder from the early 30s, down from man to man through the last 60 years to finally reach Brad Ausmus at home. Hokey but brilliant and we just gave ourselves completely to the experience.

Before this parade from the past, we had watched as home plate had been dug up and now the big screen took us to Comerica Park where the plate was being replanted and this let us show our love and affection for the old place by booing like hell with every mention of the new one. But even the boos had no edge to them. The boos seemed less an expression of anger for the new than another way of expressing affection for the old. And then one by one they dimmed the light towers, and we stood looking down on the field one last time as the men in white gravitated towards center field to say goodbye to the huge throng out in the bleachers one last time. At the time, I wondered how in the world are we going to make the five-hour drive home (Sam had a full day of classes on Tuesday and preparation for leading his own discussion section of History 131 to prepare) after all this. But we did. We slipped out down Trumbull to Fort and on to Clark and out onto I-75 with the top down and WJR giving us an endless replay of the day's events. Sparky Anderson, via relay from California, had called it the greatest event in the history of sports in Detroit and for this moment at least his hyperbole didn't seem too far off the mark. I got us to Bowling Green, where we gassed up and got a Wendy's and Sam heroically did the last four hours through the night and we were home just before 2 AM.

What a day. Hope your future with the game produces some thrills to match this one, guys.

A few post-letter additions. The official announced attendance was 43,356 which seems small to me. Perhaps that was the paid figure. My guess is that there were 46,000 plus in the park. The total attendance for the season was 2,026,441—a great tribute to Tiger Stadium as the club languished in last place for most of the year. The line-up cards were turned in by Kaline and George Brett (#6 and #5—both members of the 3,000-hit club). Brett is one of the great good ones to have played the game and it was an honor to have him participate, as representative of all the other greats who have played here since 1912, in the little ritual at home plate which gets the game underway. In my account of the game, I almost said that Moehler's way of bearing down with runners on base was Morris-like: I should have, as Moehler was wearing #47 and some of it clearly rubbed off on him. Billy Rogell, who threw out the first pitch, is 94. His toss might have been a bit wild, but it made it all the way to Ausmus. The night before the game the 440 sign in deep dead center was taken down, replaced by a substitute, and shipped off to Cooperstown. Did the Hall think that those unruly Detroit fans might get to it? As it turned out the crowd was so in awe of the game and the moment that it was tame, emotionally drenched, rather than wild in its response to the evening's events. I also did not know that our relief pitchers have long called the ridiculous bullpen dugout down the third base line, the submarine. Appropriate as it is a long narrow cage.

Finally, Todd Jones and Brian Moehler slept this final night in the clubhouse at the Stadium. A nest worthy of the Bird.

Love,
Bops

Part 6

The 2000s

We were in no hurry to get to Comerica; we were still in mourning for Tiger Stadium. The Old English **D** on the Tiger baseball cap is white when the players are at home, orange when they are on the road. I vowed to wear my road cap to my first games at Comerica because it was not yet, for me, "home." And I did so, well into the decade. The early years of the new century in Tiger baseball were an extension of the old. Ilitch, wanting a winner in his new park, made a smart baseball move and in 2002 hired Dave Dombrowski as his president and general manager to rebuild the club, and the two of them went to work to revive the franchise. Dombrowski fired GM Randy Smith and the next year hired Alan Trammell as manager. Trammell brought fans back to Comerica, but the team he was given was sad, and in 2003 they lost the most games in Tiger history, 119. The only way was up, and the road went through free agency.

The first move, in 2004, was to lure the great longtime Texas Rangers and Florida Marlins catcher Pudge Rodríguez to Detroit. Pudge, a free agent after leading the Marlins to a World Series victory, wanted a four-year contract worth ten million a year, and the Marlins (always rebuilding or unloading) refused to give their star the contract he deserved. Ilitch was more than willing to do so and convinced Rodríguez that he was serious about rebuilding the Tigers around him. And he did. The next year he and Dombrowski added the White Sox star Magglio Ordoñez, whose bum knee turned out to still have several All-Star seasons and a batting championship (.363 in '07) left in it, and, in Dombrowski's most ingenious trade ever, he picked up Placido Polanco from the Phillies, to play second base, for a reliever, Ugueth Urbina, who was soon to be in prison in Venezuela! And in 2006 he added the aging left-hander Kenny Rogers to lead a young staff and, perhaps most crucially, brought in the seasoned veteran Jim Leyland as manager. Leyland, who chain-smoked through every game, reignited the club, as Anderson had done twenty-five years before: Sparky recreated as Smokey.

Dombrowski had already made a shrewd deal with Seattle for Carlos Guillén, who plugged the hole at short and turned out to be a clutch hitter as well. Suddenly the farm system was a help by providing a fleet center fielder, Curtis Granderson, and new strong rookie arms in Justin Verlander and Joel Zumaya to go with other young pitchers like Jeremy Bonderman (from Oakland) and Nate Robertson (from Miami). Granderson and Magglio were joined in the outfield by Craig Monroe. Monroe joined the club in 2003, played steady defense in left, and provided 25 homers a year for several seasons. Brandon Inge, who had been catching in the desperate years, moved to third base when Pudge arrived, and when at the July trading deadline in 2006 Dombrowski picked up Sean Casey from the Pirates to play first base, the new Tigers had been assembled. And Shazam, the Tigers were back.

In the eleven years from 2006 and 2016 the Tigers went on a winning run that surpassed their work in the 1980s, with one stark, sad exception: they failed to win a World Series. They went twice, in 2006 and 2012, and unexpectedly were spanked each time after being the dominant team in the playoffs and the clear favorites to win it all. The level of Tiger baseball rose exponentially, starting with the surprise season of 2006, when they dashed out of the gate and proved early on that there was a new threat in the AL Central Division. For the first time since the new park was opened, it was fun to be in Comerica, and Detroit responded by packing the place in August and September when it realized it had a winner. And I started wearing my cap with the Old English white 𝔇 on it. In a season of surprises, after the strong start was sustained into July and August, the team swooned in September, as I discovered from afar as Susan and I and several friends were prowling the Hermitage in St. Petersburg and the theaters in London. We returned just in time to see them lose, via TV, the division championship to the Twins on the last day of the season. But their record was strong enough to secure them an invitation to the playoffs, and they were at last back in the postseason after two decades in the wilderness. Their tragic late-season collapse was rescued and transformed into something of a comedy by a term we might find useful in talking about Shakespeare: the Wild Card.

SHAKESPEARE AND BASEBALL IX

For those skeptical about the role of professional sports in the revival of downtown urban areas, I recommend a study of what has happened in Detroit between the opening of Comerica Park in 2000 and the present. A trip to Tiger Stadium was an in-and-out experience with perhaps a stop at the Designated Hatter or Sports Land before the game and then a beer at Hoots or Nemo's. There were no hotels, no restaurants, almost no street life. Nothing to explore or enjoy in the immediate neighborhood. Corktown was not Wrigleyville. Something similar held in the first years after the move to Comerica, but at least it was only a three- or four-block walk to Greektown, the one area in downtown Detroit that had maintained some flavor and night life, recently boosted by the addition of a casino.

Shakespeare has been exalted by scholars as the supreme English poet, and even further esteemed in the people's polls as England's Man of the Millennium. But it is prudent to remember than he was first a man of the commercial theater. He was deeply involved with all the workings of the Globe Theatre and received income as an actor, a playwright, and a shareholder in the theater. He also undoubtedly received income from at least some of the editions of his plays published in his lifetime. Even more than the Burbage family, he was the economic engine of Globe Enterprises.

Ilitch's relocation of the Tigers' ballpark was something akin to the Burbage family's move of the theater (tearing it down one oaken beam and plank after another) from Shoreditch, north of the London city wall, to the South Bank of the Thames in 1599. The deconstructed theater was transported to the river, ferried across, and reconstructed and rechristened as the Globe. Think of the chutzpah of that name. Rival theaters in Shoreditch and across the Thames in Bankside were more modestly named the Rose, the Curtain, the Swan, and the Fortune. Shakespeare and Richard Burbage would now perform in the Globe, its very name a realization of Jaques's poetic declaration that "all the world's a stage, / And all the men and women merely players."

The theater district was known as the Liberties because it was beyond the reach of the laws of the City of London. It was a "liberty," a free space where the imagination could play and the seamy, exciting, underside of urban living could thrive. It became the home of all those institutions necessary to city life—theaters, sports entertainment (bear- and bull-baiting pits), houses of prostitution, prisons, hospitals, monasteries, leper colonies—but not deemed worthy of inclusion within the formal boundaries of civil society. But the new name of Shakespeare's theater placed it at the center, not the margins, of English civilization.

Something similar was stirring in Detroit four hundred years later. Ilitch already had brought and restored Detroit's Fox Theater, a former movie palace transformed into a concert venue, which stood across Woodward from the location of the new ballpark. Soon the Ford family relocated the Lions from their suburban home at the Silverdome in

Pontiac to the new Ford Field built right behind Comerica Park. And eventually the Ilitch organization built a new arena for the Red Wings and the Pistons (who had moved north to Auburn Hills years before) just down Woodward from the Fox Theater.

The area was transformed. Within a decade half a dozen hotels sprouted up within walking distance of Comerica Park; new bars and pubs and restaurants materialized. Derelict buildings began to grow scaffolding rather than weeds. Street life returned. The city added a new tram line that runs right by these sports venues transporting passengers up and down Woodward Avenue from the Detroit Opera, the sports arenas, the homes of the Detroit Symphony and the Detroit Institute of Art (with its magnificent murals by Diego Rivera), and a revitalized neighborhood surrounding Wayne State University. It is hard to imagine another American city which has so much elite, popular, and street culture in such proximity. Ilitch and the Tigers did not do it all, but even if they could not deliver a World Series champion, they did restore a franchise and revive a blighted downtown neighborhood and help reinvigorate a city long on its knees. Not bad for Detroit or for baseball. I write this with the understanding that Detroit's population has shrunk from 1.6 million in 1950 to something like 640,000 in 2020. The next two decades will reveal if the revitalization of the downtown area (where several major companies have also relocated their home offices) will lead to a population influx.

At the risk of committing overreach by analogy, I would argue that something similar, promoted by culture rather than sport, has happened to London's Bankside (now commonly referred to as the South Bank) in the past forty years. When Oliver Cromwell's Puritan revolution succeeded in 1642, one of its first acts was to pull down the theaters, the source of idle entertainment and social corruption. When Charles II and his court returned from France to reestablish the monarchy in 1660, they built indoor theaters, modeled on those they had attended in France, within London proper. In the eighteen brief years from 1642 to 1660 all knowledge of the unusual architecture and interior space of the Elizabethan theater had vanished. The South Bank retained its shady, seedy past but now became attached to the great commercial globe itself by becoming the site of riverside warehouses connected with the shipping trade, the engine of England's burgeoning commercial empire.

When Susan and I and the kids tried to walk the South Bank along the Thames between Waterloo and London Bridges in 1975, it was impossible. Before the National Theatre and the reconstructed Globe there was no uninterrupted pathway connecting the two sites. The area was still a maze of creaky ancient warehouses (where Fagin might have presided), a great cathedral (Southwark), a fine riverside pub (the Anchor), and an enormous example of Brutalist architecture (the Bankside Power Station). Today, with the opening in the mid-1970s of the National Film Institute and the National Theatre nestled next to Waterloo Bridge, the new Globe in the late nineties, and the Tate Modern art museum (fashioned out of the former Bankside Power Station) soon after, there is now a wonderful open continuous walkway filled with strollers, joggers, music and film and theater and art lovers, and yes, even natives enjoying their city.

Baseball in Detroit and Shakespeare in London are both drawing crowds and revitalizing the urban landscape. I should mention the first and last arrivals to the revival of London's South Bank. The first was the Royal Festival Hall in the early 1950s as the home for London's major symphonies and chamber groups, and then the London Eye, the giant Ferris wheel that now dominates the skyline of the South Bank much as Big Ben does just across the Thames to the north at the Houses of Parliament.

If the first decade of the new millennium was good for the Tigers and Detroit, it was also good for me. I published three books, including a comprehensive treatment of Shakespeare on film commissioned by W. W. Norton, one of the major New York publishers of both academic and trade books, to accompany the release of the second edition of The

Norton *Shakespeare*. The book was written in what was for me something of a mad dash between 2005 and 2007 just as the Tigers were surprising the baseball world with their renaissance. It was the first (and only) book I ever wrote that had to meet a publisher's deadline, and with the aid of a young editor at Norton, we made it. Joe Barber, and our mutual failure forty years earlier to deliver the introductions and notes on Shakespeare's comedies for *The Riverside Shakespeare*, was much on my mind as the deadline loomed. As a way of thanking his ghostly presence, which has loomed so protectively and productively over my career, I dedicated the volume to him and my Hamilton College Shakespeare professor, Edwin Barrett. Huge debts acknowledged if not fully repaid.

THE 2006 PLAYOFFS AND WORLD SERIES

In 2006 the Tigers also went to work to repay a debt—to their fans. Just two years distant from losing a club record 119 games, they surprised the baseball world by getting off to a strong start and leading the American League Central for most of the season. They fell apart in the last two weeks of September and let the Twins slip by them for the division title, but their record was strong enough to make them the Wild Card team, and they quickly rebounded in the playoffs from their poor finish to the regular season.

The Tigers, as decided underdogs, squared off in the first round of the playoffs against the mighty Yankees. They split the two games in Yankee Stadium, with Verlander and Zumaya combining to win a beauty, 4–3, in game 2. Back they came to Comerica, where Sam and I caught up with them. They had the big bad Yanks huffing and puffing, and there was no swooning as first Rogers and then Bonderman polished them off to win the series 3–1. The first game in Comerica was Rogers versus Randy Johnson, the first playoff game in history to feature two starting pitchers over forty. And both left-handers. Rogers wasn't sharp but managed to wriggle his way out of jam after jam, while the aging Johnson tired in the sixth and the Tigers pounced, increasing their early lead to 5–0. Rogers pitched into the eighth and then turned it over to Zumaya and Todd Jones, who mopped up.

The Tiger pitchers had held the mighty Yanks scoreless for fourteen straight innings. Alex Rodriguez, Jason Giambi, Derek Jeter, and Johnny Damon were all baffled by Rogers. None more so than Giambi, who struck out on three straight fastballs from the normally soft-tossing Rogers in the fourth, and ARod, who continued his postseason slump by going 0 for 3. The next day Joe Torre lowered him from cleanup to the eighth spot in the order, a devastating demotion for the two-time MVP. As his troubles continued against Jeremy Bonderman, I thought back to a game versus Seattle in the 1990s at Tiger Stadium, when I was surrounded by young Detroit teenyboppers all clutching his photo and chanting, "Alex . . . Alex . . . Alex," whenever he came to the plate. No such devotion was on display on this late October afternoon from the Yankee fans (and there were plenty of them) in Comerica.

Bonderman, perhaps inspired by Rogers, pitched his strongest game of the season, and had those powerful Yankee hitters under the sway of his fastball, curve, and brilliant slider. He dispatched the first fifteen hitters on forty tosses: pitching mastery. The Tigers won the game 8–1 and the series. They were on a roll as they flew out to face the A's in Oakland for the American League championship. Verlander and Nate Robertson had strong outings, and a kid named Alexis Gómez, a September call-up from the Toledo Mud Hens, hit a home run (Leyland too was on a roll). The Tigers returned to Detroit up 2–0 and ready for the Rogers-Bonderman tandem to do its work.

Sam and I dashed to Detroit to welcome them back to Comerica, where we were again rewarded with excellent baseball. Rogers pitched a 3–0 beauty in game 3, at one point retiring seventeen A's in a row, and Bonderman battled the A's the next day, giving up three early runs but hanging in until the seventh, allowing his club to come back and tie the score. In the bottom of the ninth, with two outs and the A's ace reliever Huston Street on the mound, Monroe and Polanco singled, bringing Ordoñez to the plate. Maggs had already hit the homer that tied the game back in the sixth. Now he laced Street's second pitch—the ball's lovely arc passing right by our eyes, as Sam had managed to get us our favorite Terrace Box seats down the left field line—over the fence and the Tiger bullpen and several rows deep into the seats in left. A "sayonara home run" to welcome the Tigers back to the World Series after a two-decade absence. Here's the Tiger Letter with all the exciting details on the American League Championship Series with the A's to the youngest Tiger fans.

TIGER LETTER # 4

16 October 2006

Dear Charlie, Aidan, Theo, Audrey, and Miles:

Here's a report on our club's winning performance in the second round of the AL playoffs. **World Series** here we come and after a long wait of twenty-two years: how sweet it is. Sam and I hit the road at 10 am as the game-time had been moved up four hours from 8:30 to 4:30. More blue sky but temps in the mid-40s kept the top up as we sped north. Hit the clouds at Toledo and rolled into the Hilton Garden Inn, just two blocks from Comerica, under a cool grey October sky. Hit the streets to unload some extra tickets but we didn't find the same hot market Sam found the week before against the Yanks. A's fans evidently don't travel. The early start on a Friday afternoon and the weather contributed to a decline in pregame ticket exchange activity and we got a little lesson in the economics of the street, but Sam still managed to unload his extra four and we came back to the Hilton to change into our game gear and snuggle into our newly purchased (again on the street) Zoom/Zoom stocking caps named in honor of the Tigers' rookie relief pitcher, Joel Zumaya, who consistently hits 100 plus on the pitch speed gun.

Into the park just at game time so we missed Mickey Lolich (hero of the 1968 World Series who won three games and out pitched Bob Gibson on two days rest in game seven after the Tigers had found themselves down 3–1) throw out the first pitch and the Temptations sing the National Anthem. Mickey and the Temptations. What a combination. We slipped into our Terrace seats in 116A and a couple of big Labatt's Blues just as the old master Kenny Rogers was finishing his warm-up pitches. Rogers was up against the A's young 25-year-old hard thrower, Rich Harden who had missed most of the season with assorted arm and back injuries but had come back in September to win four starts in a row. Temp at 42 degrees as Rogers gave up a lead-off single to Jason Kendall. Hard to think that the old man could pitch an even stronger game than a week ago against the Yanks and this was an inauspicious start. But he quickly got Mark Kotsay to pop one up down the left field line that Brandon Inge made a sensational play on tumbling into the stands and managing to keep the ball tightly wrapped in his glove. Inge would go on to make a series of excellent plays at third in the two games; twice keeping potential A's rallies from developing by taking what looked like sure doubles down the line and turning them into outs, once by starting a fine 5-4-3 double play.

Rogers was in complete command and gave the A's only one more hit, a harmless single by Marco Scutaro in the 5th that was immediately erased when Jimenez bounced into an inning ending double play. At one point Rogers retired 17 in a row. The white towel waving crowd got into the game early responding to Rogers's mastery from the 2nd inning on with the now familiar chants of "Ken-ny . . . Ken-ny . . . Ken-ny" every time he reached a two-strike count on the hitter. Comerica Park became a Temple to Pitching; Rogers was the high priest; and the crowd the chorus that responded loudly but reverently to his every sly but magnificent toss.

The Tigers got him two quick runs in the first on a walk to Granderson, singles by Monroe and Polanco, and a fielder's choice by Ordoñez. In the 5th Monroe led off with a homer over the Tigers' bull pen in left and that was the game. Rogers left with one on and one out in the 8th and Rodney came on and got pinch hitter Kielty to hit into yet another A's double play (they led the league in this dubious category this year) and Todd Jones set them down in order on ten pitches in the 9th and the Tigers had just won their sixth consecutive playoff game. Man, this is getting to be fun. Someone new seems to get the big hit every night with Granderson, Monroe, and Polanco leading the way. Our big guns—Ordoñez, Guillén, and Rodríguez—have been curiously silent. If they break loose, turn out the lights.

We headed back to the hotel now with the customary high fives being exchanged with the crowd as we glided down the center of Brush Street. Tomorrow, I imagine we'll see plenty of brooms on Brush Street as the Tigers go for the sweep. Had a drink, called home, changed out of our game stuff, and headed to Greektown to a late dinner at Mosaic, a new restaurant with culinary pretensions it can't quite yet match (I had a stuffed quail that was, to be gentle, over-stuffed and Sam's steak was a bit over-sauced) but we had a fine bottle of a 2002 Cakebread cabernet and all was well in Tigerland. Back to the hotel where Uncle Sam fell asleep watching the highlights on Sports Center, and I soon followed him after reading the scorecard one more time and marveling at how thoroughly Rogers dominated the A's. The Yankees, a week ago, had runners on in every inning and sharply hammered several balls but hit right at our outfielders. Tonight, Rogers had the A's baffled from the start and set them down in neat little groups of three each inning.

Saturday was bright and blue. We lazed about. Headed back to Greektown for lunch. Took a long stroll back around Comerica's environs and I came back for a short nap while Sam unloaded the extras he had for today's game. He was back in time to see Indiana seal an upset of Iowa on a great last-minute interception and head back to the park at 4. We were back in the Terrace seats down the leftfield line where we sat last Saturday. Temps in the mid-50s and we were in the sun until the 5th inning so even though a strong breeze was blowing right at us out to left, we did not feel the cold. Sam, who does like modestly to have it all, had declared at lunch that he was a bit tired of games the Tigers dominated from

the opening and for a change of pace he'd like to see them
come from behind for the sweep.

Our lads heard him and responded. Bonderman wasn't
sharp in the 1st and gave up a one out walk, then doubles
from Bradley (a major thorn in our paw throughout the series) and Chávez, and the A's had their first lead of the series,
2–0. Bonderman then found his rhythm but in the 4th he
gave up a one out home run to Payton who hit a sharp low
line drive right down the left field line that cleared the fence
by a foot or two just inside the foul pole. 3–0. Dan Haren,
pitching for the A's, had his good split-finger fastball and had
our big hitters lunging at it as it dipped out of the zone. He
was aided (and Bonderman too) by the late afternoon shadows that separated the sun-lit mound from the darkened
plate. He struck out six of the first nine Tigers he faced but
finally ran into trouble in the 5th.

Inge led off with an infield single to 3rd that Chávez threw
away trying to make an impossible play with Inge taking 2nd.
Santiago did his job by hitting the ball to the right side for
a 4–3 out but moving Inge to 3rd. Granderson (who got as
many key hits in the series as any Tiger) hit a line shot into
center that he turned into a double when Kotsay took his
time getting to the ball knowing that Inge would score easily
from 3rd, but forgetting Granderson's speed. Then Monroe
followed with a double and we had cut the lead to 3–2. Polanco worked Haren to a full count and then hit a smash but
right at the second baseman Jimenez who doubled Monroe
off 2nd.

Bonderman put the A's down in order in the top of the 6th
and then Magglio went to work. He lined Haren's first pitch
into the seats in left leading off the 6th and when Guillén followed with a single, Macha went to the mound and removed
Haren. The Tigers then stranded two runners in the 6th and
two more in the 7th. The sun was setting behind the first base
upper deck stands and created a rose and orange painterly sky
that seemed to say the A's were dying and on their way back
to the west from which they had come. But it turned out they
were not quite dead yet. Bonderman was lifted with two outs

in the 7th when Kendall singled, and Jamie Walker came on
to pitch to the lefty Kotsay who slammed a 3–1 change-up
about ten feet foul down the right field line that would
have been a home run had it stayed fair. Then Walker struck
him out on the next pitch. We didn't all chant "Ja-mie . . .
Ja-mie . . . Ja-mie" but well we might have as that strikeout
was a key.

In the 8th things got even tenser. Jason Grilli came on
to pitch as Zumaya has a sore wrist. He gave up a lead-off
single to Bradley and here came Frank Thomas—the A's most
powerful hitter who has been missing in action for the entire
series having gone 0 for 12. We all breathed a huge sigh of
relief when he knocked Grilli's second pitch on two hops to
Polanco who started an easy 4-6-3 double play. High fives all
around. But Grilli wasn't done yet. Having escaped one threat,
he immediately created another by walking the next three
hitters on 12, count 'em, 12 pitches. I don't think I've ever
seen any pitcher walk three straight hitters, after getting the
first two outs, without throwing a single strike. Leyland finally
yanked him and brought in the lefty Ledezma to face Scutaro.
Scutaro was one of the A's hitting heroes in the Minnesota
series, getting several key hits to drive in crucial runs late in
each game. This time he popped a 1–1 pitch high in the air
behind the plate near the A's dugout that Pudge had enough
room to settle under, and we were out of danger and the
inning.

Macha, realizing the A's season was on the line, had
brought in their good closer and last year's American League
Rookie-of-the-Year, Huston Street in the 7th when the Tigers
loaded the bases with only one out. Street got Guillén to
ground to Chávez at 3rd who stepped on the bag for one
and then easily threw Carlos out at first. Street set the Tigers
down in order in the 8th, striking out two. He started the
9th in the same fashion by getting Thames, pinch hitting for
Santiago, to lift a harmless fly to center. Then, perhaps as an
indication Street was beginning to lose it, Granderson ripped
a line drive into right center that Bradley made a fine running catch on. Then, with two down, Monroe lined a single

to center, Polanco followed with one to right, and up came
Magglio with the crowd on its feet doing the "O . . . E . . .
O . . . MAGG . . . LI . . . O" chant adapted from *The Wizard of Oz*
by the White Sox fans when he was one of their big guns.

With white rally towels fluttering in a frenzy and the
noise level building, Maggs took ball one, low and away. The
second pitch was a fastball down and in and he nailed it.
The ball took off on a long arc high into the October night.
I wasn't sure it had enough to get out though a good breeze
was blowing directly out to left, but a quick glance back at the
plate revealed that Magglio knew it was gone. He stood and
admired it, putting one and then two arms in the air before
beginning his slow and graceful trot around the bases. The
ball danced right by our eager happy eyes and over the Tigers'
bull pen and landed six or seven rows deep into the left field
seats. A blast of baseball beauty. Is Kirk Gibson in the house?
The Tigers had struck, quickly and fatally. Huston Street said
after the game: "They are amazing. I was cruising along and
then suddenly in just five pitches I had lost the game 6–3."

Pandemonium. We hugged, kissed, high fived each other
and most of the fans in our area, though I drew the line at
doing more than getting my hand bruised by the loud lady
from Toledo with a mouth saltier than mine who sat behind
us and brayed in our ears for most of the game. Fortunately,
she had pretty much shouted herself hoarse by the time the
dramatic late innings drama unfolded, and we were able to
enjoy their wonders without her inappropriate admonitions.
The big man with the big bat had finally come through in a
big way with homers in the 6th and 9th; the first to tie the
score; the second to win it and the series and send the Tigers
to the World Series for the first time since 1984. Magglio felt
good and we felt good for Magglio. And for all his teammates
who gathered at the plate to welcome the man with the mop
of black curls spilling out from under his cap: the prodigal
son circles out but returns to home in glory.

No champagne bottles on the field this time, just the
standard championship hats and tee shirts and, once so
decorated, the Tigers, led again by Pudge, circumnavigated

Comerica moving from left field to right, meeting Leyland, who had graciously made his first move to the A's dugout to commiserate with Macha and his team, who was moving with a small cohort in the opposite direction. Perhaps the only time in the season, and certainly in the postseason, that manager and team weren't on the same page moving in the same direction. We yelled and cried and pointed out various players as they were joined by their families and gathered around a quickly assembled podium out at 2nd base for the presentation of the American League Champions trophy and the Most Valuable Player Award: "Polanco" had been Sam's prediction ten minutes before, and he was right. We lingered for ten or fifteen minutes after the ceremonies and then wended the familiar path back to the Hilton this time with the crowd singing out "O . . . E . . . O . . . MAGG . . . LI . . . O" as it made its way to the Greektown watering holes.

We came back to a well-deserved large whiskey, phone calls home and elsewhere to share the joy, and then to Greektown ourselves where Fishbones was packed with a long line waiting to be seated for dinner, so we hit the street, found a taxi, and headed to Carl's Chop House—Detroit's old steak house about five minutes from downtown on Grand River. It was curiously quiet; about half full, with the Michigan–Penn State game the center of attention. Sam had a Bombay gin and tonic and I a Bombay mart and we ordered the huge porterhouse for two and Lyonnaise potatoes and had a victory feast. The steak was great, but the Raymond cab couldn't hold a candle to last night's Cakebread. Ah, well, you can't always perfectly match the meal with the wine. But our sweet victory made them work handsomely together. Carl's had a shuttle which delivered us back to the hotel and the happy news that our Bobcat football team had upset Illinois in Champaign–Urbana 20–17. We hit the sack and were dead by midnight. Hard to believe that this rich unexpected postseason experience might well extend over two more weekends.

The Tigers have now won seven straight postseason games and have done so playing almost all varieties of the game: 6–0 and 3–0 shutouts; a 4–3 squeaker; 8–3, 5–1, and 8–5 displays of power and pitching; and finally, a 6–3 come-backer topped by a ninth inning two out three run walk-off home run. Only three of these games were probably riveting to the average fan but for the faithful Tiger followers they were like manna from heaven: one beautiful bountiful gift from the baseball gods after another. Now let's hope they can keep the Leyland machine running smoothly for one more series. Because of their pitching woes either the Cards or the Mets are likely to be regarded as the underdogs in the World Series. This too will be a new role for the Tigers to have to play: the favorites. May they play it and the games yet to come with the same style and grace they have mustered thus far in their remarkable performance in defeating the Yankees and the A's. Stay tuned my Tiger fans: More is yet to come. "O . . . E . . . O . . . MAGG . . . LI . . . O"

Love,
Bops

The Tigers beat the Yanks in four and swept the A's in four. That gave them a week off to await the winners of the exhausting seven-game series between the Cards and the Mets. The Tigers were on a roll, they were rested, they had Sean Casey back from a hamstring injury, but they had lost their mojo. They rolled over for the weary Cardinals in five games with only Kenny Rogers holding serve in a fine 3–2 victory (with the two runs being given up by Todd Jones in the ninth) in game 2 at Comerica. Sam and I were back for both games in Detroit and were joined for the Rogers game by Sandy Elsass, who flew in from Boston to join us. But the weather had turned nasty in Detroit, more appropriate for football than baseball. I shivered through the Comerica games in need of a scotch, not a beer. The playoffs provided our postseason euphoria, but the World Series itself was a massive disappointment. After the great triumphs in '45, '68, and '84, 2006 was a dud.

Verlander literally threw away game 1 with a throwing error and the disastrous decision to pitch to Pujols in the third with two outs and a runner on second with first base open and those of us in Comerica crying out "put him on . . . put him on." He didn't, and Albert sent a JV fastball on a sharp line into the right field stands and that was the game. Kenny's beauty the next night evened the series as it moved to St. Louis, where in '68 the Tigers had burned bright. Not in 2006. The next three games, which we caught on television, were all versions of game 1 with the Tigers seemingly anxious to give them away with too many errors, poor decision-making, and most crucially the failure to get any clutch hits. Sam and I were perplexed, especially after their brilliant play versus the Yankees and the A's in the playoffs. We consoled ourselves that with a few exceptions ours was a young club sure to only improve in the next few seasons and be back in the hunt. We turned out to be right, it wasn't a hard call, but for all their great play a World Series championship eluded them.

The team improved almost immediately when in December of 2007 Dombrowski pulled off the best trade in Tiger history. He moved six prospects, including Cameron Maybin and Andrew Miller, who eventually would have solid major league careers, to the Miami Marlins for the once-dazzling pitcher Dontrelle Willis and the finest young hitter in baseball, Miguel Cabrera. Cabrera, only twenty-five, was already being touted as a future Hall of Famer, and his subsequent achievements with the Tigers only confirmed that judgment.

Ilitch had struck out when he brought in Juan González, but now he had brought a younger, better bat to Detroit and Comerica Park. In the next dozen years Cabrera did everything but win a World Series for the Tigers. In 2012 he became the first Triple Crown winner since Carl Yastrzemski in 1967. Cabrera's back-to-back years in 2012 and 2013 were the best by a Tiger hitter since Hank Greenberg's numbers in '37 and '38. The eleven years from 2006 to 2016 were an exciting time for Detroit and Tiger baseball, as the city underwent an interesting renaissance, driven by the young and creative who swooped in to reclaim and refashion abandoned buildings, transforming them into studios for artists of all kinds and into interesting ethnic restaurants. Comerica Park was packed each season as the Tigers, particularly in August and September, played to full houses of forty thousand passionate fans.

Back at the beginning of this chronicle I mentioned that Al Kaline got me from my teenage years into graduate school, marriage, and fatherhood, and then Trammell and Whitaker took me into my teaching career, years as a dean, and emergence as a Shakespeare scholar. Now Justin Verlander and Miguel Cabrera were tasked with seeing me through the golden years and into my dotage. Good companions all. I have never met any of them in the flesh, nor did I yearn to. What do you say except "Thanks"?

The actual pressing of heroic Tiger flesh has fallen to one of our grandsons, Theo Pistner. Theo, a recent graduate of the University of Michigan, caddied as a young man at the Oakland Hills Country Club. He once carried Dan Petry's (a seventeen-game winner back in '84) bag at a charity golf tournament at Oakland Hills, featuring many former Tigers. When Petry's foursome came off the eighteenth green, there was Al Kaline greeting each player, and Petry graciously introduced Theo to Mr. Tiger. Their handshake consummates the companionship the Tigers have provided over the years to many members of the family and the impact it has had on my relationship with our own kids and now our grandchildren. Baseball was something we could share, in conversation and in print in and out of the ballpark, and sharing Shakespeare, especially in performance, followed. Our own kids saw their first Shakespeare performance (As You Like It at Ontario's Stratford Festival in the summer of 1972) before they had been to see a baseball game, and they have remained regulars at both. Their kids have followed a similar path, being equally at home in the theater and ballpark and all twelve of us have shared several rich Shakespearean weekends at the Stratford Festival, and at baseball games at Comerica Park over the past decade.

TIGER LETTER #5

24 August 09

Dear Tiger Fans:

Last week brought a series of firsts: first trip by Boppo and Sushi to Miranda and Bill's new home at Cranbrook; first Tigers game at Comerica Park for Charlie, Theo, Miles, and Bill; first burgers at the Hunter House for Bops; first 6th birthday for Miles; and the first full exploration of the Cranbrook campus (including the Owl House) by B&S. All were splendid. I wonder what Eliel Saarinen would have thought of Comerica Park. I sure was impressed by the ways in which his architecture of the two campuses talked to each other. What a treat to be able to live and work in such a handsome environment. Now to the more important stuff.

The Tigers had rallied to beat the M's 5–3 on Tuesday night with the boys relaying the late inning events from the TV watching place to the rest of us still having good conversation at the dinner table. When the Tigers pulled it out, I thought: "Great. Verlander goes tomorrow night against Ian Snell who has a 2–9 record. Should be in the bag." Then I remembered what Sparky Anderson used to call a "reverse-lock." How often in baseball when the odds seem to heavily favor one team in a particular game, the underdog leaps up and takes a large rip out of the other guy's pants. Well, that turned out to be the case on Wednesday. We caught the first few innings at the Memphis Barbeque place in Royal Oak. The Tigers got an early 1–0 lead but then in the 3rd Verlander gave up a single, then after an out a double chased that runner home, and then Ichiro hit a homer for a 3–1 lead and that's the way the game ended an hour or so later after we were back at home. Not good and made Thursday's game critical.

The day was overcast with thunderstorms brewing as the Tiger Van pulled out of Cranbrook with Charlie, Theo, and Miles decked out in the Detroit home whites with the old English Ð. We travelled in and out of rain on the trip to Detroit, but the downtown seemed relatively dry as we swung around on I-75 and got off on Rosa Parks Boulevard and over to Michigan to make a sad pass by the remains of Tiger Stadium. The old elevator shaft is still standing but all else is just rubble. Then on down to Cass and over to free street parking about three blocks from the stadium; day still overcast but no rain yet.

Snapped the required photos of the merry band under the giant tiger which presides over the front entrance and then we found Charlie and Theo's brick at the very top of the central bank of bricks right in front of the main gates. Reminded Miles that, like Audrey and Emerson, he wasn't born when the Park was being built and that I owe him a brick in some famous public place someday. Picked up a scorecard and headed for a trip on the Merry-go-Round. Only 12:30 but the lads were already lobbying to get to our seats so in and down we went. Row 11 in section 116 right on the aisle as promised. Labatt Blues for Bops and Bill. Some of the Mariners (but not Ichiro) were warming up right and front of us and Charlie, Theo, and Miles went down to the field and hung across the railing to watch them do their sprints and leg exercises. Washburn (our starter, acquired from the M's before the trading deadline to bolster the rotation) was playing long toss in left field. He kept backing up into center but never reached the warning track as Kenny Rogers used to do in getting his arm fully extended and loose. Washburn had been having a great year with the M's but has only pitched well in one of his three starts since coming to the Tigers.

He didn't exactly improve on that record today. Ichiro led off with a double, moved to 3rd on a sacrifice bunt, and came on a sacrifice fly: The very type of manufactured run the Tigers seem incapable of achieving. The M's starter was a youngster from Australia, Ryan Rowland-Smith, a tall left-hander. He easily went through our order in the first three innings giving up just a single to Ryan Raburn. Meanwhile Washburn walked Gutierrez in the 3rd and López, the M's young second baseman who is hitting .300 with 15 HRs and 72 RBIs, immediately added to those totals by slamming Washburn's second pitch on a line into the seats in left. Bill had left at the start of the inning to fetch hotdogs and got back just as López was heading for home. In the 4th Johjima, the M's catcher, hit one into the bull pen in left and we were down 4–0 and hadn't shown any signs of offensive life yet.

That changed in the bottom of the inning as Raburn hit one into the stands in right and two batters later Inge did the same to left. The sharp crack of the ball off both bats immediately suggested that they had hit them solidly and they had. The skies looked ominous, the wind was blowing stiffly from right to left, and down came a shower. We zipped into rain jackets, but the pour increased, and I was about to say "Let's head up for cover" when the rains eased and then vanished. It appeared we were in for one of those Macbeth afternoons: "So foul and fair a day I have not seen." But at least Raburn and Inge had us back in the game.

But Washburn just didn't have it and in the top of the 6th he gave up solo shots to Sweeney and Branyan. Branyan's was a monster that landed in the last row in the seats in right just below the Pepsi Porch. Magglio (in his customary spot in right) never moved but just slowly turned and watched it disappear over his head. 6–2. In the bottom of the 6th Rowland-Smith was tiring. Miguel Cabrera led off with a double and the rains began to fall again. Maggs walked on a 3–2 count and the rain became stronger. Inge fanned and then the heavens opened again, but we played on until Thomas also walked. Then the umps called for the tarp, and we got poured on as we waited to make the slow ascent from the field level to cover up above. By the time we got there the rain had begun to abate and after 15 minutes or so they stopped, and the sun reappeared.

Back to our seats we went and within another 15 minutes the grounds crew came out and began to remove the tarp and squeegee the water down the drains built into the field. We were back in action by 3:35 after about an hour delay. Bases loaded and one out. The M's brought in a righty reliever and Leyland countered by sending up the newly acquired Aubrey Huff to pinch hit for Laird. Huff hasn't done much for us since coming over from the Orioles last week and here he worked the count to 3–2 and then hit a slow roller to 2nd.

López didn't try for the DP but settled for throwing Huff out at 1st with Cabrera scoring and the runners moving up to 2nd and 3rd. Here was a situation all too familiar to Tigers fans this year. Runners in scoring position with two outs and no hitters in sight. Too often we have failed to get a key hit at such crucial moments. Leyland sent the kid catcher Avila up to pinch hit for Everett and after fouling off a few pitches he bounced one up the middle and into centerfield for two runs and suddenly we have a 6–5 game. Just what the baseball doctor ordered.

Miner came in and pitched a 1-2-3 7th and 8th. His best outing of the year. And Seay came on and did the same thing to the Mariners in the 9th. With one out in the 8th we got something going as Thomas and Santiago (in to play short after Everett was lifted) singled and Avila came up as the crowd really got into it. He hit a wicked line drive that we were all sure was into the gap in left center, but Gutierrez managed to make a sensational play by reaching out at the last moment and snagging it. Then Polanco lifted a little blooper into center that the shortstop Wilson raced out for and with his back to the infield managed to snare in his webbing for the third out and the Tigers were twice bitten and still trailed by a run. Charlie and I just shook our heads in disbelief.

This is a good spot to mention that the Tigers also got two terrific defensive plays from Brandon Inge who has played a great third base this season. In the 2nd inning Jack Hannahan lifted a high pop in foul territory back of 3rd. The wind kept carrying it towards the stands, but Inge kept his bead on it and lunged into the stands at the last minute to make the grab as he completed a back flip into the front row. We didn't know he'd held onto the ball until a fan raised his fist making the ump's OUT sign. In the 5th he made a similar grab, without the back flip, of another towering pop-up, this time hit by Ichiro. In fact, after his first inning double, we kept Ichiro off the bases which was one key to our ultimate victory. Inge is fighting a torn meniscus in his left knee, but he keeps on making great defensive plays and smashing key home runs though his offensive numbers have really tumbled since the All-Star break.

But the Tigers roared right back. Guillén led off the 9th by working a walk, on a 3–2 pitch, from the Mariners' closer David Aardsma. Then Bill and I rolled our eyes as Leyland, down by just a run, didn't have Raburn bunting. In fairness to Leyland, Raburn was 3 for 4 with a home run but now he popped one up in foul territory to the catcher. Cabrera helped to take Leyland and Raburn off the hook by lining an Aardsma fastball down into the corner in right for a double with Guillén stopping at third. Crowd back into it now. The Mariners walked Maggs to load the bases with Inge up. Inge took Aardsma deep into the count and then lifted a medium deep fly ball into right center that Gutierrez came over to handle (even though Ichiro with the superior arm was closing in on the ball too) and rifled a throw home that looked good from my angle, arriving just as Guillén slid in. He's out I thought and then I saw the ball squirt out behind the catcher and the ump make an emphatic safe sign. 6–6. I pounded a smiling Charlie and said, "let's finish this off now."

The crowd was on its feet as Clete Thomas came to the plate. He too worked the count and continued to foul off several more. Bill noticed that Branyan was still guarding the first base line even though there was no need now to protect against a double as anything that got through the infield would score Cabrera with the winner. Which is precisely what Thomas accomplished on the next pitch as he hit a sharp two bouncer just to the right of Branyan's extended glove (no third time defensive miracle for the M's here) and into right field as Cabrera came bouncing home. The Tigers rushed to pummel Thomas at first base and Leyland even sprinted out, grabbed him around the shoulders, and spun him around in glee. Gleeful pups too in our row, I'd say, as we all high-fived and cheered the Tigers as they mauled Thomas out by the mound.

What a way to begin their careers in Comerica for Charlie and Theo and Miles. Old Boppo was ever so pleased for them and for the Tigers who managed to keep this crazy season alive and hang onto first place in the Central in the only real race still alive in MLB this summer. We took in the victory looking out at a field now flooded with sunshine and Tigers retreating to the dugout and then made our slow way up the steps as the big happy crowd made its way out. Several stops for Charlie and Theo to pick out the hats they wanted, courtesy of Sushi. Miles had already popped, during the rain delay, for a blue miniature Tigers bat and batting helmet.

We danced back to the car; listened to post-game chatter on 1270 AM; and made the trip home to Cranbrook through the 5 o'clock rush hour traffic. The Tigers won both Tuesday and Thursday's games by late inning rallies just as they had in several of the games we saw earlier against the Brewers and the Orioles. The hope was that this victory would send them to Oakland with the impetus to end their inability to win on the road. Unfortunately, as I write this on Monday the 24th they have already lost two of three to Oakland, the last place team in the West, which means they have now dropped ten straight series on the road. Now they head for LA and the mighty Angels who have the next best (after the Yankees) record in baseball. Winning at home is swell but we need to be able to at least break even down the stretch on the road or we won't win the Central. The sweet thing is that the Tigers are now 6–0 this season when I am in the house—perhaps I'd better start catching some road games. Cleveland in late September anyone? Oh. And one last "first": a soaked score card which has dried out nicely and now looks like one of the Dead Sea Scrolls.

Love,
Bops

Part 7

The 2010s

The Tigers have almost always fielded a competitive club. They have rarely languished at the bottom of the American League, but neither have they dominated. In their long history of over twelve decades, they have only approached extended excellence in four approximately ten-year periods: 1905–17, 1934–45, 1981–91, and 2006–16. The early decade was defined by one of team's great managers, Hughie Jennings, and the emergence of its defining star, Ty Cobb. They finished in the top three in the American League seven times and won the pennant three times. Unfortunately, they lost all three of their World Series appearances.

That would change in their run from 1934 and 1945, when, under the leadership of Mickey Cochrane and Del Baker and Steve O'Neill, they again finished in the top three seven times and won four pennants and the World Series twice. They won the crown for the first time in 1935 and repeated as champs in 1945. Those clubs were led by the Tiger legends I inherited: Cochrane, Hank Greenberg, Charlie Gehringer, Goose Goslin, Rudy York, Schoolboy Rowe, Tommy Bridges, Dizzy Trout, and Hal Newhouser. The 1960s produced a World Series championship in 1968, which followed a strong season in '67, but the decade did not feature a consistent American League winner.

The third period extended from 1981 to 1991, the prime period in Sparky Anderson's seventeen-year tenure as manager. Now the initial competition was in the divisional race, and the Tigers finished in the top three nine times, winning the division twice and dominating the 1984 World Series versus the San Diego Padres. The 1980s were particularly rich baseball years for father and son. Miranda had gone off to college (including a year in Paris) with her mind engaged with new challenges, while the early years of the decade were her brother's high school years when being a fan, especially of a talented and winning club, takes on added significance.

These were also the early years of my deanship, when, as I mentioned earlier, I was fully engaged with implementing a new comprehensive set of common core requirements for a university with approximately fifteen thousand undergraduates. The requirements were meant to parallel students' work in their majors and, unusual for general core requirements, included courses in the junior and senior years. Major curriculum reform is common in small liberal arts colleges, but much rarer at large comprehensive public universities. Putting such a new program in place and getting it to work was an inviting but challenging opportunity, and I gave my Shakespearean energies to the task with relish. Fortunately, the Tigers, revived (by Anderson's arrival) and restocked (by the farm system and a few wise trades), were suddenly competitive again and a welcome tonic for my administrative responsibilities. Sam and I both feasted upon their new vitality.

We found our way to Detroit several times a summer and watched the strongest squad in the team's history (1984) come together over a period of years. It was built from the ground up, with the core of its players coming up through the farm system: Trammell and Whitaker and Parrish; Morris and Petry and Gibson. These talented youngsters were mixed with a few veterans acquired through judicious trades and one free agent signing by Bill Lajoie, the club's general manager, responsible for building the team: Chet Lemon, Larry Herndon, Willie Hernandez, Dave Bergman, and Darrell Evans. We thought '83 was going to be the year. We even had the surprise of seeing them play, and beat the Dodgers, in spring training in our only visit to Joker Marchant Stadium in Lakeland.

The Ohio University basketball team, under coach Danny Nee, won its conference tournament and was off to play in the NCAA first-round regional games at the Sun Dome in Tampa. Sam and I were invited by our athletic director to fly with the team to Tampa on a charter arranged by the NCAA. On landing we headed straight for Lakeland and a Tiger victory with Gibson hitting a mammoth homer over the fence in right. We were twice rewarded when the next night (a Thursday) our Bobcats beat Illinois State 51–49 on a last-second off-balance fifteen-foot jumper by freshman guard Robert Tatum. On Saturday we came up against Kentucky with its fabled "Twin Towers" and played them almost even in the first half before wilting in the second.

Nineteen eighty-three had genuine pleasures for both father and son, but '84 exceeded our wildest dreams as the Tigers raced out to their miraculous 35–5 start, maintained their momentum then through the heart of the season, polished off the Royals 3–0 in the playoffs, and dominated the Padres in the World Series as we rooted them on in the final three games in Tiger Stadium. Though the Tigers (and Bobcats) would continue to provide continuing pleasures and often even thrills in the next four decades, including both clubs finding their way back to the Big Dance (and Sweet Sixteen for the 2012 Cats) and the World Series (in 2006 and 2012), father and son sharing those three games in Tiger Stadium that clinched the World Series remains a pinnacle experience for me.

The Tiger teams between 2006 and 2016 were perhaps the strongest in their history. Not only baseball fans, but many players as well, marvel that they never won it all during those years. In 2013, for example, they had a rotation that featured three (present or future) Cy Young Award winners (Justin Verlander, Max Scherzer, and Rick Porcello), an ERA winner (Aníbal Sánchez), and a reliever who saved 42 of 43 chances that year (José Valverde). During the ten-year period, they also had two smooth-fielding center fielders (Granderson and Jackson), a power-hitting right fielder (J. D. Martinez), steady shortstop play (Carlos Guillén and Jhonny Peralta), the best DH in the league (Victor Martinez), and, as earlier noted, the greatest hitter of his generation, Miguel Cabrera, who won the Triple Crown in 2012 and back-to-back MVP Awards, as well as a bevy of impressive left fielders, including Craig Monroe, Gary Sheffield, Johnny Damon, Torii Hunter, Justin Upton, and Yoenis Cespedes. But two former catchers, a wise old one (Jim Leyland, a baseball lifer who went to school in the minor leagues) and a smart young one (Brad Ausmus, who went to Dartmouth and couldn't make big winners out of two strong teams, the Tigers and then the Angels), could not find a way to lead them to a world championship even when the baseball they provided to Detroit and Tiger fans each summer was terrific. They won with pitching; they won with power hitting; they won with clutch hitting; and sometimes they won with defense, especially when Inge played third, Placido Polanco played second, and Granderson or Jackson roamed out in Comerica's huge center field.

Each year Dombrowski and Ilitch thought one more trade or expensive free agent would be the trick that turned the tide. But Gary Sheffield, Johnny Damon, Torii Hunter, Prince Fielder, Justin Upton, Ian Kinsler, and several others failed to provide the necessary spark to put them over the top. These were all impressive players, most of them power hitters, while I thought what the Tigers really needed was a dirtbag like Boston's Dustin Pedroia or the Mets' Daniel Murphy to light their fire. I wanted a player who did all the little things: bunting, moving runners over, hitting to the opposite field, running the bases with shrewd abandon, literally willing his club to win. Such players are almost as rare as Miguel Cabrera but just as necessary. Dick McAuliffe filled such a role for the 1960s Tigers; Alan Trammell and Chet Lemon (plus hitting for power when necessary) did it in the 1980s; Tony Phillips in the 1990s; but alas, no such figure emerged after Miggy joined the team in 2008. I thought Ian Kinsler might have been the man; he had the required intensity, but something about the chemistry was missing.

However, the 2006–16 period matched the great decades of Tiger baseball in the sixties and eighties. I was surprised to discover that there were more Tiger victories in the sixties (882) than either the eighties (839) or in the slightly faux decade I've sliced out in the new century (864), but because of division play the Tigers in the Verlander-Cabrera years dominated previous Tiger teams in postseason appearances, finishing second, third, first, first, first, first, fifth, second, and fifth. And Miguel Cabrera was a wonder. He hit for power; he hit for average; he drove in runs; and he was a much more agile and steady defensive first baseman than is acknowledged. He was a smart baserunner but not fleet. What man his size is?

He was a pleasure to watch not only for his talent but because he took such obvious joy from the game. He has a shy, sweet grin that spreads into a lovely smile when he is horsing around with his teammates. He and Prince Fielder provided a special thrill when they greeted each other at the plate after big bombs: two bull elephants giving each other their personal version of high fives and hip bumps. And, even better, he tamed a drinking problem that threatened to derail his career a few years after he moved to Detroit. In his final season, 2023, Cabrera joined one of baseball's most exclusive clubs by achieving at least 3,000 hits, 500 home runs, and 600 doubles. The only other members are Hank Aaron and Albert Pujols.

Justin Verlander was a reincarnation of Jack Morris as the very definition of an ace. He had a fastball that could reach 98–100 and a wicked slow curve. More importantly, he had Morris's determination and stamina without his ill temper. Like Jack, Verlander wanted the ball every fifth day; he wanted to pitch complete games even in an era that relied upon the pen for the eighth and ninth innings; and he had no trouble throwing 110–125 pitches if needed. He was not only an ace, but a horse. When he won, he did not gloat; when he lost (and to my mind his team too often failed to score for him in close games), he did not whine. He did not apologize, either. Leyland used to get mad at him because he refused to say after a bad outing, "I stunk." He was always looking for the positive in his postgame recap with the reporters, and I think they respected him for it. The only flaw in Verlander's game was an odd one. Even with his arsenal of pitches, he often had trouble finishing hitters off, especially with the fastball. They might not be able to put it in play, but they often could repeatedly foul it off. This is what drove his pitch count up, and I think frustrated him. On the other hand, he was able to gain speed on his heater as the game progressed, so that if he started off in the mid-90s he might be hitting close to 100 mph by the seventh or eighth, a remarkable feat.

I have a special affection (who doesn't?) for great players who, even in the age of free agency, like Trammell, Whitaker, George Brett, Barry Larkin, Chipper Jones, Mike Schmidt, Tony Gwynn, and Derek Jeter, play their entire careers with one team. I wished the same for Verlander, but it was not in the cards once the team Dombrowski and Ilitch built began to hit the skids. Verlander agreed to be dealt to the Astros at the trading deadline in 2017 and then helped lead them to the World Series victory he had failed to achieve with the Tigers. Sadly, he was off his normal form in both World Series games he pitched for the Tigers: the opening games of the 2006 and 2012 championships. Verlander was his usual dominant self in his playoff appearances, but something strange happened to his effectiveness in his two World Series starts for the Tigers.

TIGER LETTER #6

                                          22 June 2010
Dear Tiger Fans:
    Just a brief report on the past weekend for the record, as the two Tigers-Diamondbacks games are still, I am sure, firmly planted in your memories. The weekend was the first gathering of the entire clan at Miranda and Bill's new digs at Cranbrook and, if memory serves me right, Sunday became the first time all twelve of us had attended at Tigers game together: an historic occasion.

The Athens contingent left home late Friday morning and arrived a bit past 5 having had to battle some early weekend traffic south and north of Detroit. The adults and Emerson had a nice dinner at Toast in the heart of Birmingham while the kids saw the remake of the *Karate Kid* several blocks away. We kept an ear and an eye on the Tigers game which was something of a roller coaster: Tigers up by four; DBacks rally to tie. DBacks go up by one, Tigers rally to tie. Then in the 7th Inge tripled to bring home Maggs and a sac fly brought Inge in for a 7–5 lead and the eventual win after Zumaya set them down in the 8th and Valverde in the 9th. Those two make for a powerful set-up/closer combination. As we were enjoying a late evening ice cream cone after the movie let out, a big storm whipped up (no one on the street paid any attention to the odd warning siren that went off) and we had to make a mad dash to the cars as the wind swirled and the rains came. Home safe to the Radisson about 11.

The rain took the humidity out of the air, and we awoke to a bright blue moderate Saturday. Breakfast at Miranda and Bill's apartment on the Kingswood (the Cranbrook Girls' School) campus and then a long walk and tour of the two campuses with some splashing in the Cranbrook fountain (one of many by the famed Swedish sculptor Carl Milles on the grounds) by Miles and Audrey. Back for a late lunch. Miranda took the kids swimming and Bops headed back for a nap. We all reassembled at 5 or so and by six everyone but Miranda and Sushi were headed to Comerica. Lovely evening with a big breeze blowing out to left. Rick Porcello has skipped a start to work on his sinker and the youngster hasn't fixed it yet. He gave up a two-run home run in the 2nd and was in and out of trouble over the next three innings but kept the Snakes off the board. But in the 6th he gave up another home run and then a single and double and Leyland pulled him. Ni Fu-Te (who is the first player from Taiwan to pitch in our big leagues) came in to face the lefty Parra who promptly hit the first pitch for a triple. Out went Ni and in came the new guy just called up from Toledo, González, who gave up a sacrifice fly but then shut them down the rest of the way.

At this point the score was 6–2 as the Tigers had gotten one in the first and another in the second, but then Edwin Jackson (last year's #2 starter for us) set us down in the 3rd, 4th, and 5th. We got one in the 6th and another in the 8th but couldn't get a two out hit to make for a big inning. In the 9th Ruben Santiago popped to left field, Donnie Kelly singled, Johnny Damon (who hasn't been any help at all in the past ten days) also popped out. But Maggs drove a double deep into the right field gap to bring Kelly home. Cabrera strolled to the plate. Just the man you want up there with the game on the line. 40,681 on their feet, yelling, whistling, vuvuzela-ing [plastic South African horns played by fans at soccer matches]. He worked the count to 3–2 and then the mighty Miggy struck out on a pitch that looked down and away and all the great crowd energy just evaporated. Ever so fortunately we still had a wedding to celebrate at home plate and fireworks to watch before heading home. An eight-game winning streak snapped. Home by 11. Mother and daughter still out on the town but they came rolling in shortly from too much *Sex and the City* 2.

Back for more the next day as all of us headed for the game about noon. Another big crowd was filing in and collecting their Charlie Brown in a Tiger cap bubblehead dolls. Hope I have one to look forward to under the tree in December as the distributor failed to be impressed by my attempts to be 14 or under. Today, under a bright and hot Sunday sun, we got a gem of a game. Max Scherzer vs. Ian Kennedy; two pieces of the big three-way Tigers-Yankees-Diamondbacks trade of last winter. Scherzer's got a big arm and can consistently hit 95–96 mph with his heater, but can he pitch? Does he trust his slider and change to mix them in effectively with the heater? Kennedy is more like Porcello. He throws four pitches with his fastball topping out at 90–92 mph. He needs to keep hitters off balance with lots of curves and sliders and change of pitch locations. Scherzer started strong getting the first two hitters easily. Then he lost it. He walked Upton, gave up a single to Montero, and a run-scoring double to Young. He'd gone to a full count on 4 of the first 5 hitters. Then came what might have been the play of the day. LaRoche hit a bouncer wide of the bag at first that seemed headed for right field, but Cabrera took two quick steps to his right, gloved it, and made the throw to Scherzer at first to nip the runner. If that ball had trickled into rightfield it would have meant two more runs for Arizona putting the Tigers in a deep hole.

Scherzer righted himself and while he continued to run up his pitch count, he settled into a good routine retiring the last twelve batters he faced in a row including striking out the side in the 7th. The Tigers played solid defense behind him, and Brennan Boesch made a nice running catch in foul territory in deep left to close out the 4th. Kennedy was just as effective. The Tigers got base runners in the 1st and 2nd but that was it as Kennedy also set down twelve in a row from the 3rd through the 6th. But he ran out of gas in the 7th and the Tigers pounced. Miggy led off with a line single up the middle and then Boesch hit a hanging curve on a giant parabola up into the cloudless sky (as I heard the now sadly departed Bob Trevas—Ohio University philosophy prof and golf fanatic—say, "That ball is so high it's got stewardesses on it") and twenty rows deep in the right field stands.

Before all 41,417 of us could settle back into our seats, Guillén hit Kennedy's next offering with equal force but not quite the same majesty into the same stands and suddenly we had the lead 3–1. That was it for Kennedy. We got two more runners on but couldn't bring them home (Damon again missing a chance to contribute). The Friday night relief story repeated itself. Zumaya got 'em 1-2-3 in the 8th and Valverde (Papa Grande now to the insiders) did the same thing in the 9th. Nice tight well-played game in two hours and thirty-five minutes with the Tigers eventually getting the timely hits. It should be noted that the tide turned when Miranda took over scorecard keeping duties from her brother. She and her blue beach hat might have played herself into a starting place in the line-up.

Other quick notes. First time that I have seen our rookie wonder boy, Brennan Boesch, in person. He could well be the next great homegrown Tiger. He's big: 6'6" and 210. Has a lovely power swing (and can hit lefthanders) though it is interesting to see how knock-kneed his stance is when looking at him from our perspective down the right field line. And he seems to love playing the game. Who wouldn't with the rookie year he's having? We need to get Porcello straightened out or find another starter at the trading deadline. Sorry to have missed Austin Jackson, though Leyland did put him in for defensive purposes in the 9th on Sunday so he must be healed. Looks like another Tigers-Twins race down to the wire (though the White Sox are surging).

I wrote this on the 22nd but didn't get back to polishing and printing until a week later. The White Sox won ten in a row before losing to the Cubs yesterday and have closed the gap. We are lined up in order: Twins 41–34; Tigers, 40–34; White Sox, 39–33. We start a three-game series at Target Field vs. the Twins tonight. A crucial series and it isn't even July. Wow. That's it.

Love to all,
Bops

THE 2012 PLAYOFFS AND WORLD SERIES

Though it looked like those 2010 Tigers would rather quickly find themselves back in contention and the playoffs, it did not happen until 2011, when they started a run of four consecutive appearances in the postseason. In 2011 they again polished off the Yankees in the Divisional Series 3–2, with all the Tiger victories taut, tense affairs (5–3, 5–4, 3–2) and the Yankee wins blowouts (9–3, 10–1). Doug Fister pitched a gem in the fifth and final game, which was decided by first-inning home runs by Delmon Young and Don Kelly. The club bore little resemblance to the 2006 crew except for Justin Verlander hitting his stride and Magglio Ordoñez playing his final season. New names proliferated, including kids like Andy Dirks, Omar Infante, Robert Raburn, Austin Jackson, and Max Scherzer, coupled with older veterans picked up through trades or free agency like Jhonny Peralta, Delmon Young, and Victor Martinez. The offense was still anchored by the great, steady Miguel Cabrera. We watched the Yankee games on television but headed north for the games in Detroit in the Championship Series games versus the Rangers.

The series opened in Arlington, where the Rangers won both games and established the pattern: rain and Nelson Cruz. Cruz won game 1 with a home run in the fourth off Verlander and game 2 with a grand slam off Ryan Perry in the eleventh. The first game had a long rain interruption and the second had to be postponed a day because of the threat of rain, which never came. The move from Texas to Michigan brought some life to the Tiger offense but did not slow down Cruz's dominating performance or the rain. All three Detroit games were played in weather inhospitable to the game, cool and wet, but the Tigers bounced back in game 3, 5–2, with Cabrera, Martinez, and Peralta hitting home runs as Doug Fister cruised to the win. We huddled against the chill but were sparked back to life by our team's play. Perhaps being back in Comerica was the answer.

The next day gave us our answer. The game began with temps in the low forties and then had a two-hour rain delay before starting up again in weather unfit for ducks, let alone tigers. The two teams stayed close and went to extra innings tied 3–3. Then Cruz did it again in the eleventh, hitting a three-run shot into the seats in left: 7–3 Rangers. I was wet, cold, tired, and depleted. We had been shivering in the ballpark for over six hours. Is this baseball? Two marts and a steak did not revive my spirits, though Sam remained on his usual even keel. The next day went far to restore my spirits and featured another once-in-a-lifetime baseball experience. The Tigers won the game with four runs in the sixth, created by four straight batters contributing to hitting for a communal cycle: Raburn singled, Miggy doubled, Victor Martinez tripled, and Delmon Young homered. Our lead was big enough to withstand another Nelson Cruz home run in the eighth as the series headed back to Texas for game 6. Scherzer didn't have his stuff: Texas scored nine in the third and coasted to an easy

15–5 win, sending us home mumbling, once again, "Wait till next year."

In this instance, "next year" was the year when the Tigers did return to the World Series and Miguel Cabrera won the Triple Crown, the first hitter to do so since Carl Yastrzemski in 1967. And was the AL MVP for the second year in a row. In a close pennant race with the White Sox, the Tigers came from several games down in the standings, led by Miggy's clutch hitting and Verlander's staunch pitching, to win it in the final ten days of the season by going 8–2. Max Scherzer and Drew Smyly pitched a Tanana-like 1–0 beauty against the Royals in the season's finale. They had two familiar foes in the playoffs, the A's in the divisional series and the Yankees in the Championship Series.

Still shivering from last year's games against the Rangers, Sam and I decided we would make them win both and advance to the World Series before heading to Detroit. Bad decision, as we missed being in Comerica for some wonderful baseball, though we caught all the action on television. The Tigers have owned the A's in the playoffs and did so again, though only after the A's stretched the series to the full five games. In game 1 Verlander gave up a leadoff home run to Coco Crisp and then shut them down through the seventh, with the bullpen cleaning up for a 3–1 win. The Tigers won again the next day 5–4 and returned to Comerica looking for the sweep. We didn't get it as the A's won the two games in Detroit 2–0 and 4–3, and the teams headed back to Oakland, where Verlander again was in command and won 6–0.

The Tigers proceeded to New York to face the Yankees, another club they had dominated in the postseason. This time they swept them 4–0 on a combination of fine pitching (Sánchez and Verlander), timely hitting (Young and Cabrera), a costly error by Eric Chávez, and missed calls (in our favor) by the umps before the institution of replay. Valverde continued his collapse by squandering a 4–0 lead in the ninth inning of game 1, eventually won by the Tigers 6–4 in the twelfth. Sánchez and Phil Coke shut them out

3–0 in game 2, and when the games resumed in Comerica, Verlander and then Scherzer were in control, winning 2–1 and 8–1. Verlander left game 3 with one out in the ninth and a runner on first, having thrown 132 pitches. Coke successfully closed the game out and the Tigers were back in the World Series, but I later wondered whether all those pitches late in the season had left Verlander a bit weary when he faced the Giants in game 1 of the World Series and promptly gave up two home runs to Pablo Sandoval.

I fault Leyland in '06 for sending the rookie Verlander out to start the first game of the World Series when he had the veteran Rogers well rested and ready to go. And Rogers won the second game (the only one the Tigers won in either series) by pitching eight innings of shutout ball. Let the old man show the kid how to do it, I thought. Don't let the rookie have to carry the weight of getting the club off to a winning start. Get the Cards off stride with Kenny's slow stuff before giving them the flamethrower. But it was not to be. In '12, however, Verlander was the man. He had pitched brilliantly during the season and repeatedly won crucial games down the stretch of the pennant race and in the playoffs. He was our ace and clearly deserved to start game 1 of the 2012 World Series.

As in 2006, the Tigers were the betting favorites. While the A's had pushed them to five games, they had then swept the Yanks while the Giants (like the Cards in '06) had to battle through two tough series, both of which went the full five and then seven games. The Reds were the National League favorites, and of course that was who we wanted, much as we wanted the Cubs back in 1984. The Reds would have been even better as we would have gotten to the games in Cincinnati as well as Comerica. But the Giants played comeback kids to rally from an 0–2 deficit against the Reds (and having to win the final three in Cincinnati) and a 1–3 deficit against the Cards. They did it with great pitching from Matt Cain, Madison Bumgarner, Ryan Vogelsong, and Barry Zito and timely hitting from Ángel Pagán, Buster Posey, and Hunter Pence. And when the starting pitching faltered, Tim Lincecum was brilliant in long relief. But, after all, who were these guys compared to our big guns, Cabrera, Fielder, Martinez, and Young (sounds like a great law firm), and strong arms Verlander, Scherzer, and Sánchez? We were rested; the Giants should have been exhausted, but instead it was, as Yogi famously put it, "Déjà vu all over again."

Looking back, it may also have been the revenge of the baseball gods for my cocky behavior back in 1954. My Waterville pal and batterymate Tommy Dressler was an Indians fan and in our youth rooted for the superior team, with a World Series championship in 1948 and a brilliant season in 1954, when they won 111 games and were clearly the best team in baseball, with one of the game's iconic starting staffs: Bob Lemon, Mike Garcia, Early Wynn, and Bob Feller. They were the overwhelming favorites to beat the Giants in the World Series until Willie Mays made his miraculous catch of Vic Wertz's blast to dead center in the Polo Grounds in game 1, and the Giants, buoyed by Mays's genius, went on to sweep the Indians. I was overjoyed, at the expense of my good friend, by the Indians' humiliation. The gods patiently waited fifty-eight years before extracting their revenge for my callous behavior.

Sam and I were certain Verlander would dominate the Giant hitters just as he had foiled the Yankees. He had the stuff and now the savvy. But it was not to be, thanks primarily to the Giants' plump third baseman (are third basemen ever plump?) Pablo Sandoval, universally known as the Panda. The Panda took Verlander deep twice in the opener and that was it. I can't blame that one on Leyland. I think that the Tiger club thought they were invincible, largely because of their great stretch run and Verlander, and when he stumbled, they tumbled and failed to bail him out. And Sandoval, for good measure, put a cap on the opener by hitting a third homer off one of our relievers.

And then the Giant pitchers took over, with Bumgarner and Vogelsong each pitching 2–0 shutouts in games 2 and 3. We were in Comerica for Vogelsong's beauty. Game 4 was played in 42 degree Michigan fall weather with occasional rain showers that several times looked like snow to me. I am a cold-climate guy, but as in '06 and '11 baseball is not suited for such conditions, says a fan of the losing team. The Giants surely loved it. We were more competitive and even had the lead for the first and only time in the series when Miggy hit a two-run shot that carried into the stands in right in the third for a 2–1 lead. The huge, cold crowd warmed up with chants of "MVP . . . MVP . . . MVP." But the Giants' fine catcher, Buster Posey, matched it in the sixth to regain the lead, 3–2. In the bottom half Delmon Young hit his own dinger and the game remained tied through the ninth.

After Phil Coke pitched a perfect ninth, he was sent back out for the tenth, where two singles sandwiched around a sacrifice bunt and a strikeout put the Giants up again, and their quirky closer, Sergio Romo, who twists and turns and whirls his body as he delivers a variety of off-speed stuff, struck out the side in the bottom of the inning, finishing Miggy and the Series off with an 86-mph fastball that caught the inside edge of the plate. I wonder if Tommy Dressler even noticed or noted what the Giants now had done to my team.

I was numb from the weather and our play. What happened to our bats, except Delmon's and Cabrera's? Sam and I dejectedly retreated to our favorite sports bar in Greektown, where we tried to revive our spirits with a few Johnny Walker Blacks on the rocks, followed by a Labatt's and a few sliders. Back over the scorecards we roamed, and the results were astonishing. Peralta and Fielder, who had sustained us in the playoffs, were a combined 2 for 29. Often in a World Series when the big bats disappear unexpected little ones pick up the slack and prosper. Not so for the Tigers. Avila, Laird, Berry, and Dirks went 2 for 31. Such numbers do not a World Series win, or even a single victory, make. As we were bemoaning our fate, a fellow fan, noticing the names of Whitaker and Trammell on the backs of our Tiger jerseys, wondered, "Where's Fryman?" We laughed, turned on our barstools, and discovered a longtime Tiger fan who went to Western Michigan and now worked for Quicken Loans.

Chatting with him began to salve our wounds, for the moment. Then, in Hemingway fashion, we walked back to the hotel in the rain.

Plays, like games, are created to be performed. While this is obvious for baseball, it has often been less so for Shakespeare. I was fortunate that my first Shakespeare professors were regular theatergoers (though they were often dismissive of filmed versions of his plays), but they taught Shakespeare not as a playwright but as a poet. The major Shakespeare critics they referenced were influenced by the tenets of the New Criticism, which approached the plays as self-contained poems ripe with irony and ambiguity, not as scripts for performance. C. L. Barber's classroom device of asking students to pick out a short passage from the play and expand upon its relevance to the entire work mirrored the work of New Critics in books and articles. Ed Barrett was a dramatic and expansive classroom presence and often asked us to read passages out loud, but I don't recall his ever asking us how a specific exchange or soliloquy might be enhanced by the way it was staged.

The academic revolution in restoring Shakespeare to the theater was begun in the early twentieth century by theater scholars and directors (William Poel, Ben Iden Payne, Walter Hodges, Tyrone Guthrie, and Andrew Gurr most conspicuously) determined to rediscover and recreate the theater for which he wrote. They were archaeologists of the dramatic imagination, trying to unearth a theatrical space that had disappeared for almost three hundred years. Rediscovering Shakespeare's theater was not the work of literary critics but of theater directors and theater historians. A movement that began at the beginning of the century gained substantial momentum at midcentury with the building of Tanya Moiseiwitsch's revolutionary thrust stage at Canada's Stratford, followed by England's Chichester Festival Theatre, the National Theatre's Olivier stage, and finally came to full fruition in the reconstructed Globe on the South Bank of the Thames near where Shakespeare's original theater had stood. In America these efforts were joined by the outdoor Angus Bowmer Theater at Ashland in Oregon, the Chicago Shakespeare Theater on Navy Pier in Chicago, and finally the American Shakespeare Company's version of Shakespeare's indoor Blackfriars Theatre, home of the American Shakespeare Company, in Staunton, Virginia.

This effort to reexamine the plays in the theatrical space which originally gave them life ran parallel to the ever-expanding (in productions and length of season) repertory of plays at Canada's Stratford, Peter Hall's creation of the Royal Shakespeare Company at Stratford-upon-Avon, Laurence Olivier's leadership of England's new National Theatre in London, and Joseph Papp's creation of the New York Shakespeare Festival in the 1960s. Suddenly, Shakespeare in Performance had new energy in the English-speaking world. I was fortunate to be in the group of young English Department Shakespeareans who helped establish Shakespeare in performance on stage and screen as a lively subfield of Shakespeare studies in the 1970s and '80s. In these years the Shakespeare game underwent a profound change. For several centuries Shakespeare had been produced (in America as well as England) by actor-managers. Now the major Shakespeare theaters were led by university-educated (many read English at Cambridge) directors like Peter Brook, Peter Hall, Trevor Nunn, Richard Eyre, Robin Phillips, Adrian Noble, and Nicholas Hytner, rather than actors. Olivier was the last of the great actor-managers, though somewhat sporadically Kenneth Branagh and Mark Rylance have kept the idea and role of the actor-manager alive in our time.

Something similar happened in the world of film. English-language film versions of Shakespeare from the 1940s through the 1960s were dominated by films directed by Laurence Olivier and Orson Welles (actors turned directors). From the late sixties on, with the crucial exceptions of Kenneth Branagh and Ralph Fiennes, Shakespeare films almost exclusively have been made not by actors but by directors: Franco Zeffirelli, Roman Polanski, Peter Brook, Peter Hall, Trevor Nunn, Adrian Noble, Baz Luhrmann, Michael Hoffman, Michael Almereyda, Richard Loncraine, Josh Whedon, Michael Radford, and Joel Coen. Stage and film productions opened themselves up for intellectual analysis, which participated in the lively ongoing critical debate about the plays themselves and Shakespeare's role in contemporary culture. This brave new world emerged in the early eighties just at the moment when my baseball team was catching fire.

While the Tigers provided rich baseball thrills in the new century, so did Shakespeare. Cranbrook and Comerica Park became the natural stopping-off places for revived family trips to Ontario's Stratford, now with all twelve of us in the entourage. The first trip was in 2004, when Charlie, Theo, Aidan, and Audrey saw their first Shakespeare, appropriately *A Midsummer Night's Dream*. Though young, they were fully engaged. The production was set in the Amazon Forest and featured wonderful aerial work (evoking memories of Peter Brook's legendary *Dream*, which Susan and I had seen in London in the summer of 1971) by Oberon and Titania and Puck, colorful, exotic costumes, and, as is often the case at Stratford, an imaginative use of theatrical space. When we returned to our rented cottage on Lake Huron, we were entertained each evening for several days by their versions of key moments in the play as they unfolded in performance.

Miranda and Sam had, years before, responded similarly to their early exposure to Shakespeare. I remember well after a screening the family attended of Orson Welles's magnificent film of the Falstaff material, *Chimes at Midnight*, for my Shakespeare on Film course in 1974, glancing out the next day into our side yard to see them reenacting the play and the film's killer scene: Hal's rejection of Falstaff at his coronation as Henry V. First Sam was on his knees while his sister shook her head and pointed her arm at him, and then Sam, like Hal in the "play extempore" with Falstaff during the first great tavern scene, insisted that they change roles and places so he could play the King-as-rejector.

By our next trips in 2010, 2014, and 2017 they were old theatrical hands, having already appeared in several plays themselves. *The Tempest, As You Like It, King Lear,* and *Romeo and Juliet* were added to their collection of Shakespearean productions along with several fine versions of classic musical comedies like *Guys and Dolls* and *Kiss Me, Kate.* The baseball games we saw as bookends to these trips often failed to match the power and the magic of the plays, with the plays more than holding their own with the games in the imaginations of six kids between the ages of ten and eighteen. Who could ask for anything more?

The remarkable cycle of team and place came to fulfillment in the decade between 2010 and 2020. Sam and Aidan and I made one late-season jaunt to Detroit after Aidan had a late Friday afternoon soccer game in Lancaster, Ohio, which already put us on the road north. We spent the night on the road and on Saturday drove right to the Corner, where, while the stadium itself had been torn down, the playing field had been preserved by the Corktown neighborhood. The gate was unlocked, so we invited ourselves in. Father, son, and grandson then played pitch and catch from the mound (where Schoolboy Rowe, Tommy Bridges, Hal Newhouser, Frank Lary, Denny McClain, Mickey Lolich, the Bird, and Jack Morris had all toiled) to home plate (where Mickey Cochrane, Bill Freehan, Lance Parrish, and Brad Ausmus had called the game). Who needs an Iowa cornfield when life magically provides the real thing?

Aidan, who would develop into a fine high school soccer player and as a senior captain helped to lead the Athens High School team to its greatest season (19–1), losing only in the Ohio State Tournament quarterfinals, had last been out on this diamond in a backpack on his father's shoulders in 1999 when he was ten months old. His father had seen games here since 1976; his grandfather, since 1950. The three of us tossed the ball around with huge smiles dancing on our faces, scarcely believing where we were and what we were doing. Aidan ran the bases, Sam jogged, and I strolled, hearing the October 1984 cheers which had erupted in response to Gibson's mighty upper-deck blast to clinch the World Series still ringing in my ears: "Goose-buster." I was back in Tiger heaven. Several years later I got to repeat this experience with Charlie, Theo, Miles, and their father, Bill. In true Pistner fashion, they did the Athenians one better by having a race from the mound to the old flagpole, still standing, in deep center field. Bill won. This time I got the chills and thrills not from the past but from the Blakean joy of watching grandchildren sport on this hallowed ground: "Such, such were the joys / When we all—girls and boys— / In our youth-time were seen / On the echoing green."

But as we know, life, though it can often be cruel and peevish, can also work in remarkable and mysterious ways. And so it came to pass, in a family of five grandsons and one granddaughter, that it was Audrey who formed the most lasting bond with the Tigers. She inherited her love of the game from her Orioles-fan mother and her attachment to the Tigers from her father. Audrey followed her brother Aidan into soccer and was a fine defensive back and cocaptain of the Athens High School women's team in her senior year. I am sure she pays some attention to European soccer, and like all of us she is a committed fan of the great American World Cup–winning women's team, but her sports passion is reserved for the Tigers.

Born in 2001, she came of fan's age just as the Tigers became consistent winners. She is the only one of Sam and Terry's kids to see a playoff game as she and her father helped the Tigers defeat the A's in 2013. The Tigers were down 2–1 in the series when the two dashed to Comerica to watch Jhonny Peralta hit a three-run homer in a Tiger come-from-behind 8–6 victory. Verlander won the series the next day on a nifty 3–0 two-hitter. He owned the A's in the playoffs. Now, ten years later, as a recent graduate of Ohio University's Honors Tutorial College, she knows the finals of the late games well before I do and is as anxious as her grandfather and father to get back into Comerica to see if this new litter of Tiger pups can learn to roar. Audrey's younger brother, Emerson, a high school junior, may well be the best soccer player in the family, as he can pass and score and was elected a captain as a junior. Aidan and Audrey had to wait to their senior years before being so honored.

As I mentioned earlier, Miranda and Bill teach at Cranbrook in Bloomfield Hills and have raised three fine lads who developed into strong athletes. Charlie was a great lacrosse player and one of the team's leading scorers when Cranbrook won the Michigan state lacrosse championship his senior year. Several years later, he was a potent striker on the Michigan State team that won the National Club Championship in 2017 (held out in Salt Lake City), where he was named the Under Armor Player of the Tournament Week. His brothers, Theo and Miles, were basketball and baseball players. Their teams did not win state or national championships, but they may have done something equally dazzling for the purposes of this saga.

Some of the Ilitch grandchildren have attended Cranbrook and played on the baseball team. The Ilitch family has graciously invited Cranbrook to play one of its games each May in Comerica Park. So Theo (in 2017) at second and Miles (in 2019 and 2021) at third have shared the infield at Comerica with Polanco and Kinsler, Inge and Cabrera, Guillén and Peralta, and each has had his mugshot projected up on the giant scoreboard above the left field stands. Miles also pitched an inning in 2021, stranding a leadoff double at second, from the same mound where Verlander and Scherzer once dominated. Susan and I got to catch that game along with Miranda and Bill, and though it was a warm May afternoon, the chills and goosebumps appeared and reappeared for nine innings.

Thoughtfully, so as to preserve for me some of the fun and some of the glory of that day, one of my eightieth-birthday presents from my family of Tiger fans was a photo of that scoreboard carrying a birthday message for me. In this saga, King Lear ("I am a very foolish fond old man, / Fourscore and upwards, not an hour more or less") awakens not only in the company of his daughter but also on the scoreboard at Comerica Park. My baseball-loving mother stirs ever so gently in her grave with a wry smile upon her face. "What have I wrought?" she thinks.

I wanted to end this account with a celebration, but my club was again in decline. I kept thinking, in these past two decades of rich Tiger history, that they would win the World Series again and that would provide me with a fitting ending. Alas, they had two chances and badly muffed them. Then the baseball gods took pity, corrected a grave injustice, and gave me my conclusion. Finally, in 2018, the Veterans Committee elected Alan Trammell and Jack Morris to the Hall of Fame, the only Tigers from the wonderful teams of the eighties to be inducted. No Tiger had been elected to the Hall by the sportswriters since Al Kaline in 1980 (his first year on the ballot), and the Veterans Committee had not tapped a Tiger since electing Hal Newhouser in 1992.

Now two well-deserving teammates (sadly without Lou Whitaker) would go in together. Morris was the dominant right-handed pitcher of the 1980s and pitched what is regarded as the strongest (after Don Larson's perfect game) World Series game in history, an eleven-inning complete-game 1–0 victory for the Twins in 1991. Trammell is ranked as one of the top-ten shortstops in the history of the game. He played for twenty years, nineteen of them with his partner at second base Lou Whitaker, who was a smooth, steady fielder and who achieved hitting and fielding numbers to rival those of most second basemen already in the Hall. Whitaker's numbers match Trammell's, and their nineteen years together at the corner and the Corner is unlikely to be topped by another double-play duo. Their record is surely as safe as DiMaggio's 56-game hitting streak.

Trammell used his Hall of Fame acceptance speech and the one he made at Comerica in late August when his number (3) was retired to graciously lobby the Hall and the Tigers to honor Whitaker in the same fashion. I doubt the Hall's Veterans Committee will listen, but in the summer of 2022 the Tigers did and retired Whitaker's number (1) and placed it alongside Trammell's out in right field. Quiet and shy, Whitaker retired to Lakeland, the Florida home for the Tigers in spring training, and never returned to the game except for some appearances with the team at Lakeland in March. He disappeared from baseball view, and so, sadly, did his name and accomplishments. Trammell, in their playing days, was a better interview and stayed in the game after he retired, first with his hometown Padres, then managing the Tigers from 2003 to 2005, and then becoming his former teammate Kirk Gibson's bench coach when Gibson managed the Arizona Diamondbacks. Trammell never left baseball; he remained in the conversation, and gradually the baseball world began to see that his numbers were as strong as, or stronger than, most of the shortstops in the Hall and that his longevity blew everyone else away. Trammell will continue to make Lou's strong case, but will the Veterans Committee listen?

Susan and I long had interest in following the New England summer culture trail wending from the Glimmerglass Opera House in Cooperstown to music at Tanglewood in the Berkshires to Shakespeare at the Mount in Lenox, Massachusetts, to the remarkable Clark Museum in Williamstown and then on to the Marlboro Music Festival outside Brattleboro. Trammell and Morris and, unexpectedly, Bill Murray provided us with a good excuse finally to make the long jaunt from southeastern Ohio. We spent the first two days of induction week in Cooperstown and its surrounds. The opera (The Barber of Seville) was colorful and lively but distinguished only by its Figaro and a clever set. Better yet was the new-world program of excerpts from American literature (Whitman, Cooper, Hemingway, Twain, Ferlinghetti, etc.) assembled by Bill Murray and old-world classical music selected by the cellist Jan Vogler and the trio (violin and piano) he created for the occasion. The show has played all over the States and Europe, including Carnegie Hall in New York and the Royal Albert Hall in London.

Even though Cooperstown does not sport a summer Shakespeare Festival, we felt culturally complete because what other Hall of Fame setting has an opera house as an added attraction, and what other sport fits so comfortably with literary culture? Roger Angell would have loved it. W. P. Kinsella would have been thrilled to have Bill Murray come strolling out of his cornfield, and even Bernard Malamud would have produced a smile at the evening's mix of American prose and European melodies.

As I have insisted, baseball is the writer's game. No other professional sport has attracted more writers to its landscape and culture. Novelists and poets and essayists have embraced the game. It has inspired wonderful poets like Donald Hall, Tom Clark, and Dave Smith, among many, novelists like Mark Harris, Malamud and Kinsella, Philip Roth, Robert Coover, and Chad Harnish, and journalists and writers like Robert Creamer, Tom Boswell, Red Smith, George Will, George Plimpton, and the best of them all, Roger Angell, to produce remarkable work. The American writer who fashioned a career as a complete man of letters, John Updike, was working at the top of his talents when he conjured up "Hub Fans Bid Kid Adieu," an account of Ted Williams's final game at Fenway. Updike does the day, the game, and Williams's historic final at-bat with the easy compelling power and grace of Ted's last home run and his proud refusal to take a bow. Ted was baseball's Coriolanus before Pete Rose too refused to show his wounds.

Modern historians have turned their eyes and their books towards baseball and created a thriving subfield of baseball history. But they have, thus far, not turned their attention to the NFL, the NBA, or the NHL in a similar fashion. My own colleague in the History Department at Ohio University, Charles Alexander, was a leader in this movement. After producing six books on twentieth-century American social history, he turned to writing a trio of baseball biographies of Ty Cobb, Rogers Hornsby, and John McGraw and then published his comprehensive history of the sport: *Our Game: An American Baseball History*. Another historian, Doris Kearns Goodwin, fashioned her own memoir of growing up as a Dodger fan. And many others have followed in their footsteps. Baseball, as literature and history, is now in the college curriculum.

We immersed ourselves in some of that history the next day by spending almost three hours touring the Hall. The place was packed with youngsters, many wearing their Little League or American Legion team uniforms. And I was pleased to see several adult men wearing Tiger T-shirts or jerseys. Made me feel less conspicuous wearing a Lou Whitaker jersey. Susan took several shots of me looking at Trammell's Hall display case with Whitaker's name boldly printed on my back, captured in the shot. One Tiger fan passing behind me simply crooned, "Louuuuuu . . . Louuuuuu."

We passed a display case with a photo of the iconic over-the-shoulder catch Willie Mays made of Vic Wertz's mighty drive in the first game of the 1954 World Series, along with the glove Willie had used to make the catch. The story of how Willie's glove made it to Cooperstown is recounted in a recent revised edition of Arnold Hano's *A Day in the Bleachers*, his equally a-May-zing account of that game. Hano's book is the only one I know that focuses on a single game and does so from the author's seat in the bleachers at the Polo Grounds, where he had the unique perspective of watching Mays dashing, with his back to the diamond, not away from but towards Hano's rapt gaze.

The relief pitcher Don Liddle, who threw the ball Wertz hit, brought his son to the club house to meet his idol, Mays. Mays, learning that the lad was about to enter Little League play, asked him if he needed a glove. The boy nodded his head and Mays gave him the mitt, saying, "Take care of this, and it will take care of you." Mindful of Mays's advice, the boy carefully used the glove in his sandlot years and then sent it to Cooperstown, along with the story of how it came into his possession. Hano comments: "Baseball, for all its faults . . . remains our greatest game. It is also the simplest. It so often comes down to a boy, his baseball glove, and a hero."[7]

We worked our way down to the first floor and the room where all the plaques of the Hall of Fame players hang and drifted through a bevy of the game's greats, with special attention paid by me to the catchers and, of course, the Tigers. We emerged into the bright sun about 1:30 p.m., took the last photos, and walked the main street past dozens of baseball emporiums and headed out into the Cherry Valley to the Ommegang Belgian Brewery for a well-deserved Belgian ale and lunch.

Had we lingered into the weekend we would have seen Lou Whitaker, in his own unobtrusive, modest fashion, sitting on a bench a block down from the Hall quietly signing autographs for those knowledgeable fans who recognized him as he waited for the ceremony where he could celebrate his partner's induction. Trammell returned the gesture by lauding his partner and his career achievements and expressing his hope Lou would soon be joining him in the Hall.

The rest of our trip into the Berkshires and the Green Mountains of Vermont was filled with other pleasures: music, theater, and a reunion with old friends, Lewis and Susan Greenstein, from our graduate student days in Bloomington. The baseball and Shakespeare connection, however, popped up again when we went to see an outdoor production of *Love's Labour's Lost* at Edith Wharton's Lenox home, the Mount. The production, trimmed to a lively ninety minutes, began at six. The audience was seated in folding lawn chairs much like the ones we had sat in to watch our own kids and then our grandchildren, at about the same summer evening hour, play their earliest baseball and softball games. The young cast engaged Shakespeare's early language-intoxicated play with brio; perhaps they didn't hit any home runs, but there were plenty of singles and doubles to admire, but no bowling as sadly the Pageant of the Nine Worthies had been cut. But they scored some runs and gave us the pleasure of Shakespeare's early indulgence in the "sweet smoke of rhetoric." We were back at play in the green world and happy to be there.

When we returned to Athens, I was walking down Court Street, the main drag connecting the town with the university, when I saw, at some distance, a tall, robust student coming towards me with a head topped by a mass of red curls and a baseball hat. My mind flashed back almost fifty years to another robust young student who walked the campus wearing a baseball hat also perched atop a mop of red curls. He was Peter King (a New Englander) wearing a Boston Red Sox hat. King went on to a distinguished career covering the NFL for *Sports Illustrated* and NBC Sports. We both played a small role in a university promotional film in 1976 that featured a brief segment from a seminar I was teaching on *Hamlet*. Peter, wearing his Red Sox cap, was one of the students. My thoughts were jolted back to the present when the Court Street student got closer, and I saw that he was not a reincarnation of King—but even better for this account—was wearing a Tigers hat. "Nice hat," says I, "Nice shirt," says he, and, having forgotten what I was wearing, I looked down to see I was sporting my "Al Kaline 1968 Champions" T-shirt. What crazy eighty-year-old retired Shakespeare prof wears an Al Kaline shirt? This one, linking the Bard and baseball once again.

TIGER LETTER #7

Cooperstown 23 July 2018

Dear Tiger Fans:

This is the last of the "Tiger Letters." The first was written thirty years ago in April of 1988 as a means of sharing the Tigers Opening Day win over the Red Sox in Fenway with Sam and Miranda. The last comes as the heroes of that win (and many others in their years in Detroit), Jack Morris and Alan Trammell, are about to be inducted (at last) into baseball's Hall of Fame. That Fenway game was my first opener and remained the only one until I travelled up to Tiger Stadium for its last opener, before the move to Comerica, in 1999. That frame is fitting since Fenway Park and Tiger Stadium (with earlier incarnations as Bennett Field, Navin Park, and Briggs Stadium) both opened in 1912 and were the oldest remaining Major League ballparks. Now only Fenway holds that honor.

My attendance at the Fenway opener was linked, as much of my baseball-loving career has been, with Shakespeare, for the annual meeting of the Shakespeare Association of America happened to take place in Boston that Easter weekend. Once again baseball mingled with the Bard and Boston's rich cultural attractions: the Copley Plaza Hotel, The Boston Museum of Fine Arts, the Celtics (my only trip to the old Boston Garden), a Sunday performance of *Macbeth* starring Christopher Plummer and Glenda Jackson and Clemens vs. Morris on opening day in Fenway, these last two pairings the stuff of myth as well as memory. I should add that the Celtics game (I can still see that amazing front line of Bird, Parish, and McHale streaming down the floor as the Garden crowd's roar mounted, zipping the ball back and forth between them before a Bird bomb from the corner or a Parish slam finished the fastbreak) and Monday's opener were courtesy of my good pal, avid sports fan, and devoted Ohio University alum, Sandy Elsass.

My good fortune of being in Cooperstown thirty years later was also tied to the arts. Susan and I had long wished to attend an opera at Glimmerglass just up gorgeous Lake Otsego from baseball's home and to experience the rich joys of music, theater, and the fine arts a few hours East in the Berkshires and southern Vermont. As a bonus, Glimmerglass had booked, for one performance only, *New Worlds* a program of excerpts from American writers from Cooper to Twain to Whitman to Hemingway to Ferlinghetti read/performed by Bill Murray accompanied by a selection of European classical music played by the piano trio led by the noted cellist, Jan Vogler. Given Bill Murray's passion for baseball and the Cubs it was perhaps no surprise that he should show up in Cooperstown's opera house during Induction Week. We went and the evening provided more hits than *The Barber of Seville* the previous afternoon, though the Rossini production was lovely to look at, had a fine Figaro, and was delivered with gusto. But it was no match for Murray who read from the works of American authors noted above and sang renditions of "Jeanie with the Light Brown Hair," "I Feel Pretty," "The Banks of

Loch Lomond," and "My Girl." Terrific stuff, but I was disappointed that, given the location and the moment, he didn't sing "Take Me Out to the Ballgame." Only in Wrigley, I guess.

I had long looked for an appropriate moment to put a large exclamation point on this odyssey of our family's connection with the Tigers. I had hoped that a World Series victory in 2006 or 2012 would have provided the occasion. But though the Tigers were favored in both encounters, the baseball gods were otherwise engaged, and two strong teams floundered unlike their predecessors in 1968 and 1984. I wanted to end with a bang, not a whimper. And then those gods woke from their slumbers, rubbed their eyes, and realized that the sadly negligent sports writers had failed to elect Jack Morris and Alan Trammell to the HOF. They went to work on the Veteran's Committee, and it came to pass that Alan and Jack were elected to enter the Hall in the same summer: virtue, finally, rewarded. Or at least partially. Full justice will not be achieved until Lou Whitaker rejoins his partner of nineteen years and he has the numbers (at the plate and in the field) to stack up against all the other second basemen already enshrined. _

Cooperstown is a madhouse on induction weekend so it seemed a good idea to visit early in the week when we could enjoy the various pleasures of the little village and not have to fight the crowds at the Hall and the induction ceremony itself. Susan, who honors her family's devotion to the Tigers more in the breach than the observance, was a great companion on our tour. We started on the third floor and worked our way down. Though I had been to Cooperstown once or twice in the past twenty years I had only toured the Hall twice, with my parents, back in 1952 and with Sam in 1992 when he joined me for my 30th reunion at Hamilton.

And, with a nod to that family tradition, perhaps the best part of touring the Hall again was observing how many parents and kids were enjoying the experience together. We came upon a father and son (perhaps 10 or so) gazing up at a large photo of Jose Altuve (the great Astros second baseman who, like Joe Morgan in his era, is pound for pound, the greatest player in today's game). The father was reminding his son that baseball players come in all shapes and sizes and that he too might become a future Altuve. Speaking of fathers and sons. Prior to the 2006 World Series (Sam and I had seen the Tigers dominate the Yankees and the A's at Comerica to clinch the AL championship) Sam presented the two of us with Detroit Tiger uniform jerseys, his with Trammell's name and number (#3) across the back, mine with Whitaker's (#1). I've only worn mine to that World Series and then again to the playoffs and WS in 2012. But I wore it at the Hall and Susan took several pictures of me standing in front of the display case honoring Tram and as she clicked her tablet, I could hear more than one visitor behind us exclaim, "great shot," "wonderful," "Louuuuuuu," and "send it to Tram." Some Tigers fans had already arrived.

We loved the gallery of old photographs and were most taken with a photo from 1889 of a group of travelling ball players in uniform standing and sitting on the Sphinx. The juxtaposition was startling and a reminder that baseball, though it had a head start, never colonized the world of sport as soccer did. There was also a fine print of Charles Conlon's famous photo of Ty Cobb sliding into third, perhaps the most reprinted photo in the history of the game, and I later learned it was taken 108 years before on the very date we were now admiring it: July 23, 1910. Isn't baseball history sweet? A fellow observer noted what I had missed: "He's no slasher in that shot, his spikes are down not up." The Cobb-as-nasty-player revisionism continues.

As to be expected given its New York location, the Hall is heavy on the Yanks, but I was surprised by how much attention is still given to the Dodgers, including a continu-ous video loop of action at Ebbets Field and not one but two giant photos of Kirk Gibson, fist pumping the air, after his big home run in the first game of the 1988 World Series. What about Gibson's similar pose after his three-run blast in the 8th inning of the final (not the first) game in 1984? And for that matter while there are loving photo portraits of Fenway and Wrigley and Forbes and even old Crosley Field in Cin-cinnati, there is nary a mention of Tiger Stadium, surely their historical rival. Neither is there any attention given to the great 1968 Cardinal-Tiger World Series, a remarkable one and the last before the beginning of divisional play.

On the other hand, there was a nice corner devoted to the Tigers of 1934–45 with pictures of Mickey Cochrane, Schoolboy Rowe, Charlie Gehringer, Hank Greenberg, and Prince Hal. There is a large exhibit honoring Hank Aaron's career and another reminding us of the great contributions of the Latin players (including Miguel Cabrera's jersey) who have come to dominate the game in the last forty years. The artifact that grabbed my attention was the mitt Willie Mays was wearing when he made his iconic over-the-shoulder catch of Vic Wertz's drive to deep center field in the Polo Grounds in the 1954 World Series. I took note because it looked just like the baseball glove I used in the mid-50s when I wasn't catching. And I thought to myself: "He made **that** catch with **that** mitt?"

We worked our way down to the 1st floor and the room where all the plaques are displayed. They are neatly divided into decade-by-decade alcoves with the initial founding five hanging in the center niche. I lingered at Harry Heilmann's (for my mother) and Cochrane's, Yogi's, Bench's, and Pudge's (I love catchers) and Kaline's (still active in the Tigers organization and soon to arrive to see his boys inducted into the Hall), and Michael Jack Schmidt's (Ohio University's man in the Hall) and then we found the current spot where this year's inductees (Chipper Jones, Pedro Guerrero, Trevor Hoffman, Jack Morris, Jim Thome, and Alan Trammell) will join the others. In a nice touch the outline of the spots on the wall where their plaques will be placed had been signed by each of them, so only those visiting in the few weeks leading up to the ceremony will ever see this piece of the tradition. Appropriately Susan put her handy tablet to work again. And then into the gift shop for souvenirs and those unique HOF post cards featuring the plaque of each member; I remember picking up Cobb and Gehringer back in '52. Sadly, they have gone the way of my baseball card collection which I carelessly told your great-grandmother to pitch when they moved from Waterville to Springfield back in 1964.

We emerged about 1:30 having spent almost two and a half hours (just the length of a well-paced game) in the museum. A few more snaps and clicks with the Hall in the background and then to the car and out into the Cherry Valley countryside to the Ommegang Brewery for a cold Belgian ale and lunch. I had bratwurst in a bun to honor the simple joy of baseball food after a tour of the Hall. The ale and the sandwich were hugely restorative, and we congratulated ourselves on the morning's work. We also proved to be prescient when the fans began to stream into the tiny town the next morning as we headed to the Berkshires and Tanglewood. On Sunday, as reported by the New York Times, a crowd of 53,000 gathered for the ceremony itself. In his remarks, Trammell looked out at Lou Whitaker in the audience and commented: "It's my hope that you will be up here someday," thus generously putting the words to our little tableau on Tuesday morning in front of Tram's shrine in the shrine.

And what of Morris? He's mellowed over the years but his path to the Hall was probably slowed by his inability to play Tom Seaver or Sandy Koufax with reporters. He gave fits to the Detroit writers who covered the Tigers. But his irascibility, like Bob Gibson's, was part of his bulldog essence as a pitcher. And thirty years ago, in that wonderful opening day game at Fenway he bested Clemens. Clemens went nine, Morris ten. Clemens threw 136 pitches and Morris 122 (can you imagine that now? No way. Even Verlander is done at 105 or so). Clemens struck out the side in the 2nd (and had eleven strikeouts); Morris, even more impressively, struck out the side in the 9th with the game tied 3–3.

Boston brought their newly acquired, from the Cubs, closer Lee Smith in to pitch the 10th. Spike Owens let a little roller from Gary Pettis squirt away from him for an error; Lou sacrificed him to second base, Evans flied out deep to right; and then, you guessed it, Morris's Hall partner, Trammell, hit a Smith fastball into the screen ten feet above the Green Monster in left. 5–3 Tigers. Trammell had provided similar heroics (then hitting two two-run homers, with Lou on base for both) in Morris's second complete game World Series win in 1984. Now the two are linked as a pair in the Hall. They await the arrival of their deserving teammate to make it a trio of Tigers.

Thus ends seventy years of watching and thirty-five years of writing about the Tigers. The letters will end but briefer email accounts (as the old letter writer finally joins the new millennium) will continue whenever we all find ourselves once again in Comerica Park or other playing fields. This stream of letters was unplanned but took on a life of its own and has delivered the pleasures of reliving the games (equally weighed in delight and dole) and then sharing their details both with my fellow observers and those of the now expanded circulation list, some of whom, brave souls, have never seen a Tigers game in person but who nevertheless dig the fine madness of the enterprise. And perhaps Charlie or Aidan or Theo or Audrey or Miles or Emerson will be inspired by this sweet folly, as Sam was in writing the "Ripken Letters," to keep the tradition going or better yet start a new one of their own. Just make sure Sushi and I are on the list and in the loop.

Love,
Bops

SHAKESPEARE AND BASEBALL XI

I conclude this Odyssean narrative with three examples of the fortuitous and fateful linkages between Shakespeare, baseball, and our lives in Athens and Ohio University. One is a final flight of an old professor's imagination, another is a happy coincidence worthy of the final pages in a Dickens novel, and the third is a sweet gift from the baseball gods.

Shakespeare's image is commonly represented by three portraits: the Martin Droeshout engraving that serves as the frontispiece to the 1623 First Folio of his complete works, the limestone sculpture of his bust by Gheerart Janssen that marks his grave in Stratford's Holy Trinity church, and the oil painting that has become known as the Chandos portrait, which hangs in the National Portrait Gallery in London, and slightly amended graces this book's cover. This portrait, while probably the least authentic, is the most reproduced because it is the most romantic. It is how we want him to look: serious (his somber gaze), natural (the simple black jersey covering a white blouse open at the neck with the collar wings extending down over the jersey), intelligent (the high forehead), and dashing (the beard, tumbling locks, and tiny gold earring in his right ear). It's the portrait of an actor as a mature playwright.

But look more closely and "on your imaginary forces work." Isn't the Chandos portrait a brilliant composite image of a twentieth-century baseball player? The black jersey and white collar could have been worn by a turn-of-the-twentieth-century player, complete with mustache and modest beard. The shoulder-length hair and that tiny gold hoop earring in his left ear entered baseball's fashion almost a hundred years later and are still with us. And what position would he have played? As much as I'd like to claim him for the catchers, he surely was a pitcher. He's Walter Johnson, Cy Young, Dizzy Dean, Bob Feller, Nolan Ryan, Justin Verlander. He's Prince Hal or would be if he was a lefty. As everything in the theater starts with the playwright, so everything in baseball starts with the pitcher. He sets the game's narrative in motion and, if he has his good stuff, controls its tempo and dictates its outcome. So, gaze at sweet Mr. Shakespeare's picture and indulge your fantasies (for that is what fans do) and think how good that face and jersey would look on a Topps baseball card and in a Tigers uniform.

I was surprised to discover that history has not provided us with a major leaguer named Bill Shakespeare. Even if he existed, he would not be a distant relative, as Shakespeare's only son, Hamnet, died when he was eleven and none of Shakespeare's brothers had children. If there was a ballplayer who shared some of the Shakespeare bloodline, he would carry the name of Hart. Shakespeare's sister Joan married William Hart (a hatter), and their line is still alive. When Park Honan, the noted biographer of Robert Browning, Matthew Arnold, Jane Austen, and Christopher Marlowe, was researching his excellent biography of Shakespeare, he engaged in correspondence with what he believed was an American descendant of the Hart line, Alex Hart.

Hart's daughter Mimi was a fellow member of our English Department. Honan was a scholarly colleague of Susan's, as they were both members of the editorial board of the Ohio-Baylor Complete Works of Robert Browning. Honan was pleased to discover a possible Hart descendant at a university he often visited when the Browning editors gathered in Athens. He and Mimi's father (an amateur genealogist) traced the American Hart line back as far as was clearly possible. Their research finally determined that the Hart-Shakespeare connection was improbable but not impossible given a few gaps in the eighteenth century, which made their search inconclusive. My reaction to this implausible news, as you might imagine, was linked to the sly way Shakespeare's subtitle for *Henry VIII* and Kenneth Branagh's title for his film of Shakespeare's last years in Stratford mingled fact and fiction by declaring, *All Is True* when, of course the titles should have read *All Is (Almost) True*.

Susan and I were delighted to learn of this connection, since we had known Mimi as a student when she moonlighted as the lead singer in an Athens rock band known as Mimi and the Bobcats, then as a fine graduate student who wrote her dissertation on music in Jane Austen's novels, then as a member of our faculty where she once again moonlighted, singing in a trio called the Local Girls. Early in her career she spent lots of time on the road with her own band and as a backup singer for many major groups like the Allman Brothers. Some of her possible Shakespeare genes were clearly at work as she combined the talents of a performer and writer. The Shakespeare affiliation became even more manifest when the Local Girls were invited to sing at court, in a manner of speaking.

Hillary Clinton visited Athens campaigning for her husband in 1996, heard the Local Girls sing, and when her husband was reelected she invited the group to come and sing at the White House as part of the entertainment at her fiftieth birthday celebration. Their performance so dazzled that they were invited back to perform at several other White House events. Virginia Woolf's imagination was seized by thinking about Shakespeare's sister. It turns out she did not die unfulfilled, but lived on, like many talented and creative women, in Athens, Ohio.

Baseball can also provide unexpected surprises, as it did for this Tiger fan in the spring of 2022 when Miguel Cabrera collected his three thousandth hit and ensured his spot in the Hall of Fame and as the best all-round hitter in Tiger history. Cabrera's single to center was smartly struck on April 23, which just happened to be Shakespeare's 458th birthday. Miggy's timing was as exquisite for his own career as it was for this little book. "Tiger, Tiger burning bright / In the ballparks of the night."

Notes

All quotations from Shakespeare are from *The Norton Shakespeare*, ed. Stephen Greenblatt (New York: W. W. Norton, 1997).

1. Donald Hall, *Fathers Playing Catch with Sons* (San Francisco: North Point Press, 1985), 11.
2. Ernest Hemingway, *The Old Man and the Sea* (New York: Charles Scribner's Sons, 1952), 22.
3. C. L. Barber, *Shakespeare's Festive Comedy* (Princeton, NJ: Princeton University Press, 1958), 221.
4. James Cox, *Recovering Literature's Lost Ground* (Baton Rouge: Louisiana State University Press, 1989), 2.
5. Roger Angell, *Season Ticket* (Boston: Houghton Mifflin, 1988), 149.
6. A. Bartlett Giamatti, *A Great and Glorious Game* (Chapel Hill, NC: Algonquin Books of Chapel Hill, 1998), 7.
7. Arnold Hano, *A Day in the Bleachers: 50th Anniversary Edition* (Cambridge, MA: Da Capo Press, 1995), 169.